ASIA BOND MONITOR
JUNE 2022

ASIAN DEVELOPMENT BANK

ADB

Contents

Emerging East Asian Local Currency Bond Markets: A Regional Update

Executive Summary

Recent Developments in Financial Conditions in Emerging East Asia

Persistent inflationary pressure has led to the tightening of monetary stances in major advanced economies and several emerging East Asian economies.[1] Financial conditions in emerging East Asia weakened between 28 February and 9 June amid ongoing monetary tightening and headwinds facing the global and regional economies that are being driven by continued inflation, rising commodity prices, a slowdown in economic growth in the People's Republic of China due to coronavirus disease (COVID-19) containment measures, supply chain disruptions, and the Russian invasion of Ukraine.

Weakened financial conditions in emerging East Asia were evidenced by currency depreciations, a retreat in equity markets, portfolio outflows, and widened risk premiums in most regional markets. During the review period, emerging East Asian currencies posted a simple average depreciation versus the United States (US) dollar of 3.2% and a gross domestic product (GDP)-weighted average depreciation of 5.1%. Most regional equity markets reported declines, recording a weighted average loss of 4.6%. Risk premiums, proxied by credit default swap spreads, posted a GDP-weighted average increase of 4.7 basis points. From 28 February to 9 June, aggregate portfolio outflows of USD4.3 billion were recorded in regional equity markets, mainly concentrated in the Republic of Korea. From March to May, aggregate portfolio outflows of USD21.9 billion were observed in regional bond markets. Local currency (LCY) government bond yields in emerging East Asia rose, tracking higher yields in major advanced economies and escalating domestic inflationary pressure.

The risks to regional financial conditions remain tilted to the downside. Faster-than-expected monetary tightening in the US and the region is a key risk. Meanwhile, heightened downside risks to the global and regional economic outlooks—including persistent inflation, a further increase in commodity prices, a slower-than-expected recovery in the People's Republic of China, prolonged supply chain disruptions, and the protracted end to the Russian invasion of Ukraine—could further weaken financial conditions.

Recent Developments in Local Currency Bond Markets in Emerging East Asia

Emerging East Asia's LCY bond market reached a size of USD23.5 trillion at the end of March, with bond issuance in the first quarter (Q1) of 2022 falling 6.5% quarter-on quarter (q-o-q) to USD2.2 trillion. Association of Southeast Asian Nations (ASEAN) member economies' aggregate LCY bond stock reached USD2.0 trillion at the end of March, accounting for 8.6% of emerging East Asia's LCY bond market. Bond issuance in ASEAN markets stood at USD393.5 billion in Q1 2022, decreasing 6.7% q-o-q from the fourth quarter of 2021 and representing 17.8% of total issuance in emerging East Asia. The drop in bond issuance in Q1 2022 was partly driven by weakened financial conditions, heightened downside risks to the economic outlook, and fiscal consolidation in some regional economies.

At the end of March, 62.6% of the outstanding LCY bonds in the region were government bonds, totaling USD14.7 trillion. LCY government bond issuance recorded USD1.3 trillion in Q1 2022, contracting 2.2% q-o-q on fiscal consolidation in several regional economies, monetary tightening, as well as heightened uncertainty in the global growth outlook. Meanwhile, outstanding corporate bonds in emerging East Asia reached USD8.8 trillion at the end of March and issuance totaled USD902.8 billion in Q1 2021, contracting 12.1% q-o-q amid weakening financial conditions and increasing uncertainties in the economic outlook.

Medium- to longer-term maturity LCY government bonds account for around half of emerging East Asia's bond market. At the end of March, 55.0% of the region's LCY government bonds carried maturities of over 5 years or longer, while 48.6% of the region's LCY government

---

[1] Emerging East Asia comprises the People's Republic of China; Hong Kong, China; Indonesia; the Republic of Korea; Malaysia; the Philippines; Singapore; Thailand; and Viet Nam.

bond issuance in Q1 2022 had a maturity of more than 5 years. Domestic financial institutions—particularly banks, pension funds, and insurance companies—continued to hold a majority share of emerging East Asia's LCY bonds.

The sustainable bond market in ASEAN+3 saw solid expansion in Q1 2022 to reach a size of USD478.7 billion at the end of March.[2] Unlike conventional bond markets, the majority of the region's sustainable bond markets carried a maturity of less than 5 years, both in terms of outstanding stock at the end of Q1 2022 and issuance during the quarter. The private sector dominates the regional sustainable bond market, with the financial sector playing a key role.

Special Topics on Local Currency Bond Markets in Emerging East Asia

The June 2022 issue of the *Asia Bond Monitor* presents two special boxes.

United States Monetary Policy News and Financial Market Reactions in Developing Asia

The Federal Reserve's monetary policy decisions have been found to have a significant influence on global financial conditions and emerging financial markets. This box comprehensively examines the impacts of both conventional and unconventional Federal Reserve monetary policy tools on exchange rates, equity market performances, bond yields, and portfolio flows in developing Asia. It finds that developing Asia's currency, equity, and bond markets consistently, persistently, and significantly respond to conventional US monetary instruments such as changes in the federal funds rate, but they respond to a much lower extent to unconventional monetary tools such as changes in securities holdings. Moreover, both conventional and unconventional monetary tightening by the Federal Reserve weaken financial conditions in developing Asia. As the Federal Reserve is expected to further hike the policy rate and start unwinding its asset holdings, developing Asian central banks must closely monitor financial conditions and make the necessary policy adjustments to safeguard financial stability in the region.

Sovereign Bond Yield Spreads and Pandemic-Related Asset Purchase Programs in Four ASEAN Economies

During the pandemic, some emerging market economies conducted asset purchase programs (APPs) to facilitate market liquidity and stabilize bond prices. This box examines the impact of APPs on government bond yield spreads in four ASEAN economies: Indonesia, Malaysia, the Philippines, and Thailand. Using central banks' APP claims as shocks, the evidence shows that APPs effectively compressed bond yield spreads in these markets, with the impacts being statistically significant in all markets except the Philippines. This evidence highlights the effectiveness of APPs in relieving pressure in ASEAN bond markets, with improved institutional and financial development and enhanced central bank credibility since the global financial crisis.

---

[2] For the discussion on sustainable bonds, ASEAN+3 includes ASEAN members Indonesia, Malaysia, the Philippines, Singapore, Thailand, and Viet Nam plus the People's Republic of China; Hong Kong, China; Japan; and the Republic of Korea.

Global and Regional Market Developments

Financial conditions weakened in emerging East Asia amid monetary tightening and headwinds to the economic outlook.

Financial conditions in emerging East Asian markets weakened from 28 February to 9 June.[1] Persistent inflationary pressure has led to monetary tightening in major advanced economies as well as in a few economies in emerging East Asia. Central banks in the Republic of Korea, Malaysia, the Philippines, and Singapore tightened their respective monetary policies during the review period to address inflationary concerns. While monetary stances in the region remained largely accommodative, regional financial conditions weakened amid expected further monetary tightening as well as uncertainty in the economic recovery associated with persistent inflation, rising commodity prices, a slower-than-expected recovery in the People's Republic of China (PRC) due to coronavirus disease (COVID-19) containment measures, supply chain disruptions, and the Russian invasion of Ukraine. The weakening was evidenced by the retreat in equity markets, portfolio outflows from the region, widening risk premiums, and the depreciation of emerging East Asian currencies against the United States (US) dollar (**Table A**). Higher inflation also pushed up bond yields in both advanced markets and emerging East Asia.

Continued inflation in major advanced markets and emerging East Asia pushed up bond yields and led to monetary tightening (**Figure A**). During the review period, 2-year and 10-year government bond yields in the US rose 138 basis points (bps) and 122 bps, respectively, following rising inflation and consecutive rate hikes in March and May. Consumer price inflation in the US continued to rise, with May posting an 8.6% year-on-year (y-o-y) uptick, following an increase of 8.3% y-o-y in April

Table A: Changes in Financial Condition in Emerging East Asia and Major Advanced Economies

	2-Year Government Bond (bps)	10-Year Government Bond (bps)	5-Year Credit Default Swap Spread (bps)	Equity Index (%)	FX Rate (%)
Major Advanced Economies					
United States	138	122	–	(8.1)	–
United Kingdom	82	91	1	0.2	(6.9)
Japan	(5)	6	1	5.0	(14.4)
Germany	137	130	4	(1.8)	(5.4)
Emerging East Asia					
China, People's Rep. of	4	0.9	5	(6.5)	(5.7)
Hong Kong, China	126	114	–	(3.7)	(0.4)
Indonesia	81	69	(8)	4.3	(1.3)
Korea, Rep. of	89	79	14	(2.7)	(4.3)
Malaysia	91	53	4	(6.1)	(4.4)
Philippines	112	140	1	(7.6)	(3.2)
Singapore	100	103	–	(1.0)	(2.0)
Thailand	113	68	6	(2.6)	(5.4)
Viet Nam	69	95	(13)	(12.2)	(1.6)

( ) = negative, – = not available, bps = basis points, FX = foreign exchange.
Notes:
1. Data reflect changes between 28 February 2022 and 9 June 2022.
2. A positive (negative) value for the FX rate indicates the appreciation (depreciation) of the local currency against the United States dollar.
Source: *AsianBondsOnline* computations based on Bloomberg LP data.

---

[1] Emerging East Asia comprises the People's Republic of China; Hong Kong, China; Indonesia; the Republic of Korea; Malaysia; the Philippines; Singapore; Thailand; and Viet Nam.

Figure A: Average Inflation and Changes in Policy Rates and Bond Yields in Major Advanced Markets and Emerging East Asia

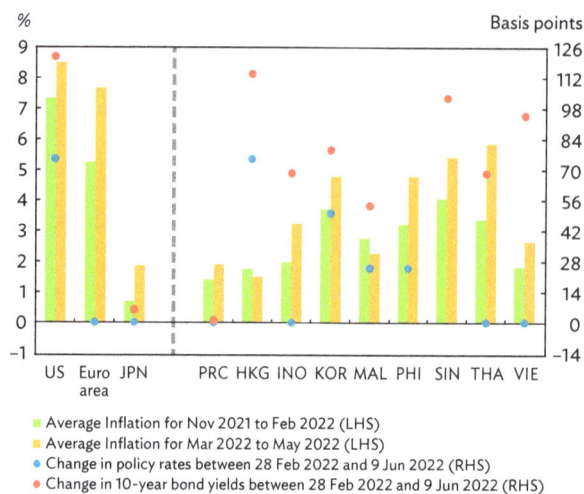

Average Inflation for Nov 2021 to Feb 2022 (LHS)
Average Inflation for Mar 2022 to May 2022 (LHS)
Change in policy rates between 28 Feb 2022 and 9 Jun 2022 (RHS)
Change in 10-year bond yields between 28 Feb 2022 and 9 Jun 2022 (RHS)

PRC = China, Rep. of; HKG = Hong Kong, China; INO = Indonesia; JPN = Japan; KOR = Korea, Rep. of; LHS = left-hand side; MAL = Malaysia; PHI = Philippines; RHS = right-hand side; SIN = Singapore; THA = Thailand; US = United States; VIE = Viet Nam.
Note: Inflation average is for the period November 2021 through May 2022 except for Japan; Hong Kong, China; Malaysia; and Singapore (November 2021 through April 2022).
Source: Various local sources.

and 8.5% y-o-y in March. Core Personal Consumption Expenditures inflation stayed elevated at 6.3% y-o-y in April and 6.6% y-o-y in March. The US economic outlook remained robust with some signs of weakening during the review period. Gross domestic product (GDP) contracted an annualized 1.5% in the first quarter (Q1) of 2022, while monthly nonfarm payroll additions fell to 390,000 in May from 436,000 in April and 398,000 in March. The unemployment rate remained low at 3.6% each in March, April, and May, down from 3.8% in February. At its June Federal Open Market Committee meeting, the Federal Reserve revised the US GDP growth forecast for 2022 downward to 1.7% from its 2.8% forecast in March. The Federal Reserve also revised upward its Personal Consumption Expenditures inflation projection for 2022 to 5.2% from 4.3% in its March projections. High inflation combined with a weak GDP growth outlook led to an 8.1% loss in the S&P 500 stock index between 28 February and 9 June.

Amid high inflation, the Federal Reserve raised its 2022 forecast for the federal funds rate to 3.4% in June from 1.9% in March. Following the rate hike of 25 bps at its

14–15 March Federal Open Market Committee meeting, the Federal Reserve raised the federal funds target range by 50 bps at its 4–5 May meeting and 75 bps at its 14–15 June meeting on rising inflation. At its May meeting, the Federal Reserve also announced a "quantitative tightening" plan to reduce holdings of Treasury bonds, agency debt, and agency mortgage-backed debt in its System Open Market Account. Holdings will be reduced by up to USD47.5 billion per month for 3 months beginning in June, which would then accelerate to USD95 billion per month beginning in September. After the second and third rate hikes by the Federal Reserve in May and June, which brought the federal funds rate to 1.50%–1.75%, the federal funds rate futures index indicated more than an 80% probability of another 75 bps rate hike in July. The market expects the federal funds rate to exceed 3.25% by the end of 2022, as evidenced by a more than 95% probability (as of 16 June) of the rate to be higher than 3.25% at the end of 2022.[2]

In the euro area, GDP grew by 5.4% y-o-y in Q1 2022, up from the 4.7% y-o-y growth posted in the fourth quarter (Q4) of 2021, as the economy gradually reopened. However, inflation and economic uncertainty rose significantly due to the Russian invasion of Ukraine. Some signs of weakness were observed; for example, industrial production in March declined 0.8% y-o-y from 1.7% y-o-y growth in February, while inflation continued to rise as the flash estimate accelerated to 8.1% y-o-y in May from 7.4% y-o-y in both March and April. The European Central Bank (ECB) on 9 June affirmed the end of the Asset Purchase Programme starting 1 July. While it left its policy rates unchanged, the ECB announced that it would raise them by 25 bps in its July meeting, citing rising inflation.

The ECB also released updated economic forecasts in June from those made in March. GDP forecasts were revised downward for 2022 (2.8% from 3.7%) and 2023 (2.1% from 2.8%), while inflation was projected higher for 2022 (6.8% from 5.1%) and 2023 (3.5% from 2.1%).

Subsequently, on 15 June, the ECB held an emergency meeting to discuss its monetary normalization policy amid the market sell-off in some markets in the euro area. The ECB announced that it would provide flexibility in reinvesting redemptions under its Pandemic Emergency Purchase Program portfolio.

[2] CME Group. CME FedWatch Tool. https://www.cmegroup.com/trading/interest-rates/countdown-to-fomc.html.

Compared to the Federal Reserve and the ECB, the Bank of Japan (BOJ) maintained a relatively dovish stance amid a weaker domestic economic performance and modest inflation. Japan reported a GDP contraction of 0.5% y-o-y in Q1 2022 after an expansion of 4.0% y-o-y in Q4 2021. In April, the BOJ downgraded its GDP estimate and forecast for fiscal years 2021 and 2022 to 2.1% and 2.9%, respectively, from 2.8% and 3.8% in January. Inflation rose to 2.5% y-o-y in April from 1.2% y-o-y in March and 0.9% y-o-y in February. In April, the BOJ revised upward its inflation estimate and projection for fiscal years 2021 and 2022 to 0.1% and 1.9%, respectively, from 0.0% and 1.1% in January. At its June meeting, the BOJ left its policy rate unchanged at –0.1% and affirmed the continuation of 10-year Japanese Government Bond purchases to keep the target rate at 0.0%, as well as the purchase of exchange-traded funds and real estate investment trusts under annual caps of JPY12.0 trillion and JPY180.0 billion, respectively. Meanwhile, the BOJ indicated that it would gradually reduce holdings of commercial paper and corporate bonds to prepandemic levels of JPY2.0 trillion and JPY3.0 trillion, respectively, after having ended the purchases of these bonds in March.

While many regional central banks maintained easy monetary stances, some regional central banks started monetary tightening to contain inflationary pressure and prevent stress in financial markets amid aggressive US monetary policy tightening (**Table B**). During the review period from 28 February to 9 June, the 2-year and 10-year government bond yields in emerging East Asian economies collectively rose, largely tracking rising bond yields in the US and increasing inflationary pressure in the region. The Philippines posted the largest increase in 10-year government bond yields in the region at 140 bps, while its 2-year yield rose 112 bps, largely driven by the 25 bps rate hike by the Bangko Sentral ng Pilipinas on 19 May. The rate hike echoed sound economic growth of 8.3% y-o-y in Q1 2022 and concerns of persistent inflation, which rose to 5.4% y-o-y in May from 4.9% y-o-y in April and 4.0% y-o-y in March. On 23 June, the Bangko Sentral ng Pilipinas raised rates again by 25 bps. Bank Negara Malaysia announced a surprise rate hike of 25 bps during its 11 May monetary policy meeting, on the back of firm economic recovery and increased inflationary pressure. The Bank of Korea made two consecutive rate hikes of 25 bps each in April and May to curb rising inflation. Similarly, Singapore further tightened its

Table B: Changes in Monetary Stances in Major Advanced Economies and Emerging East Asia

Economy	Policy Rate 30-Jun-2021 (%)	Rate Change (%)												Policy Rate 9-Jun-2022 (%)	Change in Policy Rates (basis points)
		Jul-2021	Aug-2021	Sep-2021	Oct-2021	Nov-2021	Dec-2021	Jan-2022	Feb-2022	Mar-2022	Apr-2022	May-2022	Jun-2022		
United States	0.25									↑0.25		↑0.50		1.00	↑ 75
Euro Area	(0.50)													(0.50)	0
United Kingdom	0.10						↑0.15	↑0.25	↑0.25			↑0.25		1.00	↑ 90
Japan	(0.10)													(0.10)	0
China, People's Rep. of	2.95							↓0.10						2.85	↓ 10
Indonesia	3.50													3.50	0
Korea, Rep. of	0.50		↑0.25			↑0.25		↑0.25			↑0.25	↑0.25		1.75	↑ 125
Malaysia	1.75											↑0.25		2.00	↑ 25
Philippines	2.00											↑0.25		2.25	↑ 25
Singapore	–				↑			↑			↑			–	–
Thailand	0.50													0.50	0
Viet Nam	4.00													4.00	0

( ) = negative, – = not available.
Notes:
1. Data coverage is from 30 June 2021 to 9 June 2022.
2. For the People's Republic of China, data used in the chart are for the 1-year medium-term lending facility rate. While the 1-year benchmark lending rate is the official policy rate of the People's Bank of China, market players use the 1-year medium-term lending facility rate as a guide for the monetary policy direction of the People's Bank of China.
3. The up (down) arrow for Singapore signifies monetary policy tightening (loosening) by its central bank. The Monetary Authority of Singapore utilizes the exchange rate to guide its monetary policy.
Sources: Bloomberg LP and various central bank websites.

monetary policy on 14 April by recentering the Singapore dollar nominal effective exchange rate and adjusting the slope of appreciation on expected improvement in economic growth and rising inflation. Thailand also witnessed a strong rise in its 2-year yield of 113 bps, as inflation stood well above the Bank of Thailand's full-year target range of between 1.0% and 3.0% during the first 5 months of 2022.

Contrary to the tightening actions of some central banks in the region, the People's Bank of China reduced the reserve requirement ratio of financial institutions by 25 bps on 25 April and lowered the 5-year loan prime rate on mortgages by 15 bps on 19 May. With monetary easing measures, modest inflation of 2.1% y-o-y in April and May, as well as a weaker-than-expected economic outlook amid pandemic containment measures and lockdowns in several major cities, the PRC's bond yields posted marginal changes.

Continued inflationary pressure and monetary tightening by major advanced markets' and some regional central banks weighed on equity markets and weakened currencies in the region. During the review period, equity markets in emerging East Asia posted a weighted average loss of 4.6% (**Figure B**). Except for Indonesia, all regional markets recorded declines in equity markets,

with Viet Nam posting the largest loss of 12.2% amid cautious investor sentiment over increased margin calls for leveraged investors (**Figure C**). The PRC's equity market fell 6.5% on bearish sentiments due to a bleak outlook for economic recovery. Meanwhile, the Indonesian market gained 4.3%, benefiting from improved corporate and government revenues on rising commodity prices.

Figure C: Changes in Equity Indexes in Emerging East Asia

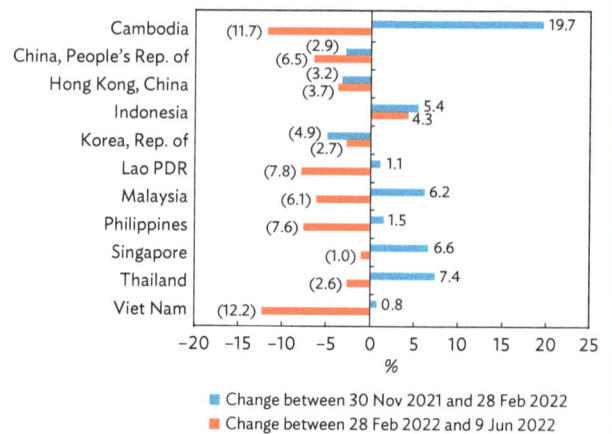

■ Change between 30 Nov 2021 and 28 Feb 2022
■ Change between 28 Feb 2022 and 9 Jun 2022

( ) = negative, Lao PDR = Lao People's Democratic Republic.
Source: *AsianBondsOnline* computations based on Bloomberg LP data.

Figure B: Equity Indexes in Emerging East Asia

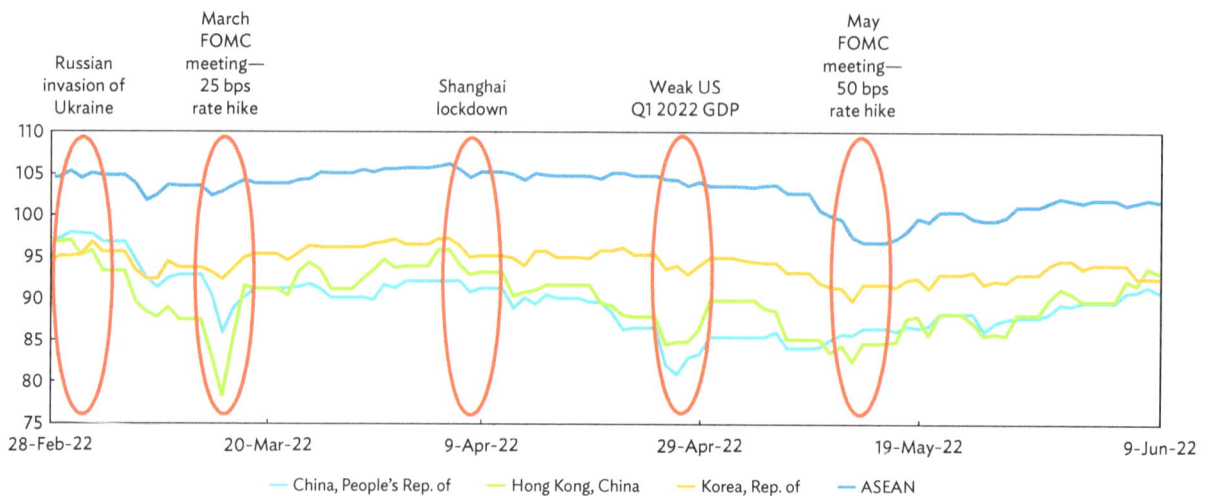

ASEAN = Association of Southeast Asian Nations, bps = basis points, FOMC = Federal Open Market Committee, GDP = gross national product, Q1 = first quarter, US = United States.
Notes:
1. 30 November 2021 = 100.
2. ASEAN comprises the markets of Cambodia, Indonesia, the Lao People's Democratic Republic, Malaysia, the Philippines, Singapore, Thailand, and Viet Nam.
3. Data as of 9 June 2022.
Source: *AsianBondsOnline* computations based on Bloomberg LP data.

Figure D: Changes in Emerging East Asian Currencies

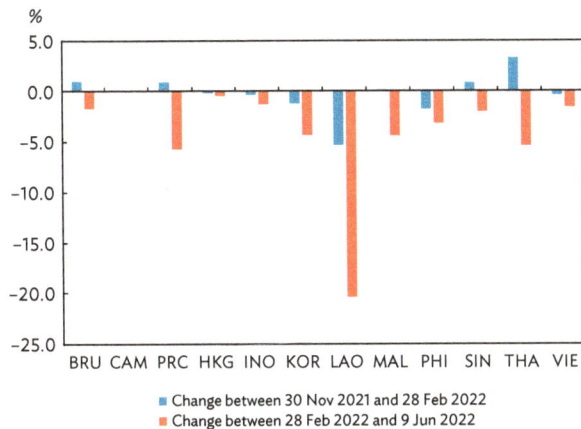

%

BRU = Brunei Darussalam; CAM = Cambodia; PRC = China, People's Rep. of;
HKG = Hong Kong, China; INO = Indonesia; KOR = Korea, Rep. of;
LAO = Lao People's Democratic Republic; MAL = Malaysia; PHI = Philippines;
SIN = Singapore; THA = Thailand; VIE = Viet Nam.
Note: A positive (negative) value for the FX rate indicates the appreciation
(depreciation) of the local currency against the United States dollar.
Source: *AsianBondsOnline* computations based on Bloomberg LP data.

Figure E: Changes in Credit Default Swap Spreads in Select Emerging East Asian Markets (senior 5-year)

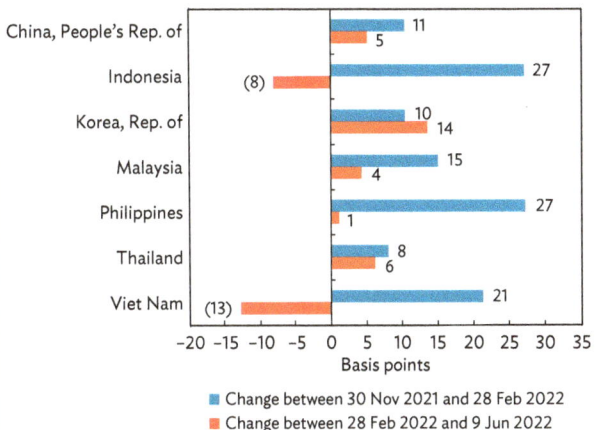

Basis points

■ Change between 30 Nov 2021 and 28 Feb 2022
■ Change between 28 Feb 2022 and 9 Jun 2022

( ) = negative.
Source: *AsianBondsOnline* computations based on Bloomberg LP data.

Figure F: Capital Flows into Equity Markets in Emerging East Asia

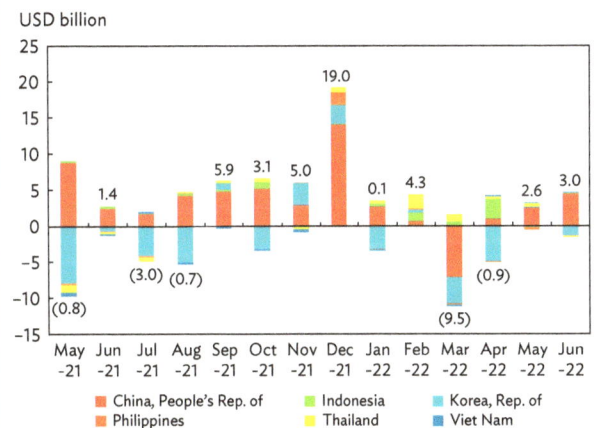

USD billion

■ China, People's Rep. of   ■ Indonesia   ■ Korea, Rep. of
■ Philippines   ■ Thailand   ■ Viet Nam

( ) = outflows, USD = United States dollar.
Notes:
1. Data coverage is from 1 May 2021 to 9 June 2022.
2. Figures refer to net inflows (net outflows) for each month.
Source: Institute of International Finance.

All emerging East Asian currencies depreciated against the US dollar amid continued monetary normalization by the Federal Reserve and increased uncertainty in regional economic recoveries (**Figure D**). Regional currencies posted a simple average depreciation of 3.2% and a GDP-weighted average depreciation of 5.1% during the review period. The Chinese yuan experienced the region's largest currency depreciation at 5.7% on a weakening economic outlook amid uncertainty related to pandemic containment measures. This was followed by the Thai baht, which fell 5.4% versus the US dollar after the current account deficit widened to USD3.4 billion in April, the largest amount in 9 years. Risk premiums in the region, proxied by credit default swap spreads, posted small and mixed movements, with a simple average hike of 1.4 bps and a GDP-weighted average increase of 4.7 bps during the review period (**Figure E**). While most markets witnessed widened risk premiums during the review period, Viet Nam's credit default swap spread narrowed by 13 bps on improved creditworthiness, as S&P Global Ratings upgraded Viet Nam's long-term foreign currency debt rating by one notch to BB+ on 26 May. Indonesia's credit default swap spread also declined 8 bps on improved government revenues due to rising commodity prices. The Indonesian finance ministry expects revenue collection to be 17.0% higher than the target set in the 2022 state budget.

Portoflio capital flows in emerging East Asia's equity markets weakened during the review period, tracking market-specific patterns. Aggregated equity market capital outflows of USD4.3 billion were recorded from 28 February to 9 June, largely concentrated in the Republic of Korea (USD9.8 billion) over concerns of slowing growth after the Bank of Korea revised downward its 2022 growth forecast to 2.7% in May from 3.0% in February (**Figure F**). Meanwhile, some

Association of Southeast Asian Nations (ASEAN) markets like Indonesia and Thailand witnessed portfolio inflows in their equity markets from March through May on sound economic performances.

Foreign portfolio outflows were also observed in emerging East Asia's bond markets in March and April (**Figure G**). The PRC bond market recorded net outflows of USD14.1 billion amid a weakened economic outlook. Major ASEAN markets such as Indonesia, Malaysia, the Philippines, and Thailand collectively witnessed net foreign selling of USD8.0 billion in their bond markets. The Republic of Korea received small net foreign bond inflows of USD0.3 billion following its series of policy rate hikes. In May, ASEAN bond markets recorded net bond outflows of USD1.2 billion, largely concentrated in Indonesia. The overall negative sentiments in the region's bond markets led to an overall decline in the share of foreign holdings from January to April (**Figure H**). The foreign holdings share in Indonesia fell to 17.0% in April from 19.0% in January, while in the Philippines

the foreign holdings share slipped from 1.8% to 1.1% during the same period. Nevertheless, bond markets in emerging East Asia demonstrated resilience to foreign sell-offs as domestic investors, particularly banks, continued to support local currency government bond markets (**Figure I**).

The risks to regional financial conditions are tilted toward the downside. Major risks include faster-than-expected monetary tightening in both the US and the region to contain persistent inflationary pressure; and heightened uncertainty in economic outlooks associated with rising commodity prices, a weaker-than-expected economic performance in the PRC, prolonged supply chain disruptions, and more-than-expected adverse spillovers from the Russian invasion of Ukraine. **Box 1** shows that Asian financial markets are significantly affected by US monetary policy news. On average, a 1 percentage point expected policy rate increase implied in the federal funds rate over the next 12 months is associated with regional currency depreciations of 0.7%, a 1.8% decline in major equity indexes, and a 7 bps increase in 10-year government bond yields on the day of a monetary policy announcement. Such impacts are statistically significant and persistent during the months after the announcement. As the Federal Reserve continues tightening its monetary policy, regional central banks need to monitor financial conditions closely to safeguard domestic financial stability.

Figure G: Foreign Capital Flows in Local Currency Bond Markets in Emerging East Asia

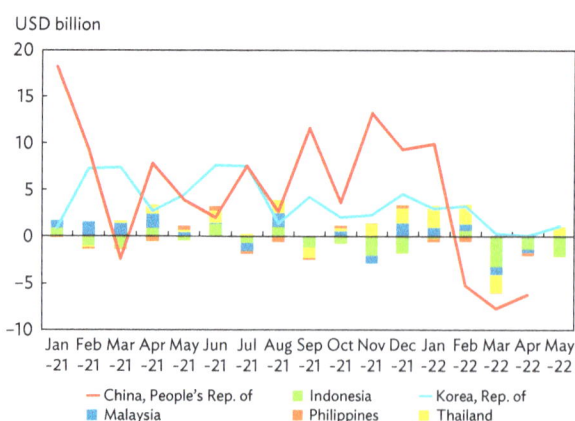

USD = United States dollar.
Notes:
1. The Republic of Korea and Thailand provided data on bond flows. For the People's Republic of China, Indonesia, Malaysia, and the Philippines, month-on-month changes in foreign holdings of local currency government bonds were used as a proxy for bond flows.
2. Data are as of 31 May 2022 except for the People's Republic of China (30 April 2022).
3. Figures were computed based on 31 May 2022 exchange rates and do not include currency effects.
Sources: People's Republic of China (Bloomberg LP); Indonesia (Directorate General of Budget Financing and Risk Management, Ministry of Finance); Republic of Korea (Financial Supervisory Service); Malaysia (Bank Negara Malaysia); Philippines (Bureau of the Treasury); and Thailand (Thai Bond Market Association).

Figure H: Foreign Holdings of Local Currency Government Bonds in Select Emerging East Asian Markets (% of total)

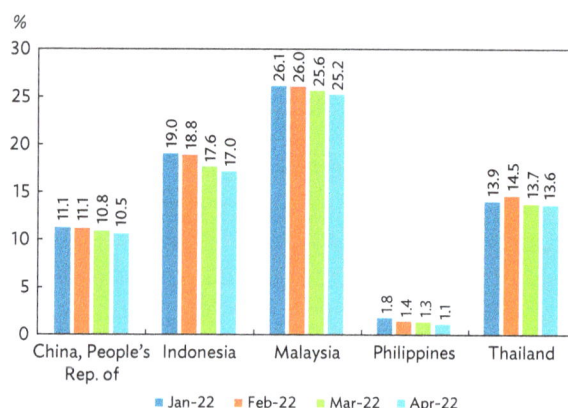

Sources: People's Republic of China (Bloomberg LP and CEIC Data Company); Indonesia (Directorate General of Budget Financing and Risk Management, Ministry of Finance); Malaysia (Bank Negara Malaysia); Philippines (Bureau of the Treasury); and Thailand (Bank of Thailand).

Figure I: Investor Profiles of Local Currency Government Bonds in Select Emerging East Asian Markets

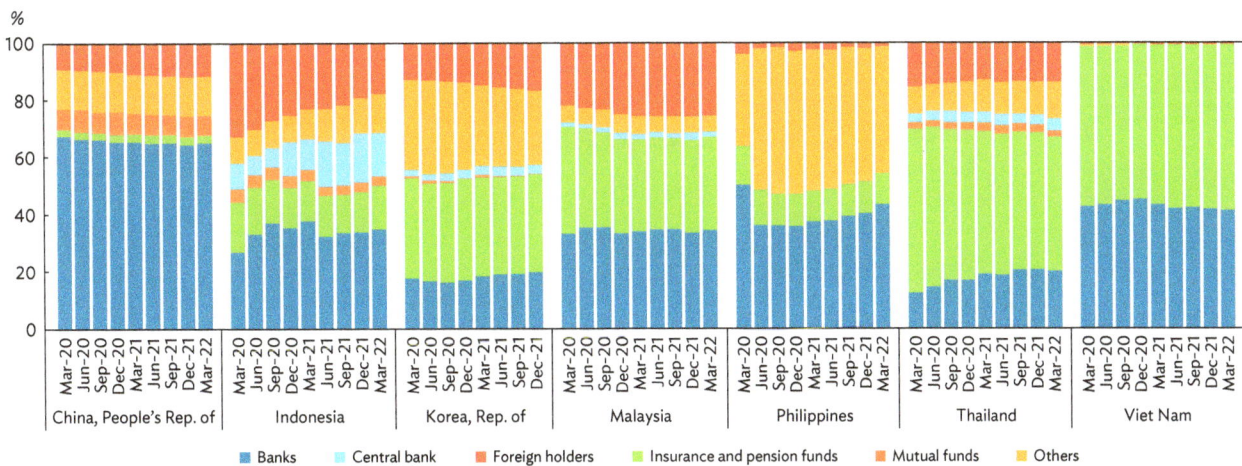

Notes:
1. Data for the Republic of Korea are up to December 2021.
2. "Others" include government institutions, individuals, securities companies, custodians, private corporations, and all other investors not elsewhere classified.
Source: *AsianBondsOnline* computations based on local market sources.

Meanwhile, several ASEAN central banks conducted asset purchase programs for the first time during the COVID-19 pandemic by buying domestic government bonds to facilitate market liquidity and foster low financing costs. **Box 2** examines the impact of these asset purchase programs on bond yield spreads in four ASEAN economies that implemented such operations—Indonesia, Malaysia, Thailand, and the Philippines—and finds that these programs contribute to a persistent decline in bond yield spreads, measured as the difference between 10-year government bond yields in these markets over that of US Treasuries. While these programs have so far shown to be effective in achieving their original objectives, regional central banks need to be cautious when they unwind asset holdings as they normalize monetary stances.

Box 1: United States Monetary Policy News and Financial Market Reactions in Developing Asia

With the importance of the United States (US) dollar in the global economy and close economic ties with much of the world, shifts in US monetary policy not only affect domestic financial conditions but also the financial conditions and investment sentiment in global economies and financial markets.[a] Prior to the 2007–2008 global financial crisis, the US Federal Reserve mainly adopted the federal funds rate as a conventional instrument to influence output, employment, inflation, and other macroeconomic variables. Then, on 25 November 2008, the Federal Reserve announced its first-ever program to purchase USD600 billion worth of obligations and securities to help improve financial conditions in financial markets (Federal Reserve 2008). Since then, the Federal Reserve has implemented asset purchase programs as an unconventional instrument to conduct monetary policy and guide market expectations.

The Federal Reserve's monetary policy decisions—whether through a conventional instrument like changes in the federal funds rate or an unconventional instrument like changes in the asset holdings of its System Open Market Account (SOMA)—have been found to significantly influence global financial conditions and generate strong reactions in emerging financial markets. For currencies, Albagli et al. (2019) show that—among emerging markets like India, Indonesia, the Republic of Korea, and Thailand—US monetary tightening through rate hikes led to greater currency depreciation after the 2007–2008 global financial crisis compared to before the crisis. Mueller, Tahbaz-Salehi, and Vedolin (2017) use changes in the federal funds rate and eurodollar futures as impacts of monetary easing measures to show that G10 currencies generally appreciate against the US dollar following Federal Open Market Committee (FOMC) meeting announcements of policy easing.[b] In equity and bond markets, Neely (2015) illustrates that international long-term bond yields decline after Federal Reserve announcements of large-scale asset purchases. Using changes in the 2-year US Treasury yield on announcement dates, Bowman, Londono, and Sapriza (2015) find that, in emerging markets globally, stock prices and exchange rates react positively and bond yields react negatively to announcements of asset purchase programs. Aizenman, Binici, and Hutchison (2016) find that news of quantitative tightening in 2013 led to negative reactions in emerging market stock indices and exchange rates versus the US dollar, but such news had an insignificant effect on emerging market sovereign spreads.

For portfolio flows, Banegas, Montes-Rojas, and Siga (2022) associate quantitative tightening with portfolio outflows from both equity and bond markets in the US. Anaya, Hachula, and Offermanns (2017) show that expansionary monetary shocks significantly increased portfolio outflows from the US, with corresponding portfolio inflows to emerging markets in Latin America, Asia, and Europe.

This study empirically estimates developing Asian financial markets' reactions to both conventional and unconventional US monetary policy shocks. It contributes to existing literature with new and comprehensive evidence on the magnitude and speed of market reactions across four indicators: (i) exchange rate changes, (ii) equity market performances, (iii) bond yields, and (iv) foreign portfolio flows. This paper also sheds new light on how conventional and unconventional US monetary policy shocks may lead to different financial market reactions in developing Asia. The findings provide useful policy implications for developing Asian central banks on how strong and how fast different financial assets react to different types of US monetary policy changes. Such knowledge is particularly important to safeguard regional financial stability as the Federal Reserve rapidly tightens monetary policy in 2022 to curb inflation, while many central banks in emerging East Asia maintain their relatively easy monetary stances.

To capture conventional US monetary policy shocks, the literature widely adopts the change in the federal funds rate futures on the day of a policy announcement as the measure of a conventional monetary policy shock (see, for example, Kuttner 2001, Gertler and Karadi 2015, Dahlhaus and Vasishtha 2020). This paper follows Dahlhaus and Vasishtha (2020) to use the daily change in 12-month federal funds rate futures on the day of an FOMC meeting announcement to account for conventional monetary policy shocks. In empirical models, the study follows Gertler and Karadi (2015) to use cumulative daily changes on policy announcement days over a 6-month horizon to capture forward guidance after US policy announcements.

To gauge unconventional monetary policy shocks, the literature either uses dummies for announcement dates to reflect asset purchase decisions or employs changes in SOMA holdings to capture the magnitude of asset purchases. Fratzscher, Lo Duca, and Straub (2018) argue that the latter measurement is more informative when examining market

---

[a] This box was written by Resi Ong Olivares (consultant) and Shu Tian (senior economist) in the Economic Research and Regional Cooperation Department of the Asian Development Bank.

[b] The G10 refer to the following: Australia, Canada, the European Union, Japan, New Zealand, Norway, Sweden, Switzerland, the United Kingdom, and the US.

continued on next page

Box 1 *continued*

reactions. This study thus follows the spirit of Banegas, Montes-Rojas, and Siga (2022) to use log differences in the Federal Reserve's SOMA holdings over the 6 months following an FOMC meeting announcement.

This study then examines how US monetary policy changes influenced exchange rates, portfolio flows, equity indexes, and 10-year government bond yields from January 2004 to November 2021 in 12 developing Asia economies: Bangladesh, the People's Republic of China, India, Indonesia, the Republic of Korea, Malaysia, Pakistan, the Philippines, Singapore, Sri Lanka, Thailand, and Viet Nam.[c]

To gauge the direction and magnitude of financial market reactions, the study adopts panel regression to a month-economy panel by regressing changes in the financial market indicators on conventional and unconventional US monetary policy shocks, after controlling for current levels of the federal funds rate, US inflation, the US volatility index, and foreign exchange reserves and inflation in developing Asian markets, as well as time and market fixed effects. To understand the timing of transmission of US monetary policy shocks to developing Asian financial markets, this study follows Dahlhaus and Vasishtha (2020) to construct a common factor for each financial market indicator across developing Asia, using a principal-component method, and to visualize how conventional and unconventional US monetary policy shocks trigger financial market reactions in developing Asia, using impulse-response functions estimated from vector autoregression.

Empirical evidence from the panel regression shows that conventional US monetary tightening, in the form of a rate hike, leads to significant currency depreciation, negative equity market returns, and increased 10-year government bond yields in developing Asian markets on the announcement day (**Figure B1.1**). Specifically, a 1 percentage point increase in the federal funds rate over the next 6 months, implied in the 12-month futures contracts, is associated with an average currency depreciation of 0.73%, a 1.84% loss in equity indexes, and around a 7 basis points (bps) increase in 10-year government bond yields on the day of announcement in developing Asia. Meanwhile, unconventional monetary policy instruments, as proxied by changes in SOMA account holdings, are only significantly associated with a change in the exchange rate on the announcement day. On average, a 1 percentage point increase in SOMA holdings (quantitative easing) over

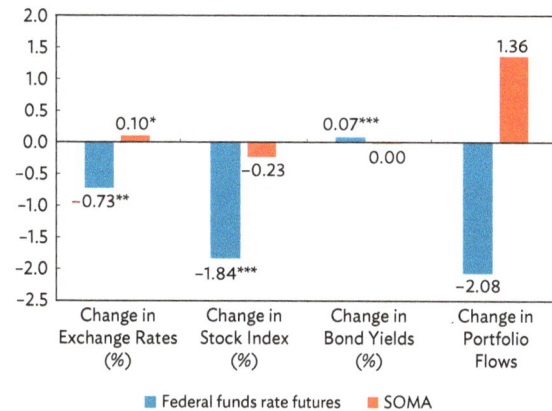

Figure B1.1: Impact of United States Monetary Policy News on Developing Asian Financial Markets

Notes: The blue bars represent the reactions of developing Asian financial markets to a 1 percentage point increase over 6 months after the announcement, implied in the 12-month federal funds rate futures, while the orange bars represent the impact of a 1 percentage point increase in securities holdings in the System Open Market Account (SOMA) on developing Asian financial markets. The financial indicators examined include percentage change in exchange rate against the United States dollar (USD), portfolio flows, and equity index, and the yield change on 10-year government bonds. Sample developing Asian markets comprise Bangladesh, the People's Republic of China, India, Indonesia, the Republic of Korea, Malaysia, Pakistan, the Philippines, Singapore, Sri Lanka, Thailand, and Viet Nam.
***, **, and * denote significance levels of 0.01, 0.05, and 0.10, respectively.
Source: Authors' calculations based on data from Bloomberg, CEIC, and the Institute of International Finance Capital Flows Database.

the 6 months after the FOMC meeting announcement is associated with a 0.1% currency appreciation on the day of announcement. Neither type of monetary policy shock is linked to significant reactions in capital flows to developing Asia on the announcement day.

Using impulse-response functions estimated from vector autoregression, it is observed that after an FOMC announcement of conventional US monetary policy tightening in the form of a rate hike, developing Asian economies witness significant currency depreciation during the next 1–6 months, an immediate and significant negative reaction in equity markets in current month and the next month that is still observable after 3–4 months, and an increase in 10-year government bond yields over the next 3–6 months (**Figure B1.2**). Moreover, unconventional US monetary policy instruments, in the form of quantitative easing or an increase in SOMA holdings, trigger currency appreciation in the first month after the announcement and a decrease in bond yields 1–3 months after the announcement.

---

[c] Some markets do not have all four indicators due to data availability. Portfolio flow data are not available for Singapore, bond yield data are not available for Pakistan, while portfolio flow and bond yield data are not available for Bangladesh.

continued on next page

Box 1   *continued*

Figure B1.2: Responses of Exchange Rates, Portfolio Flows, Stock Returns, and Bond Yields in Developing Asia to a Standard Deviation Shock to the Federal Funds Futures Rate and System Open Market Account Holdings

a. Exchange Rates

Response of Exchange Rate to Federal Funds Rate Futures

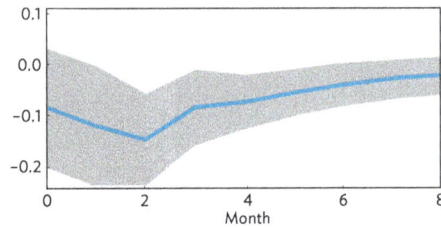

Response of Exchange Rate to SOMA

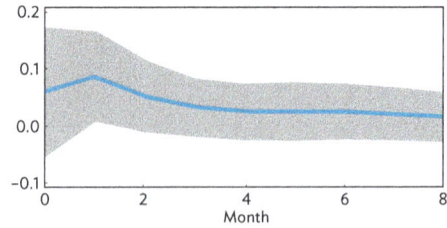

b. Capital Flows

Response of Portfolio Flows to Federal Funds Rate Futures

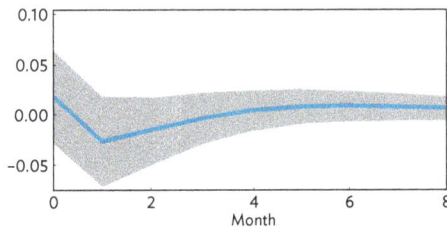

Response of Portfolio Flows to SOMA

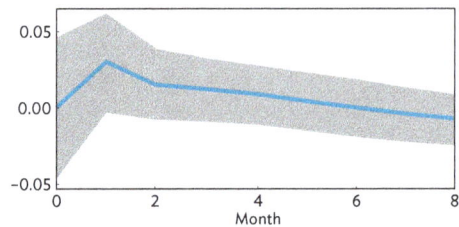

c. Stocks Index

Response of Stock Returns to Federal Funds Rate Futures

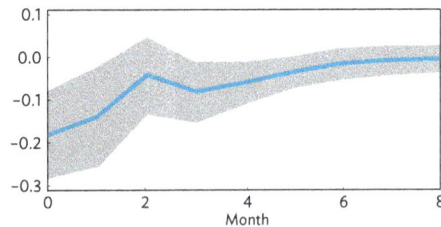

Response of Stock Returns to SOMA

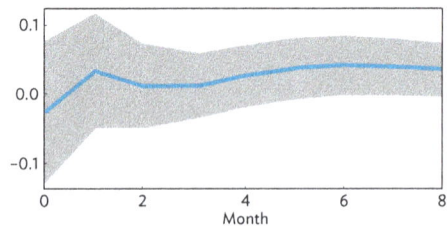

d. Bond Yields

Response of Bond Yields to Federal Funds Rate Futures

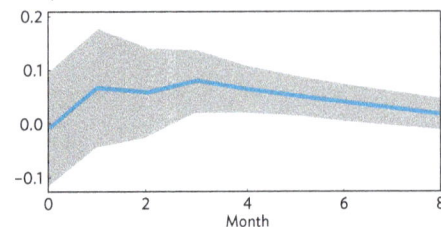

Response of Bond Yields to SOMA

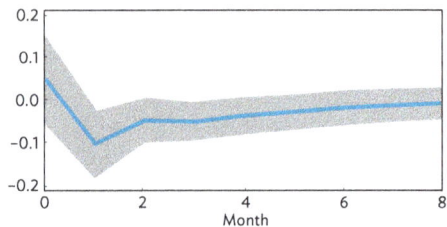

95% CI   Orthogonalized IRF

CI = confidence interval, irf = impulse-response functions.
Notes: For each panel, the left-hand side depicts the impact in developing Asia of a one standard deviation change in 12-month federal funds rate futures (cumulative for 6 months), and the right-hand side depicts a one standard deviation change in the log difference of securities holdings in the System Open Market Account (SOMA) over the 6 months after a policy announcement. Developing Asia comprises Bangladesh, the People's Republic of China, India, Indonesia, the Republic of Korea, Malaysia, Pakistan, the Philippines, Singapore, Sri Lanka, Thailand, and Viet Nam.
Source: Authors' calculations based on data from Bloomberg, CEIC, and the Institute of International Finance Capital Flows Database.

continued on next page

Box 1   *continued*

Overall, it seems that currency, equity, and bond markets in developing Asia have robust and significant reactions to conventional US monetary policy instruments relative to unconventional instruments. But both types of monetary policy tightening weaken financial conditions in developing Asia. In March, the Federal Reserve initiated a new round of monetary tightening with a 25 bps hike, which was followed by rate hikes of 50 bps in May and 75 bps in June, and is widely expected to be followed by another 75 bps rate hike in July. Asian financial conditions have weakened significantly since March. At its May FOMC meeting, the Federal Reserve announced it would begin unwinding its SOMA holdings in June. Therefore, it is important for developing Asian central banks to closely monitor changes in financial conditions in the region and make necessary policy adjustments to safeguard financial stability.

References

Albagli, Elias, Luis Ceballos, Sebastian Claro, and Damian Romero. 2019. "Channels of US Monetary Policy Spillovers to International Bond Markets." *Journal of Financial Economics* 134 (2): 447–73.

Ahmed, Shaghil, and Andrei Zlate. 2014. "Capital Flows to Emerging Market Economies: A Brave New World?" *Journal of International Money Finance* 48 (Part B): 221–48.

Aizenman, Joshua, Mahir Binici, and Michael M. Hutchison. 2016. "The Transmission of Federal Reserve Tapering News to Emerging Financial Markets." *International Journal of Central Banks* 12 (2016): 317–56.

Anaya, Pablo, Michael Hachula, and Christian J. Offermanns. 2017. "Spillovers of US Unconventional Monetary Policy to Emerging Markets: The Role of Capital Flows." *Journal of International Money and Finance* 73 (2017): 275–95.

Banegas, Ayelen, Gabriel Montes-Rojas, and Lucas Siga. 2022. "The Effects of US Monetary Policy Shocks on Mutual Fund Investing." *Journal of International Money and Finance* 102595.

Bowman, David, Juan M. Londono, and Horacio Sapriza. 2015. "US Unconventional Monetary Policy and Transmission to Emerging Market Economies." *Journal of International Money and Finance* 55 (C): 27–59.

Bräuning, Falk, and Victoria Ivashina. 2020. "US Monetary Policy and Emerging Market Credit Cycles." *Journal of Monetary Economics* 112 (2020): 57–76.

Dahlhaus, Tatjana, and Garima Vasishtha. 2020. "Monetary Policy News in the US: Effects on Emerging Market Capital Flows." *Journal of International Money and Finance* 109 (2020): 102251.

Fratzscher, Marcel, Marco Lo Duca, and Roland Straub. 2018. "On the International Spillovers of US Quantitative Easing." *The Economic Journal* 128 (608): 330–77.

Gertler, Mark, and Peter Karadi. 2015. "Monetary Policy Surprises, Credit Costs, and Economic Activity." *American Economic Journal: Macroeconomics* 7 (1): 44–76.

Kuttner, Kenneth N. 2001. "Monetary Policy Surprises and Interest Rates: Evidence from the Fed Funds Futures Market." *Journal of Monetary Economics* 47 (3): 523–44.

Mueller, Philippe, Alireza Tahbaz-Salehi, and Andrea Vedolin. 2017. "Exchange Rates and Monetary Policy Uncertainty." *The Journal of Finance* 72 (3): 1213–52.

Neely, Christopher. 2015. "Unconventional Monetary Policy Had Large International Effects." *Journal of Banking and Finance* 52 (C): 101–11.

United States Federal Reserve. 2008. "Federal Reserve Announces It Will Initiate a Program to Purchase the Direct Obligations of Housing-Related Government-Sponsored Enterprises and Mortgage-Backed Securities Backed by Fannie Mae, Freddie Mac, and Ginnie Mae." Press Release. 25 November.

Box 2: Sovereign Bond Yield Spreads and Pandemic-Related Asset Purchase Programs in Four ASEAN Economies

Central banks in some emerging market economies engaged in quantitative easing during the coronavirus disease (COVID-19) pandemic by buying domestic government bonds.[a] These asset purchase programs (APPs) aimed at reducing bond yields, thereby supporting the stability of emerging economy financial markets (International Monetary Fund 2020, World Bank 2021, Asian Development Bank 2021). This box considers the impact of central bank APPs on bond spreads in the four member economies of the Association of Southeast Asian Nations (ASEAN) that implemented such operations: Indonesia, Malaysia, Thailand, and the Philippines.

Drawing on a new paper by Beirne and Sugandi (Forthcoming), the effectiveness of the monetary policy transmission mechanism of the APPs to bond spreads is examined, both in terms of magnitude and duration over a time horizon. A counterfactual assessment is also conducted to assess the additionality of the APPs. Central bank claims to the central government are used as a proxy indicator of APPs, given that actual purchase data are not publicly available. These claims increased sharply relative to prepandemic levels, and the growth rate of the claims is assumed to be an adequate

approximation for actual asset purchases. This approach is superior to using a dummy variable for APPs, which is also consistent with our findings but fails to capture the intensity of quantitative easing purchases. The empirical work shows that APPs had a statistically significant dampening effect on bond yield spreads during the COVID-19 pandemic. To quantify the additionality of an APP in terms of transmission to bond spreads (i.e., 10-year government bond yields relative to those of United States Treasuries), the actual bond spreads were compared to spreads that would have prevailed under a scenario without an APP. The "no APP" scenario assumes a trajectory of bond spreads based on prepandemic fundamentals (**Figure B2.1**).

We find that APPs had varying degrees of bond market additionality across the four ASEAN economies that comprise our sample. For Thailand and the Philippines, we observe that actual spreads would have been higher without the APPs, while this effect takes time to materialize. The evidence supporting APP effectiveness on this basis is less prevalent in the cases of Indonesia and Malaysia. To examine the impact more rigorously, we estimate a series of country-specific vector autoregression regression models from 7 January 2010

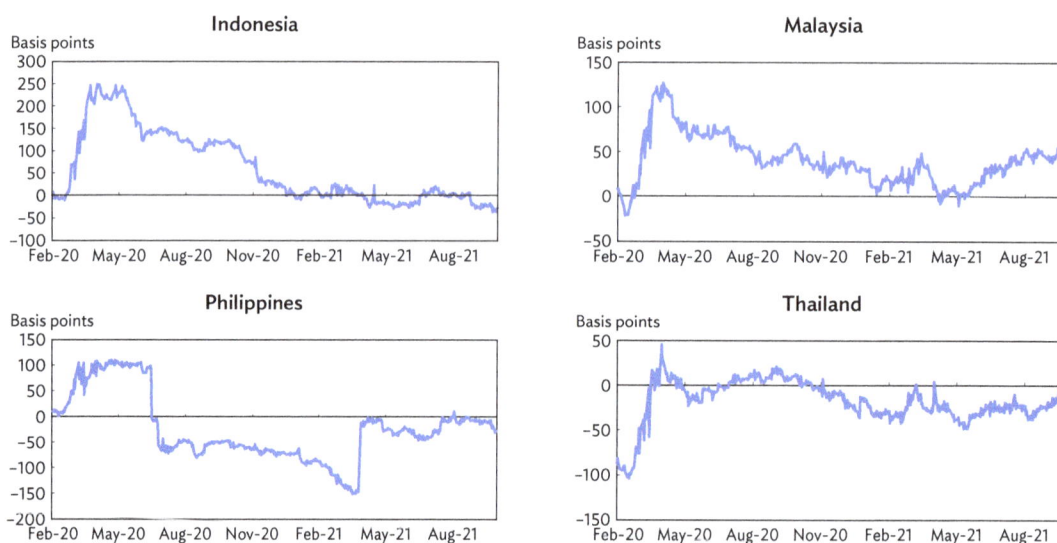

Figure B2.1: Government Bond Yield Spread Gaps

Note: Reported is the difference between the actual bond spread and the bond spread implied by prepandemic fundamentals over the period 1 January 2010 to 28 February 2020. Where the actual spread is lower, denoted in the chart as a negative gap, then the inference is that the asset purchase program was effective in compressing the bond spread.
Source: Authors' calculations based on Beirne and Sugandi (Forthcoming).

---

[a] This box was written by John Beirne (vice-chair of research and senior research fellow) and Eric Sugandi (project consultant) of the Asian Development Bank Institute.

continued on next page

Box 2   *continued*

to 1 September 2021. The responses of bond spreads, as well as exchange rates, to shocks emanating from the APPs are shown in **Figures B2.2** and **B2.3**, respectively.

APP shocks lead to compressions in bond spreads in all four ASEAN economies, although we fail to find a statistically significant result at the 95% confidence level in the case of

Figure B2.2: Impulse Responses of Government Bond Spreads to Asset Purchase Program Shocks

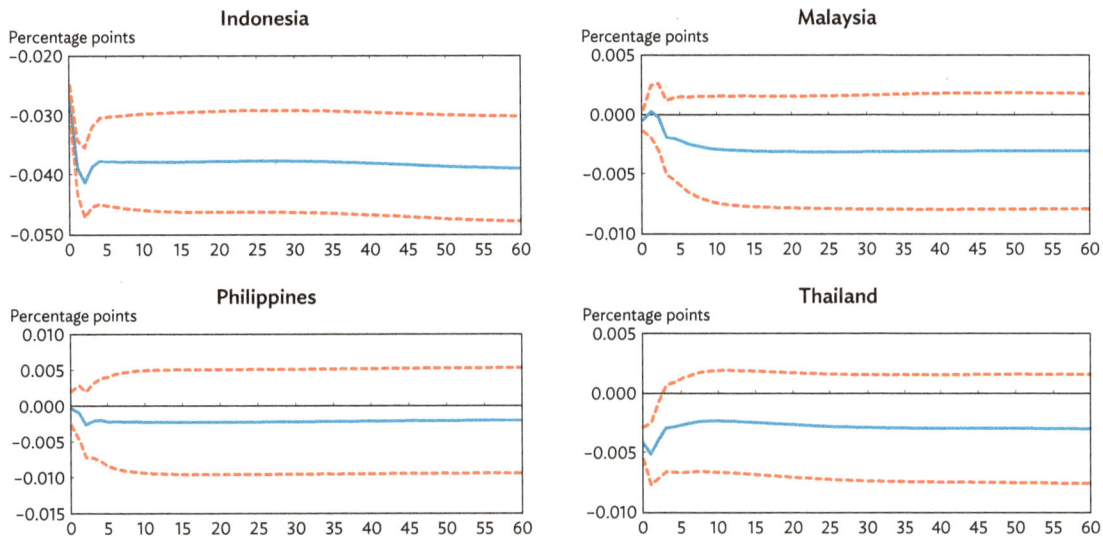

Note: Reported are the impulse-response functions based on a one standard deviation shock imposed on the APP. The dotted lines represent 95% confidence intervals. The vertical axis represents percentage points, while the horizontal axis refers to the number of days.
Source: Authors' calculations based on Beirne and Sugandi (Forthcoming).

Figure B2.3: Impulse Responses of Exchange Rates to Asset Purchase Program Shocks

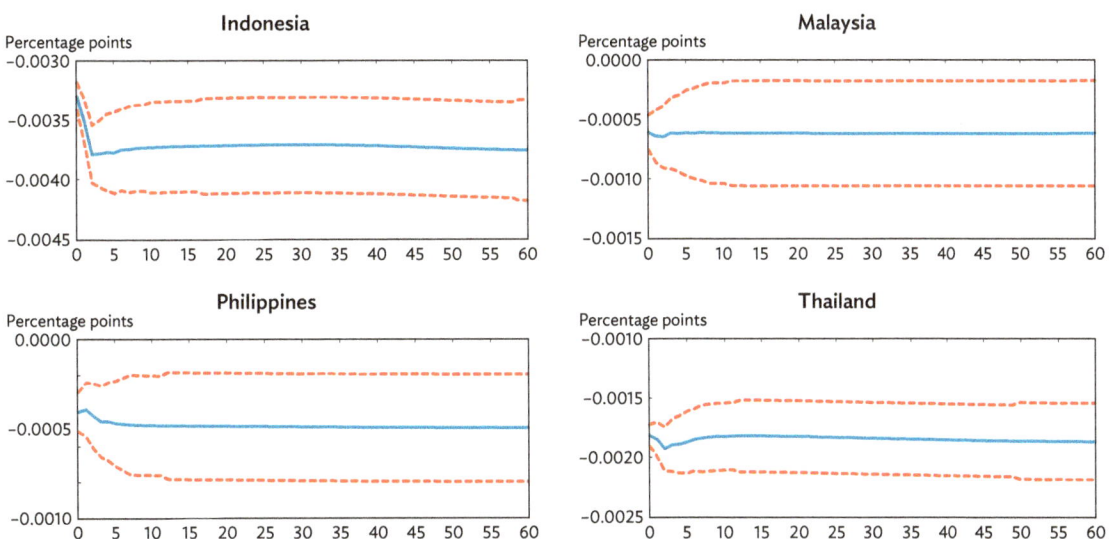

Note: Reported are the impulse-response functions based on a one standard deviation shock imposed on the APP. The dotted lines represent 95% confidence intervals. The vertical axis represents percentage points, while the horizontal axis refers to the number of days.
Source: Authors' calculations based on Beirne and Sugandi (Forthcoming).

continued on next page

Box 2 *continued*

the Philippines. The magnitude of the bond spread response and its persistence, as regards statistical significance, is most notable for Indonesia. On the other hand, the bond spread reactions for Malaysia and Thailand remain significant only in the immediate period following the shock. In the case of exchange rate reactions to APP shocks, statistically significant effects are found across all four ASEAN economies. As in the case of bond spreads, the highest magnitude of exchange rate depreciation occurs in Indonesia. The size of the depreciation is somewhat lower for Thailand, followed by Malaysia and the Philippines.

Improved institutional development and central bank credibility in the four ASEAN economies in our sample, particularly since the global financial crisis, are important factors underpinning the effectiveness of the APPs. Ample liquidity and higher levels of financial development in the period since the global financial crisis have also contributed to the improved functioning of financial markets in these four ASEAN economies, thereby supporting monetary policy transmission. Overall, the evidence suggests that bond spread compressions due to central bank APPs are persistent, while significant stabilizing effects are found on exchange rates. Further analysis by Beirne and Sugandi (Forthcoming) shows that the APPs also helped to temper capital flow volatility during the COVID-19 pandemic, while no significant effect

was found on inflation expectations. This latter point is particularly important from a monetary policy perspective. The quantitative easing measures were effective in their objective, to varying degrees, of relieving pressure on long-term bond yields and supporting stability in asset markets, while also not aggravating the medium-term inflation outlook.

References

Asian Development Bank. 2021. *Asia Bond Monitor, September 2021*. Manila. https://www.adb.org/publications/asia-bond-monitor-september-2021.

Beirne, John, and Eric Alexander Sugandi. Forthcoming. "Central Bank Asset Purchase Programs in Emerging Market Economies." ADBI Working Paper Series.

International Monetary Fund. 2020. *Global Financial Stability Report, October 2020: Bridge to Recovery*. Washington, DC. https://www.imf.org/en/Publications/GFSR/Issues/2020/10/13/global-financial-stability-report-october-2020.

World Bank. 2021. *Global Economic Prospects January 2021*. Washington, DC. http://hdl.handle.net/10986/34710.

Bond Market Developments in the First Quarter of 2022

Size and Composition

Emerging East Asia's bond market continued to expand in the first quarter of the year, reaching a size of USD23.5 trillion at the end of March.

In the first quarter (Q1) of 2022, the local currency bond (LCY) market in emerging East Asia expanded 3.1% quarter-on-quarter (q-o-q) to reach a size of USD23.5 trillion at the end of March.[3] The market's aggregate growth eased from 3.6% q-o-q in the fourth quarter (Q4) of 2021, driven primarily by slower growth in the government bond segment as authorities eased debt issuance to balance economic recovery efforts with fiscal sustainability. Expansion in the region's corporate bond market accelerated in Q1 2022 from Q4 2021, as corporates locked in prevailing interest rates in anticipation of higher borrowing costs in the future as central banks tighten their monetary policies to slow inflationary momentum.

Five of the region's nine markets experienced slower q-o-q growth in Q1 2022 than in the previous quarter (**Figure 1a**). Nonetheless, all nine LCY bond markets in emerging East Asia recorded positive q-o-q growth rates in Q1 2022. The markets of the Philippines and the People's Republic of China (PRC) posted the fastest q-o-q expansion, while the markets of Malaysia and Hong Kong, China exhibited the slowest q-o-q growth during the review period.

On an annual basis, overall growth in emerging East Asia's LCY bond market rose to 13.8% year-on-year (y-o-y) in Q1 2022 from 12.8% y-o-y in the previous quarter. All nine markets showed positive y-o-y growth in Q1 2022, with four of the nine markets posting faster y-o-y growth rates in Q1 2022 than in the prior quarter (**Figure 1b**). The LCY bond markets in Viet Nam and Singapore recorded the region's fastest y-o-y growth rates, while the markets of Malaysia and Hong Kong, China showed the weakest expansions in Q1 2022.

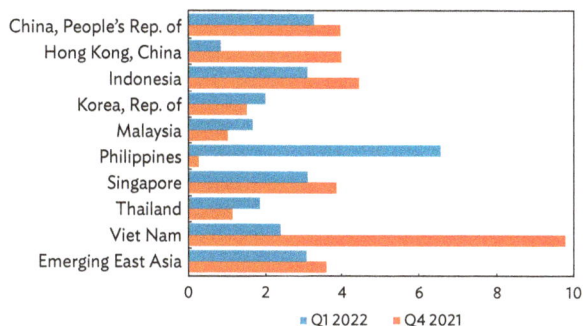

Figure 1a: Growth of Local Currency Bond Markets in the Fourth Quarter of 2021 and First Quarter of 2022 (q-o-q, %)

q-o-q = quarter-on-quarter, Q1 = first quarter, Q4 = fourth quarter.
Notes:
1. For Singapore, corporate bonds outstanding are based on *AsianBondsOnline* estimates.
2. Growth rates are calculated from local currency base and do not include currency effects.
3. Emerging East Asia growth figures are based on 31 March 2022 currency exchange rates and do not include currency effects.
Sources: People's Republic of China (CEIC Data Company); Hong Kong, China (Hong Kong Monetary Authority); Indonesia (Bank Indonesia; Directorate General of Budget Financing and Risk Management, Ministry of Finance; and Indonesia Stock Exchange); Republic of Korea (KG Zeroin Corporation and The Bank of Korea); Malaysia (Bank Negara Malaysia); Philippines (Bureau of the Treasury and Bloomberg LP); Singapore (Monetary Authority of Singapore, Singapore Government Securities, and Bloomberg LP); Thailand (Bank of Thailand); and Viet Nam (Bloomberg LP and Vietnam Bond Market Association).

The PRC's LCY bond market remained the largest in emerging East Asia. At the end of March, the PRC's outstanding bond stock reached a size of USD18.8 trillion, accounting for almost 79.9% of the region's total. Overall growth moderated to 3.3% q-o-q in Q1 2022 from 3.9% q-o-q in Q4 2021, as a slowdown in government debt growth outpaced accelerated growth in the corporate bond segment. Growth in government bonds fell to 2.7% q-o-q in Q1 2022 from 4.5% q-o-q in the previous quarter, due primarily to a contraction in Treasury bonds and other government bonds. Meanwhile, policy bank bonds and local government bonds posted robust growth, as the government continued its efforts to prop up the economy amid the spread of the Omicron variant. Growth in the corporate bond segment picked up, rising to 4.2% q-o-q in Q1 2022 from 2.9% q-o-q

---

[3] Emerging East Asia comprises the People's Republic of China; Hong Kong, China; Indonesia; the Republic of Korea; Malaysia; the Philippines; Singapore; Thailand; and Viet Nam.

Figure 1b: Growth of Local Currency Bond Markets in the Fourth Quarter of 2021 and First Quarter of 2022 (y-o-y, %)

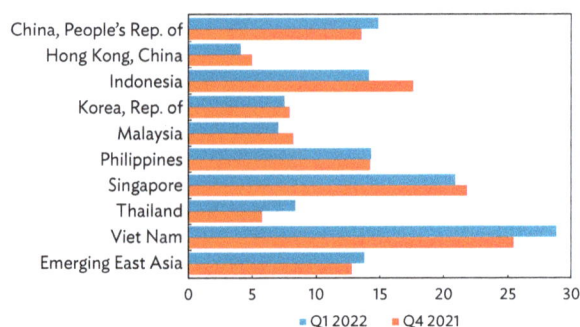

Q1 = first quarter, Q4 = fourth quarter, y-o-y = year-on-year.
Notes:
1. For Singapore, corporate bonds outstanding are based on *AsianBondsOnline* estimates.
2. Growth rates are calculated from local currency base and do not include currency effects.
3. Emerging East Asia growth figures are based on 31 March 2022 currency exchange rates and do not include currency effects.
Sources: People's Republic of China (CEIC Data Company); Hong Kong, China (Hong Kong Monetary Authority); Indonesia (Bank Indonesia; Directorate General of Budget Financing and Risk Management, Ministry of Finance; and Indonesia Stock Exchange); Republic of Korea (KG Zeroin Corporation and The Bank of Korea); Malaysia (Bank Negara Malaysia); Philippines (Bureau of the Treasury and Bloomberg LP); Singapore (Monetary Authority of Singapore, Singapore Government Securities, and Bloomberg LP); Thailand (Bank of Thailand); and Viet Nam (Bloomberg LP and Vietnam Bond Market Association).

in the prior quarter. On a y-o-y basis, the PRC's LCY bond market expanded 14.9% in Q1 2022, up from 13.6% in Q4 2021.

With an outstanding LCY bond stock amounting to USD2.4 trillion at the end of March, the Republic of Korea remained home to the region's second-largest LCY bond market. Its share of the regional bond total was little changed from 10.3% in Q4 2021 to 10.2% in Q1 2022. Overall growth picked up, rising to 2.0% q-o-q in Q1 2022 from 1.5% in Q4 2021, largely driven by faster growth in the government bond segment. Robust growth in central government bonds drove much of the expansion in the government bond segment, as the stock of central bank bonds and other government bonds contracted during the review period. Growth in central government bonds jumped to 4.8% q-o-q in Q1 2021 from 1.4% q-o-q in the previous quarter, as the government frontloaded its borrowing in line with its usual policy and to support economic recovery. Meanwhile, growth in outstanding corporate bonds dropped to 1.0% q-o-q in Q1 2022 from 2.4% q-o-q in Q4 2021 amid rising borrowing costs.

As of May, the Bank of Korea had raised its policy rates aggressively, with five rate hikes since August 2021. On a y-o-y basis, the Republic of Korea's LCY bond market grew 7.5% in Q1 2022, down from 7.9% in the previous quarter.

Hong Kong, China's LCY bond stock reached USD325.1 billion at the end of March on marginal growth of 0.8% q-o-q, the weakest growth among emerging East Asian markets in Q1 2022. The slower pace of overall growth in Q1 2022 was due to weaker growth of the government bond segment compared to the prior quarter, combined with a contraction of the corporate bond segment. The stock of Exchange Fund Bills expanded 3.6% q-o-q in Q1 2022 versus 5.7% q-o-q in Q4 2021, while outstanding Exchange Fund Notes posted zero growth in Q1 2022. The stock of Hong Kong Special Administrative Region bonds rose 1.9% q-o-q in Q1 2022, down from 2.7% q-o-q in the previous quarter. Corporate bonds outstanding contracted 1.9% q-o-q in Q1 2022, reversing the 2.7% q-o-q gain in the previous quarter, due primarily to a relatively high volume of maturities, which outpaced the growth in issuance. On a y-o-y basis, Hong Kong, China's LCY bond market expanded 4.1% in Q1 2022, down from 5.0% in Q4 2021.

The total amount of outstanding LCY bonds among members of the Association of Southeast Asian Nations (ASEAN) was generally stable between Q4 2021 and Q1 2022, amounting to USD2.0 trillion at the end of March.[4] The ASEAN member economies' share of the region's total also remained unchanged from Q4 2021 to Q1 2022 at 8.6%. Members' aggregate bond stock expanded 2.8% q-o-q in Q1 2022, up from 2.6% q-o-q in Q4 2021. On an annual basis, the aggregate bond stock grew 13.3% y-o-y in Q1 2021, down from 13.6% y-o-y in the previous quarter. At the end of March, ASEAN member economies' total government bond stock reached USD1.5 trillion, accounting for 73.0% of the ASEAN total bond market. Aggregate corporate bonds outstanding amounted to USD0.5 trillion, accounting for the remaining 27.0% share. The LCY bond markets in Singapore, Thailand, and Malaysia remained the largest among ASEAN members at the end of March.

Singapore's outstanding stock of LCY bonds amounted to USD461.5 billion at the end of March. Overall growth eased to 3.1% q-o-q in Q1 2022 from 3.8% q-o-q in

---

[4] LCY bond statistics for ASEAN include the markets of Indonesia, Malaysia, the Philippines, Singapore, Thailand, and Viet Nam.

the preceding quarter. Growth in the government bond segment rose to 4.5% q-o-q in Q1 2022 from 4.1% q-o-q in Q4 2021. The robust growth in outstanding government bonds in Q1 2022 was supported by 3.5% q-o-q growth in Singapore Government Securities and a 5.6% q-o-q rise in Monetary Authority of Singapore (MAS) bills. Meanwhile, outstanding corporate bonds posted a marginal contraction in Q1 2022 amid rising borrowing costs. MAS is among the few central banks in the region that began tightening monetary policy in the second half of 2021 to slow inflation. On a y-o-y basis, growth in Singapore's LCY bond market inched down to 20.9% in Q1 2022 from 21.9% in the prior quarter.

Thailand's LCY bond market expanded 1.8% q-o-q and 8.4% y-o-y in Q1 2022 to reach USD450.7 billion at the end of March. The rate of growth in Q1 2022 accelerated from that of Q4 2021 in both quarterly and annual terms (1.1% q-o-q and 5.8% y-o-y, respectively). Stronger growth in both the government and corporate bond segments drove the expansion in Q1 2022. Growth in outstanding LCY government bonds rose to 2.1% q-o-q in Q1 2022 from 1.6% q-o-q in the prior quarter, driven by primarily by government bonds and Treasury bills (4.1% q-o-q), as well as state-owned enterprise and other bonds (1.8% q-o-q). Meanwhile, the stock of Bank of Thailand (BOT) bonds recorded a 2.6% q-o-q contraction in Q1 2022 due to a relatively high volume of maturities. Meanwhile, growth in corporate bonds outstanding picked up to 1.2% q-o-q in Q1 2022 from 0.01% q-o-q in the previous quarter, as corporates issued debt to take advantage of prevailing rates in anticipation of interest rate hikes in the future. Renewed investor sentiment amid a nascent revival of tourism and other economic activities also boosted demand for corporate bonds.

The stock of outstanding LCY bonds in Malaysia totaled USD419.8 billion at the end of March. Overall growth rose to 1.7% q-o-q in Q1 2022 from 1.0% q-o-q in Q4 2021, largely due to accelerated growth of outstanding government bonds, which more than doubled to 2.8% q-o-q in Q1 2022 from 1.2% q-o-q in the previous quarter. The growth in the government bond stock stemmed solely from central government bonds, which expanded 2.8% q-o-q in Q1 2022. There were no outstanding central bank bills at the end of March. Meanwhile, growth in corporate bonds outstanding slipped to 0.3% q-o-q in Q1 2022 from 0.8% q-o-q in Q4 2021. On a y-o-y basis, Malaysia's LCY bond

market grew 7.0% in Q1 2022, down from 8.2% in the preceding quarter.

Malaysia's *sukuk* (Islamic bond) bond market continued to be the largest in emerging East Asia, reaching a size of USD267.0 billion at the end of March. Government *sukuk* outstanding totaled USD112.6 billion, accounting for 48.5% of Malaysia's total LCY government bond stock in Q1 2022. Malaysia's corporate bond market is dominated by *sukuk*; at the end of March, outstanding corporate *sukuk* reached USD154.4 billion, or 82.3% of total corporate bonds outstanding.

In Indonesia, the outstanding stock of LCY bonds amounted to USD381.4 billion at the end of March. Overall growth moderated to 3.1% q-o-q in Q1 2022 from 4.4% q-o-q in Q4 2021. Growth in the government bond segment dropped to 3.0% q-o-q in Q1 2022 from 4.6% in the prior quarter. Growth in central government bonds (3.2% q-o-q) and central bank bonds (8.4% q-o-q) outpaced the contraction in nontradable bonds (7.1% q-o-q). Meanwhile, growth in the corporate bond segment accelerated to 4.5% q-o-q in Q1 2022 from 2.0% q-o-q in the prior quarter, bolstered by a revival in issuance amid economic recovery and issuers taking advantage of low borrowing costs ahead of anticipated rate hikes. On an annual basis, Indonesia's LCY bond market expanded 14.1% y-o-y in Q1 2022, down from 17.7% y-o-y in Q4 2021.

The *sukuk* market in Indonesia reached a size of USD66.9 billion at the end of March, representing 17.5% of the total LCY bond market. Government *sukuk* amounted to USD64.4 billion, accounting for 18.4% of Indonesia's LCY government bond market. Corporate *sukuk* totaled USD4.6 billion, comprising 14.8% of Indonesia's LCY corporate bond stock.

The outstanding stock of LCY bonds in the Philippines reached USD201.5 billion at the end of March on growth of 6.5% q-o-q and 14.3% y-o-y. The pace of expansion in Q1 2022 surpassed the quarterly and annual rates of growth in the previous quarter (0.3% q-o-q and 14.2% y-o-y, respectively), driven by accelerated growth in the government bond segment and a recovery in the corporate bond segment. Growth in government bonds outstanding soared to 6.5% q-o-q from 0.5% in Q4 2021, as the government issued a sizable Retail Treasury Bonds and debt exchange in Q1 2022. Growth in the stock of Bangko Sentral ng Pilipinas (BSP) securities augmented overall government bond market growth in Q1 2022, posting an expansion of 57.7% q-o-q. Growth in the stock of Treasury bonds also contributed to the growth. Meanwhile, the stock of Treasury bills contracted in Q1 2022. The corporate bond segment registered 6.6% q-o-q growth in Q1 2022, reversing the 1.3% q-o-q decline in the previous quarter. Corporate debt issuance jumped 160.8% q-o-q in Q1 2022 amid the reopening of the Philippine economy—most business activities resumed after prolonged restrictions—and as corporate issuers locked in prevailing lower borrowing rates.

With a total size of USD93.6 billion at the end of March, Viet Nam's LCY bond market remained the smallest in emerging East Asia. Overall growth dropped to 2.4% q-o-q in Q1 2022 from 9.8% q-o-q in Q4 2021, as both the government and corporate bond segments recorded a slowdown. Government bonds outstanding rose 1.5% q-o-q in Q1 2022 versus 5.3% q-o-q in the prior quarter. The growth slowdown was driven by weaker growth in Treasury bonds combined with a contraction in government-guaranteed and municipal bonds. Corporate bonds outstanding grew 4.6% q-o-q in Q1 2022, down from 22.7% q-o-q in the previous quarter as issuance contracted. On an annual basis, Viet Nam's LCY bond market growth rose to 28.9% y-o-y in Q1 2022 from 25.5% y-o-y in Q4 2021.

Government bonds continued to account for a majority share of emerging East Asia's outstanding LCY bond stock at the end of Q1 2021. The region's government bond stock totaled USD14.7 trillion, representing 62.6% of the total LCY bond market at the end of March (**Table 1**). Growth in the region's government bond market moderated to 2.8% q-o-q in Q1 2022 from 4.0% q-o-q in Q4 2021. All nine government bond markets in the region posted positive q-o-q growth rates in Q1 2022. Most governments continued to raise debt during the review period to sustain economic recovery, but at a slower pace than in previous quarters as authorities started balancing economic recovery efforts with fiscal sustainability. The review period also saw higher borrowing costs compared to preceding quarters, as several of the region's central banks started tightening monetary policy to arrest inflation and in response to the United States (US) Federal Reserve's monetary policy tightening.

The LCY government bond markets of the PRC and the Republic of Korea remained the two largest markets in emerging East Asia, with a combined share of 88.8% of

the region's outstanding LCY government bond stock at the end of March. Meanwhile, the combined shares of ASEAN member economies accounted for 10.0% of the region's LCY government bond market. Among ASEAN member economies, Indonesia, Thailand, and Singapore had the largest LCY government bond markets. Viet Nam's LCY government bond market was the smallest among ASEAN member economies at the end of March.

In terms of maturity structure, emerging East Asia's government bonds remained mostly concentrated in medium- to longer-term tenors at the end of March (**Figure 2**). Apart from Hong Kong, China, all of the region's markets had over half of their government bonds concentrated in tenors of 5 years or longer. Due to strong market demand for shorter-dated securities, Hong Kong, China's government bond market was dominated by shorter-dated debt at the end of March. Meanwhile, bonds in the Republic of Korea, Thailand, and Viet Nam were predominantly concentrated in tenors with maturities of 10 years or longer. The PRC's LCY government bond market had a mixed structure: bonds with maturities of 1–3 years and 5–10 years each accounted for about 30% of the total, while bonds with maturities of 3–5 years and 10 years or longer each had about a 20% share.

The outstanding stock of LCY corporate bonds in emerging East Asia amounted to USD8.8 trillion at the end of March, comprising 37.4% of the region's total LCY bond market. Growth in the region's total corporate bonds outstanding quickened to 3.4% q-o-q in Q1 2022 from 2.8% q-o-q in Q4 2021, driven primarily by accelerated growth in the PRC's corporate bond market. Apart from Singapore and Hong Kong, China, all of the region's corporate bond markets posted positive growth in Q1 2021, as corporates issued debt in anticipation of rising borrowing costs in the future, and as the reopening of economies revived investor confidence in most of the region's markets. On the other hand, a relatively high volume of maturities outpaced issuance growth in Hong Kong, China, while the spread of the Omicron variant dampened investor sentiment in Singapore.

The PRC and the Republic of Korea were home to the two largest corporate bond markets in emerging East Asia, accounting for 76.4% and 15.7%, respectively, of the region's total LCY corporate bond stock at the end of March. The combined shares of ASEAN member economies comprised 6.2% of the region's LCY corporate

Table 1: Size and Composition of Local Currency Bond Markets

| | Q1 2021 | | Q4 2021 | | Q1 2022 | | Growth Rate (LCY-base %) | | | | Growth Rate (USD-base %) | | | |
| | Amount (USD billion) | % share | Amount (USD billion) | % share | Amount (USD billion) | % share | Q1 2021 | | Q1 2022 | | Q1 2021 | | Q1 2022 | |
							q-o-q	y-o-y	q-o-q	y-o-y	q-o-q	y-o-y	q-o-q	y-o-y
China, People's Rep. of														
Total	15,799	100.0	18,117	100.0	18,755	100.0	2.1	17.3	3.3	14.9	1.7	26.8	3.5	18.7
Government	10,102	63.9	11,701	64.6	12,051	64.3	1.6	18.5	2.7	15.4	1.2	28.1	3.0	19.3
Corporate	5,697	36.1	6,416	35.4	6,704	35.7	2.9	15.2	4.2	13.9	2.5	24.5	4.5	17.7
Hong Kong, China														
Total	315	100.0	324	100.0	325	100.0	1.7	8.4	0.8	4.1	1.4	8.1	0.4	3.3
Government	153	48.6	169	52.2	174	53.4	0.2	1.5	3.3	14.6	(0.03)	1.2	2.9	13.7
Corporate	162	51.4	155	47.8	151	46.6	3.1	15.9	(1.9)	(5.8)	2.8	15.5	(2.3)	(6.5)
Indonesia														
Total	330	100.0	373	100.0	381	100.0	6.2	36.0	3.1	14.1	2.8	52.7	2.4	15.4
Government	301	91.0	342	91.9	350	91.8	6.7	41.5	3.0	15.2	3.2	58.9	2.2	16.5
Corporate	30	9.0	30	8.1	31	8.2	1.7	(2.3)	4.5	3.9	(1.6)	9.8	3.7	5.0
Korea, Rep. of														
Total	2,382	100.0	2,388	100.0	2,391	100.0	2.4	8.9	2.0	7.5	(1.7)	17.2	0.1	0.4
Government	992	41.6	994	41.6	1,009	42.2	4.0	13.1	3.4	8.9	(0.1)	21.8	1.5	1.7
Corporate	1,390	58.4	1,395	58.4	1,383	57.8	1.2	6.0	1.0	6.5	(2.8)	14.1	(0.8)	(0.5)
Malaysia														
Total	398	100.0	417	100.0	420	100.0	2.8	7.9	1.7	7.0	(0.3)	12.5	0.7	5.5
Government	215	54.0	228	54.7	232	55.3	4.3	10.7	2.8	9.7	1.2	15.4	1.9	8.2
Corporate	183	46.0	189	45.3	188	44.7	1.0	4.8	0.3	3.9	(2.0)	9.3	(0.6)	2.5
Philippines														
Total	188	100.0	192	100.0	201	100.0	6.5	28.4	6.5	14.3	5.4	34.1	5.0	7.2
Government	155	82.7	164	85.5	172	85.5	8.4	36.5	6.5	18.1	7.3	42.6	5.0	10.8
Corporate	33	17.3	28	14.5	29	14.5	(2.0)	0.01	6.6	(4.1)	(3.0)	4.5	5.0	(10.0)
Singapore														
Total	384	100.0	449	100.0	461	100.0	3.9	12.7	3.1	20.9	2.1	19.2	2.7	20.1
Government	260	67.6	305	67.9	318	68.8	6.0	19.3	4.5	23.2	4.2	26.1	4.1	22.3
Corporate	125	32.4	144	32.1	144	31.2	(0.3)	1.1	(0.003)	16.3	(1.9)	6.9	(0.4)	15.4
Thailand														
Total	443	100.0	443	100.0	451	100.0	(0.6)	5.1	1.8	8.4	44.7	59.4	1.6	1.7
Government	325	73.3	323	72.8	329	72.9	(0.8)	8.5	2.1	7.7	43.8	56.2	1.9	1.1
Corporate	118	26.7	121	27.2	122	27.1	(0.1)	(3.3)	1.2	10.1	47.2	69.0	1.0	3.3
Viet Nam														
Total	72	100.0	92	100.0	94	100.0	(0.3)	18.8	2.4	28.9	(0.2)	21.8	2.3	30.2
Government	59	82.2	65	71.3	66	70.7	(1.1)	6.5	1.5	10.8	(0.9)	9.1	1.4	11.9
Corporate	13	17.8	26	28.7	27	29.3	3.3	156.0	4.6	112.6	3.5	162.3	4.6	114.7
Emerging East Asia														
Total	20,311	100.0	22,795	100.0	23,480	100.0	2.2	16.0	3.1	13.8	1.9	25.7	3.0	15.6
Government	12,561	61.8	14,291	62.7	14,700	62.6	2.0	18.1	2.8	14.8	2.1	28.1	2.9	17.0
Corporate	7,750	38.2	8,504	37.3	8,780	37.4	2.4	12.7	3.4	12.1	1.7	22.0	3.2	13.3
Japan														
Total	11,604	100.0	11,338	100.0	10,843	100.0	2.7	7.8	1.1	2.7	(4.2)	4.7	(4.4)	(6.6)
Government	10,793	93.0	10,515	92.7	10,067	92.8	2.9	8.1	1.3	2.5	(4.1)	5.0	(4.3)	(6.7)
Corporate	811	7.0	823	7.3	776	7.2	0.4	4.7	(0.4)	5.2	(6.3)	1.7	(5.8)	(4.3)

( ) = negative, LCY = local currency, q-o-q = quarter-on-quarter, Q1 = first quarter, Q4 = fourth quarter, USD = United States dollar, y-o-y = year-on-year.
Notes:
1. For Singapore, corporate bonds outstanding are based on *AsianBondsOnline* estimates.
2. Corporate bonds include issues by financial institutions.
3. Bloomberg LP end-of-period LCY–USD rates are used.
4. For LCY base, emerging East Asia growth figures based on 31 March 2022 currency exchange rates and do not include currency effects.
5. Emerging East Asia comprises the People's Republic of China; Hong Kong, China; Indonesia; the Republic of Korea; Malaysia; the Philippines; Singapore; Thailand; and Viet Nam.
Sources: People's Republic of China (CEIC Data Company); Hong Kong, China (Hong Kong Monetary Authority); Indonesia (Bank Indonesia; Directorate General of Budget Financing and Risk Management, Ministry of Finance; and Indonesia Stock Exchange); Republic of Korea (KG Zeroin Corporation and The Bank of Korea); Malaysia (Bank Negara Malaysia); Philippines (Bureau of the Treasury and Bloomberg LP); Singapore (Monetary Authority of Singapore, Singapore Government Securities, and Bloomberg LP); Thailand (Bank of Thailand); Viet Nam (Bloomberg LP and Vietnam Bond Market Association); and Japan (Japan Securities Dealers Association).

Figure 2: Maturity Profiles of Local Currency Government Bonds in Emerging East Asia

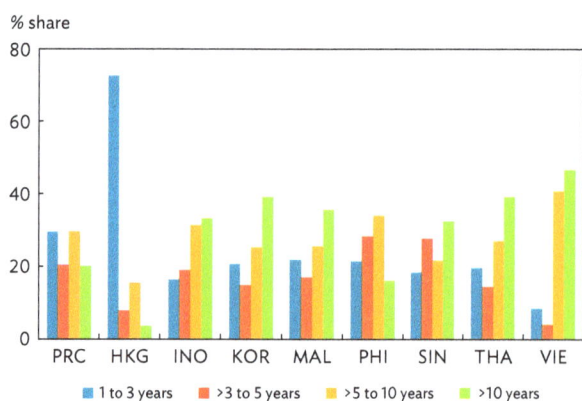

PRC = China, People's Rep. of; HKG = Hong Kong, China; INO = Indonesia; KOR = Korea, Rep. of; MAL = Malaysia; PHI = Philippines; SIN = Singapore; THA = Thailand; VIE = Viet Nam.
Notes:
1. Government bonds include Treasury bills and bonds.
2. Data as of 31 March 2022.
Source: AsianBondsOnline.

Table 2: Size and Composition of Local Currency Bond Markets (% of GDP)

	Q1 2021	Q4 2021	Q1 2022
China, People's Rep. of			
Total	98.0	100.7	102.0
Government	62.7	65.0	65.5
Corporate	35.3	35.7	36.5
Hong Kong, China			
Total	89.8	88.0	89.5
Government	43.6	45.9	47.8
Corporate	46.2	42.1	41.7
Indonesia			
Total	31.0	31.3	31.3
Government	28.2	28.8	28.7
Corporate	2.8	2.5	2.6
Korea, Rep. of			
Total	145.7	148.3	150.2
Government	60.7	61.7	63.4
Corporate	85.1	86.6	86.9
Malaysia			
Total	122.7	125.2	125.7
Government	66.2	68.5	69.5
Corporate	56.5	56.7	56.2
Philippines			
Total	51.0	50.4	52.2
Government	42.2	43.1	44.6
Corporate	8.8	7.3	7.6
Singapore			
Total	107.8	113.7	114.5
Government	72.8	77.2	78.8
Corporate	34.9	36.5	35.7
Thailand			
Total	89.0	91.0	91.3
Government	65.3	66.2	66.6
Corporate	23.7	24.8	24.7
Viet Nam			
Total	23.5	24.9	25.0
Government	19.3	17.7	17.6
Corporate	4.2	7.1	7.3
Emerging East Asia			
Total	96.6	98.6	99.7
Government	59.7	61.8	62.4
Corporate	36.9	36.8	37.3
Japan			
Total	239.9	240.8	243.5
Government	223.2	223.3	226.1
Corporate	16.8	17.5	17.4

GDP = gross domestic product, Q1 = first quarter, Q4 = fourth quarter.
Notes:
1. Data for GDP is from CEIC Data Company.
2. For Singapore, corporate bonds outstanding are based on AsianBondsOnline estimates.
Sources: People's Republic of China (CEIC Data Company); Hong Kong, China (Hong Kong Monetary Authority); Indonesia (Bank Indonesia; Directorate General of Budget Financing and Risk Management, Ministry of Finance; and Indonesia Stock Exchange); Republic of Korea (KG Zeroin Corporation and The Bank of Korea); Malaysia (Bank Negara Malaysia); Philippines (Bureau of the Treasury and Bloomberg LP); Singapore (Monetary Authority of Singapore, Singapore Government Securities, and Bloomberg LP); Thailand (Bank of Thailand); Viet Nam (Bloomberg LP and Vietnam Bond Market Association); and Japan (Japan Securities Dealers Association).

bond market. Among ASEAN member economies, the three largest LCY corporate bond markets were those of Malaysia, Singapore, and Thailand, while the smallest market was that of Viet Nam.

The value of emerging East Asia's aggregate LCY bonds outstanding at the end of March was almost equivalent (99.7%) to the region's total gross domestic product (GDP) in Q1 2022. This was up from 98.6% at the end of December 2021 and 96.6% at the end of March 2021 (**Table 2**). Economies continued to borrow from the bond market to support recovery but, at the same time, some economies experienced a slowdown in growth due to a resurgence of coronavirus disease (COVID-19) infections and/or high commodity prices that constrained consumption. The GDP equivalent of the region's government bonds outstanding rose to 62.4% in Q1 2022 from 61.8% in Q4 2021, and for corporate bonds the GDP equivalent increased to 37.3% from 36.8% over the same period.

In Q1 2022, four markets had a bond market share of GDP above 100%; the highest in the region was the Republic of Korea's at 150.2%, followed by Malaysia (125.7%), Singapore (114.5%), and the PRC (102.0%). On the other hand, Viet Nam had the smallest share at 25.0%, albeit one that has increased in recent quarters.

The bond market's share of GDP increased from Q4 2021 to Q1 2022 in all emerging East Asian markets except for Indonesia, where the share was broadly stable. For the outstanding government bonds' share of GDP, increases were seen in all markets except Indonesia and Viet Nam. For outstanding corporate bonds' share of GDP, four markets posted declines: Hong Kong, China; Malaysia; Singapore; and Thailand, while the rest of the markets posted increases.

Singapore had the largest government bonds' share of GDP in the region at the end of Q1 2022 at 78.8%, while Viet Nam had the smallest at 17.6%. For corporate bonds, the Republic of Korea had the largest share at 86.9%, while Indonesia had the smallest at 2.6%.

Foreign Holdings

Foreign investors scaled down their holdings of government bonds in most emerging East Asian markets in Q1 2022.

Declines in offshore investor ownership occurred in all emerging East Asian LCY government bond markets between Q4 2021 and Q1 2022 except Thailand and Viet Nam, where the shares were almost unchanged (**Figure 3**). Foreign investor sentiment toward the

region was weighed down by the aggressive monetary policy normalization of the US Federal Reserve, the protracted status of the Russian invasion of Ukraine, soaring global commodity prices, and the slowdown in the PRC's economy. The combined effect of these adverse developments caused uncertainty and volatility in the market, leading to a flight to safety among foreign investors.

The PRC market experienced a slight decline in the foreign holdings' share of government bonds to 10.8% at the end of March from 10.9% at the end of December 2021. This ended a string of consecutive quarterly increases in place since June 2019. The decrease can be attributed to concerns about economic uncertainty and the slowdown in the PRC amid mobility restrictions due to COVID-19. Also contributing was the domestic bond market's diminished yield advantage as the Federal Reserve began hiking benchmark interest rates while the People's Bank of China (PBOC) did the opposite. The decrease in the foreign holdings' share was notable especially as the government bond market has endured previous market stress, including market panic at the height of the COVID-19 pandemic.

In Indonesia, foreign holdings of government bonds continued to decline in Q1 2022. The share was down to 17.6% at the end of March from 19.0% at the end of December 2021, which can be largely attributed to the Federal Reserve's policy of tightening. The decline of 1.5 percentage points was the largest among the region's markets. The Government of Indonesia's reduction of bond issuance to better manage its fiscal deficit may have also contributed to the decline of foreign holdings via less supply in the market.

The global risk-off sentiment also resulted in foreign investors reducing their exposure in the government bond markets of Malaysia and the Philippines. In Malaysia, the share of offshore holdings declined to 25.6% at the end of March from 26.0% at the end of December 2021. Even with the decline in Q1 2022, Malaysia still had the highest foreign holdings' share of government securities among all markets in emerging East Asia. In the Philippines, the share fell to 1.3% at the end of March from 1.9% at the end of December 2021. Aside from the aggressive Federal Reserve action, foreign investor sentiment soured toward Philippine government bonds because of soaring domestic inflation, a large fiscal deficit, and uncertainty stemming from the pending change in government administration.

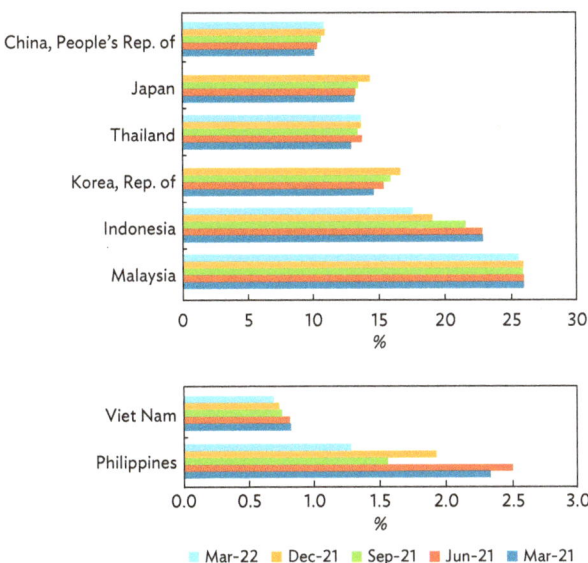

Figure 3: Foreign Holdings of Local Currency Government Bonds in Select Asian Markets (% of total)

Note: Data for Japan and the Republic of Korea are as of 31 December 2021.
Source: *AsianBondsOnline* calculations based on data from local market sources.

Meanwhile, in Thailand and Viet Nam, the foreign holdings' shares were only marginally changed during Q1 2022, settling at 13.7% and 0.7%, respectively, at the end of March.

In the Republic of Korea, foreign investors increased their holdings of government bonds as reflected in the respective share climbing to 16.6% at the end of December 2021 from 15.9% at the end of September 2021. Korean government bonds maintained their appeal as its monetary tightening measure helped maintain the rate differential with US Treasuries. From August 2021 to April 2022, the Bank of Korea raised the policy rate four times to quell inflation.

Foreign Fund Flows

Foreign fund flows diverged across emerging East Asia's bond markets in Q1 2022.

Emerging East Asia's LCY bond markets received total net inflows of USD2.4 billion in Q1 2022, down significantly from USD35.2 billion in Q4 2021 (**Figure 4**). It was also the smallest amount of net inflows since the region

Figure 4: Foreign Capital Flows in Local Currency Bond Markets in Emerging East Asia

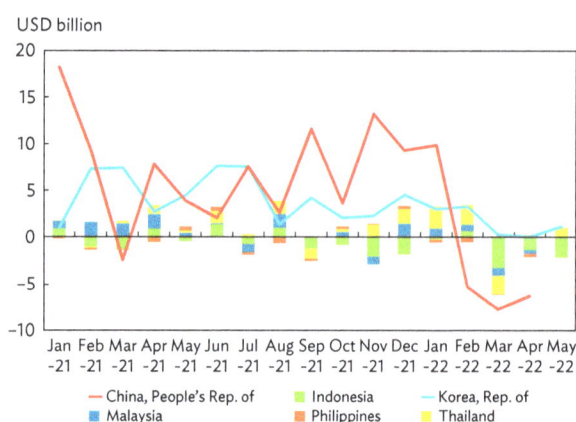

USD = United States dollar.
Notes:
1. The Republic of Korea and Thailand provided data on bond flows. For the People's Republic of China, Indonesia, Malaysia, and the Philippines, month-on-month changes in foreign holdings of local currency government bonds were used as a proxy for bond flows.
2. Data are as of 31 May 2022 except for the People's Republic of China (30 April 2022).
3. Figures were computed based on 31 May 2022 exchange rates and do not include currency effects.
Sources: People's Republic of China (Bloomberg LP); Indonesia (Directorate General of Budget Financing and Risk Management, Ministry of Finance); Republic of Korea (Financial Supervisory Service); Malaysia (Bank Negara Malaysia); Philippines (Bureau of the Treasury); and Thailand (Thai Bond Market Association).

incurred net outflows of USD4.2 billion in Q1 2020. Movements of foreign capital were mixed during the quarter: the Republic of Korea, Malaysia, and Thailand experienced net inflows into their bond markets, while the markets of the PRC, Indonesia, and the Philippines posted net outflows. In April, however, investor risk aversion resulted in emerging East Asia's bond markets to record total net outflows of USD8.2 billion, with the largest drag coming from the PRC. In May, total net outflows in the region, excluding the PRC, amounted USD0.1 billion where Indonesia had foreign sell-off that offset the net inflows in the rest of the markets.

Low foreign net inflows in Q1 2022 and the eventual offloading of funds in April in emerging East Asia occurred because of (i) the strengthening of the US dollar against regional currencies and (ii) foreign investors pricing in a quicker pace of interest hikes as the Federal Reserve embarks on aggressive policy normalization. Foreign investors became net sellers of the region's LCY bonds in March—when the Federal Reserve hiked its policy rate—for the first time since recording a monthly sell-off in February 2019. The ongoing Russian invasion of Ukraine and concerns about a further slowdown in the PRC's economy, the second largest in the world, as it sticks to its zero COVID-19 policy, also dampened foreign investor demand in the region.

Foreign investors in the PRC sold a net USD3.3 billion in Q1 2022, a sizable turnaround from net inflows of USD26.3 billion in Q4 2021. It was the first quarterly net outflows from the PRC since the sell-off in Q1 2019. During Q1 2022, the PRC recorded net inflows of USD9.9 billion in January, which were followed by net outflows in February and March of USD5.4 billion and USD7.8 billion, respectively. The PRC's bond market has long been an attractive investment destination offering a yield premium, which is why it is included in different global bond indexes. Moreover, the PRC has enjoyed a strong economy and currency. However, these advantages have diminished with the economic slowdown in the PRC and the subsequent monetary policy easing by the PBOC in January to uplift the economy. This was further exacerbated by the fresh wave of COVID-19 cases, which resulted in mobility restrictions, and the global economic impact of the Russian invasion of Ukraine. In April, foreign investors sold a net USD6.4 billion from the PRC government bond market.

Indonesia and the Philippines incurred net foreign fund withdrawals of USD3.0 billion and USD0.9 billion in

Q1 2022, respectively, as a result of uncertainty and market volatility. For Indonesia, the net outflows during the quarter were lower compared to USD4.9 billion in Q4 2021. In Q1 2022, the Indonesian bond market saw net inflows in February of USD0.6 billion, which were more than offset by the sell-offs in January of USD0.3 billion and in March of USD3.3 billion. In April, foreign investors continued to be net sellers, withdrawing USD1.4 billion from the Indonesian bond market, while in May, the net outflows nearly doubled to USD2.2 billion. In the Philippines, net outflows in Q1 2022 reversed the net inflows of USD0.7 billion in Q4 2021. From January to May, the Philippines recorded monthly net outflows ranging from USD0.03 billion to USD0.6 billion. The Philippines, including its economic center, the National Capital Region, was placed back under mobility restrictions in January due to a fresh wave of COVID-19 cases, which hit an all-time high, likely causing market worries. While the surge was short-lived, concerns over high inflation, rising debt, and (to a certain extent) uncertainty related to national elections in May kept foreign investors cautious and contributed to the capital flight.

The bond markets of the Republic of Korea, Malaysia, and Thailand were resilient in Q1 2022, despite the presence of risk-off sentiment, as they remained recipients of net foreign fund inflows during the quarter, keeping in place the observed trend in recent quarters. The bond market of the Republic of Korea saw net inflows of USD6.3 billion during the quarter. While positive, net inflows were down significantly from Q1 2021, which saw a net USD15.3 billion influx of foreign funds. Each month of Q1 2022 posted net inflows, with the largest in February at USD3.1 billion. In April, foreign investors trimmed their net allocations in the bond market to only USD0.03 billion. While the Republic of Korea's bond market remained a key destination for foreign funds in the region, the weakening domestic economic outlook and investor caution toward the region affected the bond market as evidenced by waning demand. In May, net inflows accelerated to USD1.1 billion.

In Malaysia, the bond market recorded its eighth consecutive quarter of net inflows in Q1 2022, adding USD0.8 billion. Foreign investors remained net buyers in the Malaysian bond market in January (USD0.9 billion) and February (USD0.7 billion). However, in March, the Malaysian bond market posted its first monthly net outflows (USD0.8 billion) since November 2021. The trend continued in April with net outflows of USD0.4 billion, brought about by the hawkish monetary

policy stance of the Federal Reserve. Foreign capital returned in May, recording net inflows of USD0.1 billion. Thailand also saw net foreign buying in Q1 2022 reach USD2.5 billion. Thailand's bond market has maintained quarterly net inflows since June 2020. Through May, March was the only month in which net outflows were recorded (USD2.0 billion), triggered by the rate hike in the US.

Local Currency Bond Issuance

Local currency bond issuance in emerging East Asia during Q1 2022 reached USD2.2 trillion.

Issuance in emerging East Asia's LCY bond markets continued its robust performance, albeit slightly slower than in the previous quarter. Total issuance, however, has remained above prepandemic levels and reached USD2.2 trillion in Q1 2022 (**Figure 5**).

Among regional markets, Hong Kong, China saw the largest increase in its share of the regional issuance total, rising 0.6 percentage points to 6.7%, while the Republic of Korea gained 0.2 percentage points to account for an 8.7% share at the end of March. ASEAN markets had a collective share of 17.8% of emerging East Asia's issuance total during the quarter, similar to

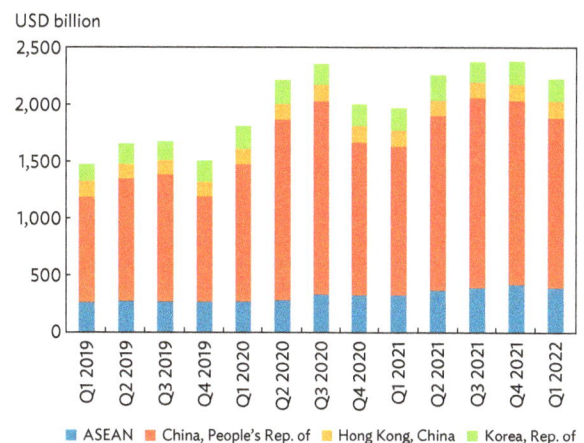

Figure 5: Local Currency Bond Issuance in Emerging East Asia

USD billion

ASEAN = Association of Southeast Asian Nations, Q1 = first quarter, Q2 = second quarter, Q3 = third quarter, Q4 = fourth quarter, USD = United States dollar.
Notes:
1. ASEAN includes the markets of Indonesia, Malaysia, the Philippines, Singapore, Thailand, and Viet Nam.
2. Figures were computed based on 31 March 2022 currency exchange rates and do not include currency effects.
Source: *AsianBondsOnline*.

that of the previous quarter. The PRC, which accounted for 66.9% of the regional issuance total during the quarter, saw its share dip 0.8 percentage points from a 67.7% share in Q4 2021.

The majority of new bonds issued in Q1 2022 comprised government bonds and corporate bonds (**Figure 6**). Government bonds accounted for a 59.2% share of the region's bond issuance total during the quarter, up from 56.7% in the earlier quarter. This is largely due to governments frontloading their fiscal funding early in the year to take advantage of ample liquidity in the market while interest rates were still low. In contrast, the share of corporate bonds slipped to a 40.8% share in Q1 2022 from 43.3% in Q4 2021, as corporates weighed their individual borrowing plans amid uncertainty in the economic outlook stemming from tightening monetary policy by the Federal Reserve, supply chain disruptions, the Russian invasion of Ukraine, and the weakening growth outlook in the PRC. Some regional markets also tightened restrictions due to the surge in COVID-19 cases brought about by the spread of the Omicron variant, thereby stalling economic activities. Meanwhile, central banks accounted for 18.9% of emerging East Asia's total issuance in Q1 2022.

On a q-o-q basis, emerging East Asia's LCY bond issuance declined 6.5% in Q1 2022, following a marginal 0.2% expansion in Q4 2021. All bond segments recorded q-o-q declines in issuance during the quarter, with corporate bonds posting the largest contraction.

Figure 6: Issuance Volume by Type of Bonds

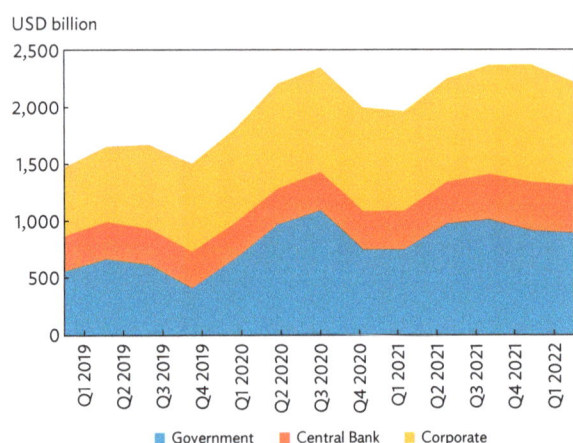

USD billion

Q1 = first quarter, Q2 = second quarter, Q3 = third quarter, Q4 = fourth quarter, USD = United States dollar.
Note: Figures were computed based on 31 March 2022 currency exchange rates and do not include currency effects.
Source: *AsianBondsOnline*.

Government bond issuance contraction slipped to a slower pace of −2.2% q-o-q compared with −4.8% q-o-q in the preceding quarter.

Treasury and other government bond issuance moderated in Q1 2022, falling 2.2% q-o-q. The decline, however, was slower than the 9.6% q-o-q contraction posted in Q4 2021. Over 45% of Treasury issuances during the quarter carried maturities of more than 5 years or longer. While most governments normally frontloads issuance at the start of each year, issuance for Q1 2022 was curtailed by negative sentiments due to the Federal Reserve's tightening stance and the Russian invasion of Ukraine. Some governments are also focused on fiscal consolidation as part of their debt management strategy. Total issuance of Treasury and other government bonds reached USD892.8 billion in Q1 2022. Only the markets of the Republic of Korea, Malaysia, and the Philippines had increased issuance of Treasury and other government bonds in Q1 2022 versus the previous quarter.

Central bank issuance during the quarter reached USD419.1 billion, a decline of 2.3% q-o-q after posting 7.1% q-o-q growth in the prior quarter. Five central banks in the region posted higher issuance volume in Q1 2022— the Hong Kong Monetary Authority, Bank of Korea, BOT, BSP, and State Bank of Vietnam—due to high liquidity in the banking system and rising inflation.

Issuance of corporate bonds in the region totaled USD902.8 billion in Q1 2022, registering a 12.1% q-o-q decline and reversing the 7.6% q-o-q gain in Q4 2021. Four out of nine markets in emerging East Asia recorded higher issuance volume during the quarter: Hong Kong, China; Indonesia; the Philippines; and Thailand. The region's corporate bond issuance during the quarter was dragged down by less issuance from the larger markets of the PRC and the Republic of Korea.

On a y-o-y basis, LCY bond issuance in the region climbed 13.0% in Q1 2022, down from an 18.8% hike in the preceding quarter. Despite both the government and corporate bond segments posting positive y-o-y growth rates, they were slower than in Q4 2021. Malaysia was the sole market in the region that posted negative y-o-y issuance growth during the quarter.

Most emerging East Asian markets saw a tapering of LCY bond issuance in Q1 2022, after record-high issuances in 2021. Six out of nine regional markets posted q-o-q contractions in issuance in Q1 2022 (**Table 3**). Only

Table 3: Local-Currency–Denominated Bond Issuance (gross)

| | Q1 2021 | | Q4 2021 | | Q1 2022 | | Growth Rate (LCY-base %) | | Growth Rate (USD-base %) | |
| | Amount (USD billion) | % share | Amount (USD billion) | % share | Amount (USD billion) | % share | Q1 2022 | | Q1 2022 | |
							q-o-q	y-o-y	q-o-q	y-o-y
China, People's Rep. of										
Total	1,255	100.0	1,598	100.0	1,481	100.0	(7.6)	14.2	(7.4)	18.0
Government	575	45.8	775	48.5	747	50.4	(4.0)	25.6	(3.7)	29.8
Central Bank	0	0.0	0	0.0	0	0.0	–	–	–	–
Treasury and Other Govt.	575	45.8	775	48.5	747	50.4	(4.0)	25.6	(3.7)	29.8
Corporate	680	54.2	823	51.5	734	49.6	(11.0)	4.5	(10.8)	8.0
Hong Kong, China										
Total	143	100.0	144	100.0	148	100.0	3.1	4.0	2.6	3.2
Government	105	73.5	118	81.7	120	81.3	2.5	15.1	2.1	14.2
Central Bank	105	73.3	117	81.1	120	81.0	3.0	15.0	2.6	14.2
Treasury and Other Govt.	0.3	0.2	1	0.7	0.4	0.3	(56.0)	22.2	(56.2)	21.3
Corporate	38	26.5	26	18.3	28	18.7	5.5	(26.7)	5.0	(27.2)
Indonesia										
Total	34	100.0	49	100.0	46	100.0	(5.3)	31.6	(6.0)	33.1
Government	33	95.9	47	95.5	43	94.1	(6.7)	29.2	(7.4)	30.6
Central Bank	12	34.5	28	57.4	26	57.7	(4.8)	120.3	(5.5)	122.8
Treasury and Other Govt.	21	61.4	19	38.1	17	36.4	(9.6)	(22.0)	(10.2)	(21.1)
Corporate	1	4.1	2	4.5	3	5.9	24.0	88.2	23.2	90.3
Korea, Rep. of										
Total	205	100.0	205	100.0	193	100.0	(4.0)	0.8	(5.8)	(5.9)
Government	91	44.3	60	29.4	81	42.0	36.9	(4.5)	34.4	(10.8)
Central Bank	29	14.3	21	10.3	25	12.9	19.7	(8.9)	17.5	(14.9)
Treasury and Other Govt.	62	30.1	39	19.1	56	29.1	46.2	(2.5)	43.5	(8.9)
Corporate	114	55.7	144	70.6	112	58.0	(21.1)	5.0	(22.5)	(2.0)
Malaysia										
Total	24	100.0	21	100.0	19	100.0	(8.6)	(18.7)	(9.4)	(19.8)
Government	14	56.9	11	53.7	12	61.4	4.5	(12.3)	3.5	(13.5)
Central Bank	0	0.0	0	0.0	0	0.0	–	–	–	–
Treasury and Other Govt.	14	56.9	11	53.7	12	61.4	4.5	(12.3)	3.5	(13.5)
Corporate	10	43.1	10	46.3	7	38.6	(23.7)	(27.2)	(24.4)	(28.2)
Philippines										
Total	44	100.0	39	100.0	46	100.0	18.8	10.9	17.0	4.0
Government	43	97.3	38	97.1	43	93.6	14.5	6.7	12.8	0.04
Central Bank	23	51.2	24	60.0	25	55.6	10.0	20.4	8.4	12.9
Treasury and Other Govt.	20	46.0	15	37.0	17	38.0	21.9	(8.5)	20.1	(14.2)
Corporate	1	2.7	1	2.9	3	6.4	160.8	159.0	156.9	142.8
Singapore										
Total	169	100.0	244	100.0	215	100.0	(11.7)	28.2	(12.0)	27.3
Government	166	98.4	240	98.2	213	99.2	(10.8)	29.2	(11.2)	28.3
Central Bank	142	84.2	211	86.3	187	87.4	(10.6)	33.1	(11.0)	32.1
Treasury and Other Govt.	24	14.2	29	11.9	25	11.8	(12.3)	6.5	(12.6)	5.8
Corporate	3	1.6	4	1.8	2	0.8	(58.5)	(33.2)	(58.6)	(33.7)
Thailand										
Total	63	100.0	62	100.0	63	100.0	3.2	6.4	3.0	(0.1)
Government	54	85.1	50	82.1	50	79.2	(0.4)	(1.0)	(0.6)	(7.0)
Central Bank	34	53.1	31	50.9	34	53.3	8.0	6.8	7.8	0.2
Treasury and Other Govt.	20	32.0	19	31.2	16	25.9	(14.1)	(13.8)	(14.3)	(19.1)
Corporate	9	14.9	11	17.9	13	20.8	19.5	48.6	19.2	39.5

continued on next page

Table 3 *continued*

	Q1 2021		Q4 2021		Q1 2022		Growth Rate (LCY-base %) Q1 2022		Growth Rate (USD-base %) Q1 2022	
	Amount (USD billion)	% share	Amount (USD billion)	% share	Amount (USD billion)	% share	q-o-q	y-o-y	q-o-q	y-o-y
Viet Nam										
Total	3	100.0	9	100.0	5	100.0	(51.4)	80.4	(51.4)	82.2
Government	2	67.8	4	42.4	3	70.0	(19.8)	86.1	(19.9)	88.0
Central Bank	0	0.0	0	0.0	1	30.4	–	–	–	–
Treasury and Other Govt.	2	67.8	4	42.4	2	39.6	(54.6)	5.3	(54.7)	6.3
Corporate	0.8	32.2	5	57.6	1	30.0	(74.6)	68.4	(74.6)	70.1
Emerging East Asia										
Total	1,940	100.0	2,371	100.0	2,215	100.0	(6.5)	13.0	(6.6)	14.2
Government	1,082	55.8	1,344	56.7	1,312	59.2	(2.2)	20.6	(2.4)	21.2
Central Bank	344	17.7	431	18.2	419	18.9	(2.3)	24.4	(2.8)	21.8
Treasury and Other Govt.	738	38.1	912	38.5	893	40.3	(2.2)	18.9	(2.1)	20.9
Corporate	858	44.2	1,027	43.3	903	40.8	(12.1)	3.5	(12.1)	5.3
Japan										
Total	664	100.0	662	100.0	463	100.0	(26.0)	(23.3)	(30.0)	(30.2)
Government	640	96.4	615	93.0	444	95.9	(23.6)	(23.7)	(27.8)	(30.6)
Central Bank	0	0.0	0	0.0	0	0.0	–	–	–	–
Treasury and Other Govt.	640	96.4	615	93.0	444	95.9	(23.6)	(23.7)	(27.8)	(30.6)
Corporate	24	3.6	47	7.0	19	4.1	(56.4)	(11.8)	(58.8)	(19.8)

( ) = negative, – = not applicable, LCY = local currency, q-o-q = quarter-on-quarter, Q1 = first quarter, Q4 = fourth quarter, USD = United States dollar, y-o-y = year-on-year.
Notes:
1. Corporate bonds include issues by financial institutions.
2. Bloomberg LP end-of-period LCY–USD rates are used.
3. For LCY base, emerging East Asia growth figures are based on 31 March 2022 currency exchange rates and do not include currency effects.
Sources: People's Republic of China (CEIC Data Company); Hong Kong, China (Hong Kong Monetary Authority); Indonesia (Bank Indonesia; Directorate General of Budget Financing and Risk Management, Ministry of Finance; and Indonesia Stock Exchange); Republic of Korea (KG Zeroin Corporation and The Bank of Korea); Malaysia (Bank Negara Malaysia); Philippines (Bureau of the Treasury and Bloomberg LP); Singapore (Singapore Government Securities and Bloomberg LP); Thailand (Bank of Thailand); Viet Nam (Bloomberg LP, Hanoi Stock Exchange, and Vietnam Bond Market Association); and Japan (Japan Securities Dealers Association).

the markets of Hong Kong, China; the Philippines; and Thailand logged positive q-o-q issuance growth during the quarter.

The PRC's overall LCY bond issuance further declined 7.6% q-o-q in Q1 2022 to USD1.5 trillion after contracting 3.2% q-o-q in the previous quarter. The q-o-q decline was seen in both the government and corporate bond segments. Government bonds contracted 4.0% q-o-q in Q1 2022, largely due to a 23.5% q-o-q drop in Treasury bonds as the government continued with their risk control policy.

In contrast, issuance of local government bonds was relatively stable in the PRC, falling 1.9% q-o-q in Q1 2022. The special bond quota was set at CNY3.7 trillion this year, the same as in 2021. However, local government bond issuance was up 108.7% y-o-y, as the government sought to frontload issuance to help prop up the economy. Issuance of policy bank bonds also gained 34.6% q-o-q, as policy banks sought to provide economic

support. Corporate bond issuance in the PRC, however, declined 11.0% q-o-q as economic weaknesses led companies to curtail issuance. On a y-o-y basis, LCY bond issuance in the PRC eased to 14.2% in Q1 2022 from 20.3% in Q4 2021.

Total issuance of LCY bonds in the Republic of Korea declined to USD192.8 billion, contracting 4.0% q-o-q in Q1 2022 after rising 14.3% q-o-q in Q4 2021. Issuance was dragged down by decreased issuance of corporate bonds, as interest rates reached prepandemic level following the Bank of Korea's series of upward adjustments in policy rates starting in August 2021. The Republic of Korea is the only market in emerging East Asia with a higher share of corporate bonds than government bonds. In contrast, government bonds rose 36.9%, fueled by strong issuance of (i) Treasury and other government bonds to fund the budget deficit and (ii) central bank instruments to help curb inflation. On a y-o-y basis, LCY bond issuance in the Republic of Korea decelerated to 0.8% in Q1 2022 from 6.6% in Q4 2021.

In Hong Kong, China, issuance of LCY bonds totaled USD147.8 billion in Q1 2022 on a modest expansion of 3.1% q-o-q. Overall growth continued to be driven by central bank issuance, which rose 3.0% q-o-q and accounted for 81.0% of Hong Kong, China's issuance total in Q1 2022. Issuance of Exchange Fund Bills, which account for nearly all central bank issuance, remained strong, buoyed by high liquidity in the market. In Q1 2022, corporate bond issuance grew 5.5% q-o-q as companies tapped the market ahead of the Federal Reserve's widely expected rate hike. In contrast, issuance of Hong Kong Special Administrative Region bonds dipped 56.0% q-o-q, albeit coming from a low base. Compared with the same period a year earlier, Hong Kong, China's LCY bond issuance swelled to 4.0% y-o-y in Q1 2022 after declining 1.1% y-o-y in the preceding quarter.

Collectively, LCY bond issuance of ASEAN member economies tallied USD393.5 billion in Q1 2022. Overall growth contracted 6.7% q-o-q, reversing the 6.8% q-o-q gain in Q4 2021. On a y-o-y basis, issuance growth moderated to 19.5% in Q1 2022 from 28.3% in the preceding quarter. Only the Philippines and Thailand had increased borrowing during the quarter, while Indonesia, Malaysia, Singapore, and Viet Nam tapered their respective issuances compared with Q4 2021. The leading ASEAN markets in terms of issuance in Q1 2022 were Singapore, Thailand, the Philippines, and Indonesia, which accounted for 54.5%, 16.1%, 11.7%, and 11.6% of the aggregate ASEAN total, respectively.

Singapore continued to account for the largest amount of bonds issued among all ASEAN markets, with issuance amounting to USD214.6 billion in Q1 2022. Overall growth, however, slipped 11.7% q-o-q, with declines recorded across all bond segments. Central bank bond issuance, which accounted for 87.4% of total issuance in Q1 2022, contracted 10.6% q-o-q. Treasury bonds also fell 12.3% q-o-q after rising 11.4% q-o-q in Q4 2021. Corporate bond issuance further slumped, falling 58.5% q-o-q in Q1 2022 following an 18.6% q-o-q decline in the preceding quarter. Singapore has tightened its monetary policy thrice since October 2021 to contain inflation, making it more costly for corporates to engage in borrowing. On a y-o-y basis, Singapore's LCY bond issuance growth moderated to 28.2% in Q1 2022 from 52.0% in Q4 2021.

In Thailand, new bond sales climbed to USD63.4 billion in Q1 2022 for a 3.2% q-o-q gain. Growth was largely driven by higher issuance of central bank instruments and corporate bonds. Central bank issuance rose 8.0% q-o-q as the BOT increased its issuance of Thai Overnight Repurchase Rate-linked fixed rate bonds to support the use of this rate in pricing financial assets and fulfill rising investor demand. Corporate bond issuance also contributed to the growth, rising 19.5% q-o-q in Q1 2022. In the same period, the issuance of Treasury and other government bonds declined 14.1% q-o-q. LCY bond issuance in Thailand rose 6.4% y-o-y in Q1 2022, a turnaround from the 8.3% y-o-y decline in Q4 2021.

The Philippines' issuance volume climbed to USD45.9 billion in Q1 2022, rising 18.8% q-o-q and posting the fastest q-o-q growth among regional bond markets. Overall government bond issuance grew 14.5% q-o-q, fueled by the 21.9% gain in the sale of Treasury and other government bonds. In addition to the regular Treasury auctions, the government sold its 27th series of Retail Treasury Bonds in March, raising PHP457.8 billion. Central bank issuance rose 10.0% q-o-q in Q1 2022, while corporate bond issuance more than doubled as firms rushed to lock-in low interest rates. Compared with the same period a year earlier, LCY bond issuance growth in the Philippines moderated to 10.9% y-o-y in Q1 2022 from 43.2% y-o-y in Q4 2021.

LCY bond sales in Indonesia reached USD45.8 billion in Q1 2022, contracting 5.3% q-o-q following a 1.4% q-o-q gain in Q4 2021. The decline in issuance stemmed from less issuance of Treasury bonds as the government plans to reduce borrowing as part of its debt management strategy in 2022. The Ministry of Finance aims to reduce the budget deficit, which based on the 2022 state budget is estimated at 4.85% of GDP. Bank Indonesia also reduced its issuance of Sukuk Bank Indonesia in Q1 2022, with issuance falling 4.8% q-o-q. In contrast, corporate bond issuance picked up 24.0% q-o-q, as corporates engaged in borrowing while interest rates remained low. On a y-o-y basis, however, growth in LCY bond issuance accelerated to 31.6% in Q1 2022 from only 4.9% in Q4 2021.

Malaysia's LCY bond issuance totaled USD19.4 billion in Q1 2022 for an 8.6% q-o-q contraction. This was a turnaround from the 2.6% q-o-q hike in Q4 2021. Corporate bonds dragged down overall growth as issuance fell 23.7% during the quarter, which more than offset the 4.5% q-o-q uptick in government bonds. Higher government bond sales were fueled by the need to support economic recovery efforts and refinance maturing obligations. Malaysia's LCY bond issuance further contracted 18.7% y-o-y in Q1 2022 after a 0.7% y-o-y decline in the preceding quarter.

Viet Nam posted the largest decline in issuance in Q1 2022 among the region's bond markets, with issuance falling 51.4% q-o-q to USD4.6 billion. Corporate bonds dragged down issuance volume for the quarter, as issuance fell 74.6% q-o-q amid tighter monitoring by the State Securities Commission. Issuance of Treasury and other government bonds fell 54.6% q-o-q in Q1 2022. In contrast, the State Bank of Vietnam resumed issuance of central bank bills with USD1.4 billion of issuance in Q1 2022, the first quarterly issuance since Q1 2020. On an annual basis, Viet Nam's LCY bond issuance swelled 80.4% y-o-y in Q1 2022 versus 25.4% y-o-y growth in Q4 2021.

Cross-Border Bond Issuance

Cross-border bond issuance in emerging East Asia totaled USD9.2 billion in Q1 2022.

Intraregional bond issuance in emerging East Asia reached USD9.2 billion in Q1 2022, more than double the USD4.5 billion raised in the previous quarter and 60% higher than the USD5.7 billion raised in Q1 2021. Six economies registered cross-border issuances in Q1 2022, up from only four in the previous quarter. In descending order of issuance volume, these include Hong Kong, China; the PRC; Singapore; the Republic of Korea; the Lao People's Democratic Republic (Lao PDR); and Malaysia (**Figure 7**). Monthly issuance volumes amounted to USD2.9 billion, USD1.9 billion, and USD4.3 billion, respectively, in the first 3 months of the year. The large issuance volume in March may be attributed to corporates intending to take advantage of relatively lower borrowing costs in anticipation of higher yields arising from expectations of further rate hikes by the Federal Reserve.

Hong Kong, China continued to dominate the region with a 77.9% share and aggregate issuance of USD7.1 billion in Q1 2022, almost double the USD3.7 billion raised in the previous quarter. Sixteen institutions issued cross-border bonds in Hong Kong, China in Q1 2022, all of which were denominated in Chinese yuan.

Figure 7: Origin Economies of Intra-Emerging East Asian Bond Issuance in the First Quarter of 2022

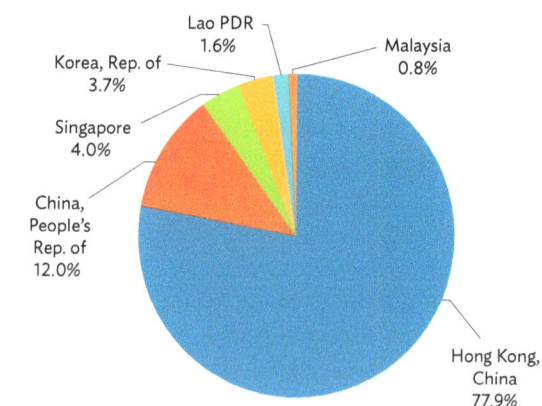

Lao PDR 1.6%
Malaysia 0.8%
Korea, Rep. of 3.7%
Singapore 4.0%
China, People's Rep. of 12.0%
Hong Kong, China 77.9%

Lao PDR = Lao People's Democratic Republic.
Source: *AsianBondsOnline* calculations based on Bloomberg LP data.

Companies from the transportation sector had the largest collective share of cross-border issuance at 37.6%, led by China Merchants Group, a PRC state-owned company based in Hong Kong, China and primarily involved in shipping and integrated transportation, which raised a total of USD2.4 billion worth of short-term bonds in February and March. The other two companies from the transportation sector that also issued notable cross-border bonds in Q1 2022 were Shenzhen International Holdings, which raised USD0.2 billion via 6-year bonds and Yuexiu Transport Infrastructure with USD0.2 billion worth of 5-year bonds. Finance companies comprised a third of all cross-border bond issuance in Hong Kong, China in Q1 2021. This sector was led by the Hong Kong Mortgage Corporation, which raised a total of USD1.7 billion worth of multi-tenor bonds ranging from less than 1 year to 3 years. China Mengniu Dairy was another one of the largest issuers of cross-border bonds in Hong Kong, China with a quarterly total of USD1.2 billion worth of short-term bonds.

The PRC registered the second-largest aggregate issuance of cross-border bonds in Q1 2022 at USD1,098 million, comprising a 12.0% share of the regional total. All cross-border bonds issued in the PRC during the quarter had tenors of 5 years and were all denominated in Hong Kong dollars. The three issuers were Smart Insight International (USD497.9 million), Sail Vantage (USD351.1 million), and Logan Group (USD249.0 million).

In Singapore, five institutions issued cross-border bonds in Q1 2022 with a total issuance volume of USD366.5 million denominated in Chinese yuan and Hong Kong dollars. The two largest issuers in Singapore were PSA Treasury Pte., a port and harbor operator, which issued USD127.7 million worth of 9-year HKD-denominated bonds, and CMT MTN Pte., a real estate investment trust with USD114.9 million worth of 9-year HKD-denominated bonds.

In the Republic of Korea, the Export–Import Bank of Korea was the sole issuer with a total issuance volume of USD335.5 million worth of multi-tenor, CNY-denominated bonds. Meanwhile, in the Lao PDR, the government raised USD150.2 million via a dual-tranche THB-denominated cross-border bond. This marks the return of the Government of the Lao PDR to the Thai bond market for the first time since 2019. Proceeds from the bond issuance are expected to be used to refinance its maturing debt.

Cagamas Global, Malaysia's state-owned mortgage corporation, was the sole issuer of cross-border bonds in Malaysia in Q1 2022, raising USD73.8 million worth of SGD-denominated 2-year bonds.

The top 10 issuers of cross-border bonds in the region had an aggregate volume of USD7.7 billion and comprised 84.1% of the regional total. Six on the list were firms from Hong Kong, China, while the rest were from the PRC and the Republic of Korea. The top three issuers were from Hong Kong, China—including China Merchants Group, Hong Kong Mortgage Corporation, and China Mengniu Dairy.

The Chinese yuan remained the predominant currency of cross-border bonds in the region in Q1 2022 with a share of 82.0% and equivalent to a total of USD7.5 billion (**Figure 8**). Firms from Hong Kong, China led the issuance in this currency. The second-most widely used currency was the Hong Kong dollar with a total volume of USD1.4 billion and a share of 15.6%. Other currencies used in cross-border issuances were the Thai baht (USD0.2 billion, 1.6% share) and Singapore dollar (USD0.1 billion, 0.8%).

In Q1 2022, issuance of cross-border bonds in emerging East Asia were largely from three major industries. Finance companies accounted for a third of all cross-border issuance in Q1 2021 with an aggregate volume of USD3.0 billion and a share almost at par with the previous quarter of 33.2% (**Figure 9**). The largest issuers from this industry include the Hong Kong Mortgage Corporation (USD1.7 billion) and the Bank of Commerce Hong Kong (USD0.4 billion). The transportation sector, with total cross-border issuance volume of USD2.7 billion, had the second-largest share at 29.3%. It also registered the biggest percentage increase, up from 14.2% in the previous quarter, largely driven by the cross-border bond issuance of

Figure 8: Currency Shares of Intra-Emerging East Asian Bond Issuance in the First Quarter of 2022

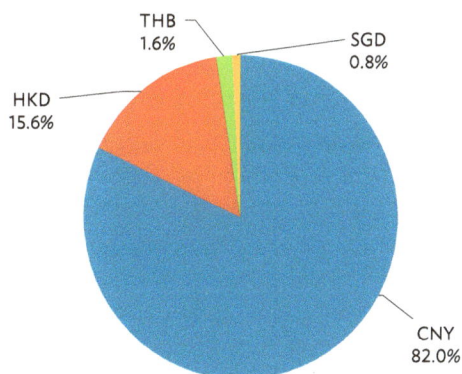

CNY = Chinese yuan, HKD = Hong Kong dollar, SGD = Singapore dollar, THB = Thai baht.
Source: *AsianBondsOnline* calculations based on Bloomberg LP data.

Figure 9: Intra-Emerging East Asian Bond Issuance by Sector

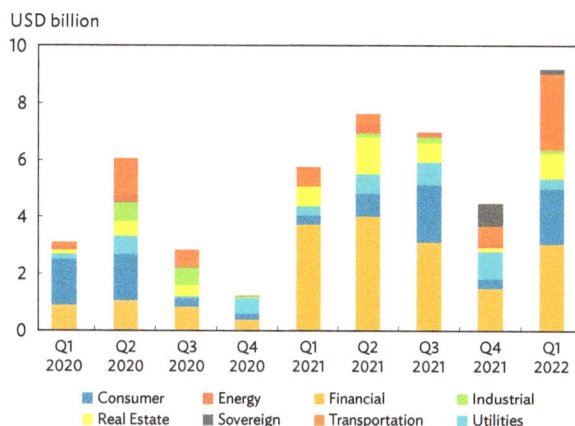

Q1 = first quarter, Q2 = second quarter, Q3 = third quarter, Q4 = fourth quarter, USD = United States dollar.
Note: Figures were computed based on 31 March 2022 currency exchange rates and do not include currency effects.
Source: *AsianBondsOnline* calculations based on Bloomberg LP data.

China Merchants Group (USD2.4 billion), which was the single-largest cross-border issuer in the region in Q1 2022. Companies involved in consumer products accounted for almost a fourth of the regional cross-border total (USD1.9 billion) during the quarter, and a higher share of 21.0% compared to 7.1% in Q4 2021. The largest issuer from this industry was China Mengniu Dairy (USD1.2 billion). The share of companies involved in real estate also increased to 9.6% (USD0.9 billion) in Q1 2022 from 3.3% in the previous quarter. Other sectors that registered cross-border bonds in Q1 2022 were utilities, sovereigns, and industrials.

G3 Currency Bond Issuance

Emerging East Asia's G3 currency bond issuance totaled USD99.5 billion from January through April.

During the January–April period, G3 currency bonds issued by emerging East Asian markets amounted to USD99.5 billion. This represented a decline of 30.7% y-o-y from the same period in 2021, when G3 currency issuance totaled USD143.5 billion (**Table 4**).[5] All economies in the region logged lower G3 currency issuance volumes during the review period compared to the previous year. Fundraisers were cautious as geopolitical concerns escalated with the Russian invasion of Ukraine, interest rates increased worldwide, and the PRC's property sector slumped. Investors were also apprehensive due to growth outlook concerns brought about by the negative US economic growth recorded in Q1 2022 and the PRC's COVID-19-related lockdowns.

Of the total G3 currency bonds issued in the region from January through April, 93.5% was denominated in US dollars, 5.6% in euros, and 0.9% in Japanese yen. Bonds denominated in US dollars totaled USD93.1 billion during the review period in emerging East Asia, a contraction of 31.6% y-o-y from the previous year due to reduced fundraising activities from all economies in the region except for the Philippines, which more than doubled its issuance in US dollars. EUR-denominated issuance amounted to USD5.5 billion in January–April, a decline of 17.4% y-o-y, as issuance activities in Indonesia, the Republic of Korea, and the Philippines declined, which may be attributed to interest rate increases in the

US and the euro area during the review period. Funds raised from bonds issued in Japanese yen amounted to USD0.9 billion, soaring 23.0% y-o-y on increased issuance in the PRC, Malaysia, and the Philippines.

More than half of the issuance of G3 currency bonds in emerging East Asia was from the PRC, which raised the equivalent of USD54.2 billion during the first 4 months of 2022. The Republic of Korea followed with USD16.3 billion, then Hong Kong, China with USD9.6 billion. The US dollar was the main currency chosen by all economies in the region in raising G3 currency funds.

From January to April, a y-o-y drop in G3 currency bond issuance was recorded in Indonesia (−57.7%); Malaysia (−51.4%); Hong Kong, China (−41.7%); Thailand (−35.0%); the PRC (−28.9%), the Philippines (−28.0%), the Republic of Korea (−8.8%); and Singapore (−3.5%). No G3 currency bonds were issued by Viet Nam during the review period after having issued USD-denominated bonds during the same period in the prior year.

For the first 4 months of 2022, 54.5% of all emerging East Asian issuances of G3 currency bonds was from the PRC: USD50.2 billion was raised in US dollars, EUR-denominated bonds totaled the equivalent of USD3.9 billion, and USD0.1 billion worth of JPY-denominated bonds was issued. Technology company Prosus issued a multicurrency, multitranche callable bond totaling USD5.1 billion. The USD-denominated tranche had tenors of 5 years, 10 years, and 30 years. The tranche denominated in euros had maturities of 4 years, 8 years, and 12 years. In January, financial institution China Construction Bank issued a 10-year USD2.0 billion callable USD-denominated bond. Funds raised will be considered as Tier 2 capital of the bank.

During the review period, the Republic of Korea accounted for 16.4% of all G3 currency bonds issued in the region: USD16.2 billion was in US dollars and the equivalent of USD0.1 billion was issued in euros. A prolific issuer of G3 currency bonds, the Export–Import Bank of Korea raised funds from 16 USD-denominated issuances during the first 4 months of 2022 totaling USD4.3 billion. It also issued one callable bond denominated in euros. The bank raised the equivalent of USD47.5 million from the

---

[5] G3 currency bonds are denominated in either euros, Japanese yen, or US dollars. For the discussion on G3 currency issuance, emerging East Asia comprises the People's Republic of China; Hong Kong, China; Indonesia; the Republic of Korea; Malaysia; the Philippines; Singapore; Thailand; and Viet Nam.

Table 4: G3 Currency Bond Issuance

2021			January–April 2022		
Issuer	Amount (USD billion)	Issue Date	Issuer	Amount (USD billion)	Issue Date
China, People's Rep. of	**217.4**		**China, People's Rep. of**	**54.2**	
Industrial and Commercial Bank of China 3.200% Perpetual	6.2	24-Sep-21	China Construction Bank 2.850% 2032	2.0	21-Jan-22
China Development Bank 0.380% 2022	2.0	10-Jun-21	Prosus 4.987% 2052	1.3	19-Jan-22
Prosus 3.061% 2031	1.9	13-Jul-21	China Cinda (2020) I Management 3.250% 2027	1.0	28-Jan-22
Others	207.4		Others	49.9	
Hong Kong, China	**39.7**		**Hong Kong, China**	**9.6**	
Hong Kong, China (Sovereign) 0.000% 2026	1.4	24-Nov-21	Airport Authority Hong Kong 2.50% 2032	1.2	12-Jan-22
NWD Finance 4.125% Perpetual	1.2	10-Jun-21	Airport Authority Hong Kong 3.25% 2052	1.2	12-Jan-22
Hong Kong, China (Sovereign) 0.625% 2026	1.0	2-Feb-21	Airport Authority Hong Kong 1.75% 2027	1.0	12-Jan-22
Others	36.1		Others	6.2	
Indonesia	**26.4**		**Indonesia**	**4.9**	
Indonesia (Sovereign) 3.05% 2051	2.0	12-Jan-21	PT Freeport Indonesia 5.315% 2032	1.5	14-Apr-22
Perusahaan Penerbit SBSN Indonesia III 1.50% 2026	1.3	9-Jun-21	Indonesia (Sovereign) 3.550% 2032	1.0	31-Mar-22
Indonesia (Sovereign) 1.85% 2031	1.3	12-Jan-21	PT Freeport Indonesia 4.763% 2027	0.8	14-Apr-22
Others	21.9		Others	1.6	
Korea, Rep. of	**43.9**		**Korea, Rep. of**	**16.3**	
Posco 0.00% 2026	1.2	1-Sep-21	Export–Import Bank of Korea 1.250% 2025	1.0	18-Jan-22
Korea Housing Finance Corporation 0.01% 2026	1.1	29-Jun-21	Korea Development Bank 2.000% 2025	1.0	24-Feb-22
SK Hynix 1.50% 2026	1.0	19-Jan-21	Export-Import Bank of Korea 1.625% 2027	1.0	18-Jan-22
Others	40.6		Others	13.3	
Malaysia	**16.0**		**Malaysia**	**4.2**	
Petronas Capital 3.404% 2061	1.8	28-Apr-21	MISC Capital Two 3.75% 2027	0.6	6-Apr-22
Petronas Capital 2.480% 2032	1.3	28-Apr-21	Bank Negara Interbank Bills 0.00% 2022	0.6	25-Jan-22
Others	13.0		Others	3.0	
Philippines	**10.8**		**Philippines**	**2.8**	
Philippines (Sovereign) 3.200% 2046	2.3	6-Jul-21	Philippines (Sovereign) 4.200% 2047	1.0	29-Mar-22
Philippines (Sovereign) 1.375% 2026	1.1	8-Oct-21	Philippines (Sovereign) 3.556% 2032	0.8	29-Mar-22
Others	7.5		Others	1.0	
Singapore	**16.5**		**Singapore**	**6.3**	
BOC Aviation 1.625% 2024	1.0	29-Apr-21	United Overseas Bank 0.387% 2025	1.6	17-Mar-22
Temasek Financial I 2.750% 2061	1.0	2-Aug-21	DBS Bank 2.375% 2027	1.5	17-Mar-22
Others	14.5		Others	3.2	
Thailand	**4.1**		**Thailand**	**1.3**	
Bangkok Bank in Hong Kong, China 3.466% 2036	1.0	23-Sep-21	GC Treasury Center 4.4% 2032	1.0	30-Mar-22
GC Treasury Center 2.980% 2031	0.7	18-Mar-21	GC Treasury Center 5.2% 2052	0.3	30-Mar-22
Others	2.4		Others	–	
Viet Nam	**1.6**		**Viet Nam**	**–**	
Emerging East Asia Total	**376.4**		**Emerging East Asia Total**	**99.5**	
Memo Items:			Memo Items:		
India	**23.7**		**India**	**6.8**	
Vedanta Resources 8.95% 2025	1.2	11-Mar-21	Reliance Industries 3.625% 2052	1.8	12-Jan-22
Others	22.5		Others	5.1	
Sri Lanka	**0.8**		**Sri Lanka**	**0.01**	
Sri Lanka (Sovereign) 7.95% 2024	0.2	3-May-21	Sri Lanka (Sovereign) 8% 2023	0.01	24-Jan-22
Others	**0.6**		**Others**	**0.001**	

USD = United States dollar.
Notes:
1. Data exclude certificates of deposit.
2. G3 currency bonds are bonds denominated in either euros, Japanese yen, or US dollars.
3. Bloomberg LP end-of-period rates are used.
4. Emerging East Asia comprises the People's Republic of China; Hong Kong, China; Indonesia; the Republic of Korea; Malaysia; the Philippines; Singapore; Thailand; and Viet Nam.
5. Figures after the issuer name reflect the coupon rate and year of maturity of the bond.
Source: *AsianBondsOnline* calculations based on Bloomberg LP data.

EUR-denominated bond, which had a tenor of 30 years. During the review period, Korea Development Bank issued a total of USD1.8 billion in bonds denominated in US dollars. The issuance included bonds with maturities from 2 years to 10 years.

Hong Kong, China accounted for a 9.7% share of bond issuances denominated in G3 currencies during the January–April period. Its G3 issuances comprised USD-denominated bonds valued at USD9.6 billion and bonds denominated in Japanese yen totaling USD0.03 billion. In January, the Airport Authority Hong Kong raised USD4.0 billion from a four-tranche, USD-denominated issuance. The 5-year tranche amounting to USD1.0 billion was a callable green bond. The other tranches (10 years, 30 years, and 40 years) were regular callable bonds, the proceeds of which will be used to finance the company's Three-Runway System project. The Hong Kong Mortgage Corporation issued several US dollar bonds amounting to USD1.0 billion from February to April.

In January to April, ASEAN member economies' issuance of G3 currency bonds plummeted 41.2% y-o-y.[6] G3 currency bonds issued in the region amounted to USD19.4 billion, which was well below the USD33.0 billion registered in January–April 2021 due to slow fundraising activities in all member economies. During the review period, ASEAN issuance was 19.5% of the total issuance of G3 currency bonds of emerging East Asia, down from the 23.0% share logged in the prior period. In the first 4 months of 2022, Singapore had the most issuance of G3 currency bonds in the ASEAN region. This was followed by Indonesia, Malaysia, the Philippines, and Thailand.

Singapore accounted for a 6.3% share of total issuance of G3 currency bonds in emerging East Asia during the review period, with issuance of USD4.7 billion in US dollars and the equivalent of USD1.6 billion in euros. In March, the United Overseas Bank issued a 3-year, EUR-denominated bond valued at USD1.6 billion. The issuance was drawn from its global covered bond program. In April, the bank issued three series of USD-denominated bonds totaling USD2.1 billion from its global medium-term note program. The series had a 3-year fixed-rate bond, 3-year floating-rate bond, and callable 11-year bond.

In January–April, issuances of G3 currency bonds in Indonesia were 4.9% of the emerging East Asian total. All issuances were denominated in US dollars and valued at USD4.9 billion. Mining company Freeport Indonesia issued a total of USD3.0 billion via a multitranche callable bond. The tenors of the issuance were 5 years, 10 years, and 30 years, the proceeds of which will be used for a smelter project in Indonesia. In March, the Government of Indonesia issued a dual-tranche callable bond. With tenors of 10 years and 30 years, and amounting to USD1.8 billion, proceeds from the issuance will be used for repurchasing some of the government's global bonds and for general budgetary purposes.

Malaysia's issuance of G3 currency bonds was 4.2% of the emerging East Asian total during the review period. The economy's USD-denominated issuances amounted to USD4.0 billion, and its JPY-denominated bonds totaled USD0.2 billion. In the first 4 months of 2022, the central bank of Malaysia issued several USD-denominated Bank Negara Interbank Bills valued at USD2.5 billion. The bills were issued to manage liquidity in the foreign exchange market. In April, shipping company MISC Capital Two issued a USD1.0 billion dual-tranche bond denominated in US dollars. Drawn from the company's multicurrency global medium-term note program, the issuance had tenors of 3 years and 5 years, the proceeds of which will be used for general corporate purposes.

For the January–April period, the Philippines accounted for a 2.8% share of total G3 currency bond issuances in the region. By currency, USD2.3 billion worth of US dollar bonds were issued, while JPY-denominated bonds amounted to the equivalent of USD0.5 billion. During the first 4 months of the year, the Government of the Philippines was the sole issuer of G3 currency bonds in its economy, issuing multi-tranche bonds both in US dollars and Japanese yen. In March, the issuance of USD-denominated bonds included tenors of 5 years, 10.5 years, and 25 years, amounting to USD2.3 billion. In April, samurai bonds totaling USD0.5 billion were issued with maturities of 5 years, 7 years, 10 years, and 20 years. For the US dollar issuance, the 25-year bond was a sustainability bond, while all tranches of the JPY-denominated issue were sustainability bonds.

---

[6] For the discussion on G3 currency issuance, data for ASEAN include Indonesia, Malaysia, the Philippines, Singapore, Thailand, and Viet Nam.

Thailand accounted for a 1.3% share of all G3 currency bonds issued by emerging East Asia during the review period, conducting fundraising activities solely in US dollars totaling USD1.3 billion. Only one firm, GC Treasury Center, issued G3 currency bonds during the first 4 months of 2022. In March, it raised funds from a dual-tranche, callable issuance with tenors of 10 years and 30 years. With growth in mind, proceeds from the issuance will be used for planned strategies and general corporate purposes.

Figure 10 illustrates the monthly issuance of G3 currency bonds in emerging East Asia for April 2021 to April 2022. With the onset of the Russian invasion of Ukraine in February 2022, issuances plummeted as economies in the region held back raising G3 currency bonds. Fundraising activities were also slow as interest rates increased due to central banks tightening monetary policies to combat inflationary pressures caused by the invasion and the gradual reopening of economies worldwide. After the dip in February, however, issuances picked up again in March, with the PRC leading the region in terms of issuance.

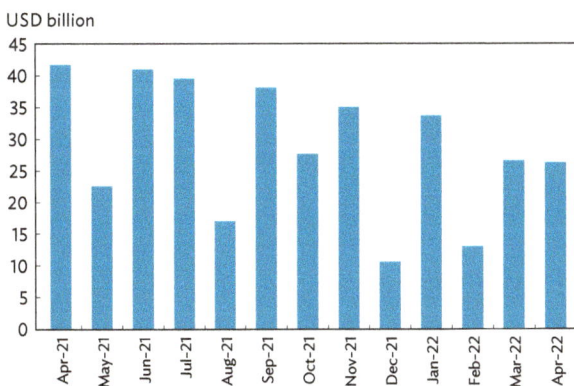

Figure 10: G3 Currency Bond Issuance in Emerging East Asia

USD = United States dollar.
Notes:
1. Emerging East Asia comprises Cambodia; the People's Republic of China; Hong Kong, China; Indonesia; the Republic of Korea; the Lao People's Democratic Republic; Malaysia; the Philippines; Singapore; Thailand; and Viet Nam.
2. G3 currency bonds are bonds denominated in either euros, Japanese yen, or US dollars.
3. Figures were computed based on 30 April 2022 currency exchange rates and do not include currency effects.
Source: *AsianBondsOnline* calculations based on Bloomberg LP data.

Bond Yield Movements

Yields in emerging East Asia rose on central bank moves to rein in inflation.

Globally, inflation has risen in 2022 due to supply shocks stemming from the Russian invasion of Ukraine as well as production disruptions in the PRC. This has led central banks in advanced economies to begin raising policy rates. The central bank that has most significantly affected global markets is the Federal Reserve, which raised its policy rate by 25 basis points (bps) during its 14–15 March meeting. This was followed by a 50 bps rate hike during its 4–5 May meeting, taking the federal funds target rate range to between 0.75% an 1.00%, while noting that inflation remains elevated.

In addition, the Federal Reserve's forecasts in March raised the projected number of rate hikes to six from a previous estimate of three made in December 2021. The Federal Reserve also unveiled its planned balance sheet reduction program, which is set to begin on 1 June. The Federal Reserve said as part of its balance sheet reduction program, that it would reinvest principal maturities in excess of a monthly cap. The cap for Treasury bonds will be USD30.0 billion for the first 3 months of the reduction program and increase to USD60.0 billion per month thereafter. For agency debt and mortgage-backed securities, the cap would be set at USD17.5 billion and increase to USD35.0 billion after 3 months. In its 14-15 June meeting, the Federal Reserve raised the federal funds target rate by 75 bps.

The Bank of England has also been steadily raising interest rates, having raised rates four times this year with the last rate hike of 25 bps on 4 May, taking the bank rate to 1.0% to arrest inflation. Meanwhile, the European Central Bank (ECB) has yet to raise policy rates. However, on 14 April, while its policy rates were left unchanged, the central bank affirmed that its Asset Purchase Programme would likely end in the third quarter of 2022 based on current economic conditions. The current trajectory of the Asset Purchase Programme is EUR40 billion in April, EUR30 billion in May, and EUR20 billion in June. In a later interview, the ECB president indicated that the central bank's first rate hike could come in July.

In contrast, the Bank of Japan (BOJ) has remained largely dovish. During its 28 April meeting, the BOJ largely left its monetary policy unchanged. The BOJ also affirmed that it would continue to purchase government bonds without limits to keep the 10-year government bond yield at zero. However, the BOJ announced that it would begin a facility offering to purchase 10-year bonds at a fixed-rate of 0.25% to help prevent yields from rising, reinforcing the BOJ's dovishness.

Emerging East Asia's yields also rose, tracking closely the impacts of central bank actions both in advanced economies and regionally, between 28 February and 31 May. One exception has been the PRC, whose rise in its 2-year yields have been relatively muted (**Figure 11a**). The PRC's yield movements have been capped by weakness in the PRC's economy. All other economies showed a strong rise in their respective 2-year yields, with the largest increase coming from Hong Kong, China as it closely tracked US yield movements. The next was Thailand after briefly experiencing the highest inflation in the region in March (**Figure 11b**). While nearly all markets had their yields trending upward, there was a slight downward movements after 10 May as US yields had a brief decline over recession concerns.

Across the region, movements in 10-year yields were similar, with nearly all markets showing a strong rise in yields following the Federal Reserve's rate hikes. The exception again was the PRC, with its 10-year yield

remaining relatively stable during the review period (**Figure 12a**). The Philippine had the highest rise in its 10-year yields following uncertainties from the results of the presidential elections (**Figure 12b**). The 10-year yields also exhibited a brief downward drop similar to 2-year yields after 10 May.

Emerging East Asia also witnessed a steepening of yield curves between 28 February and 31 May (**Figure 13**). Singapore recorded the steepest increase, with a rise of 86 bps, followed by Viet Nam at 84 bps. Singapore's yields rose due to quickening inflation, which led to two tightening measures by its central bank since the start of the year.

Most 2-year versus 10-year yields spreads fell between 28 February and 31 May with the exception of the Philippines and Viet Nam (**Figure 14**). The steepest decline was noted in Malaysia, where the yield spread shrank 37 bps, followed by Indonesia and Thailand at 36 bps each.

The PRC's divergence in yield movements in contrast to other markets in the region was largely due to the economic headwinds currently being faced. While the PRC's GDP growth rose to 4.8% y-o-y in Q1 2022 from 4.0% y-o-y in Q4 2021, it was lower than the 18.3% y-o-y posted in Q1 2021 and the 7.9% y-o-y posted in Q2 2021.

Figure 11a: 2-Year Local Currency Government Bond Yields

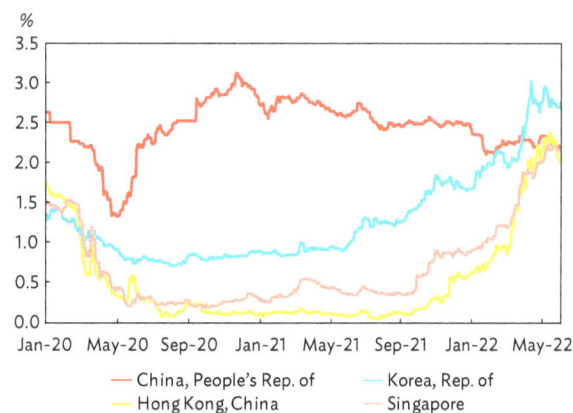

Note: Data coverage is from 1 January 2020 to 31 May 2022.
Source: Based on data from Bloomberg LP.

Figure 11b: 2-Year Local Currency Government Bond Yields

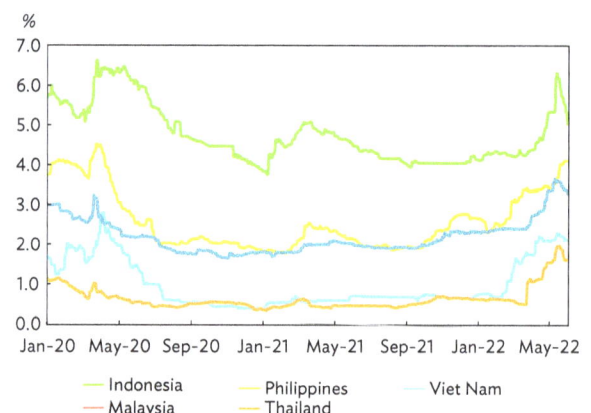

Note: Data coverage is from 1 January 2020 to 31 May 2022.
Source: Based on data from Bloomberg LP.

Figure 12a: 10-Year Local Currency Government Bond Yields

Note: Data coverage is from 1 January 2020 to 31 May 2022.
Source: Based on data from Bloomberg LP.

Figure 12b: 10-Year Local Currency Government Bond Yields

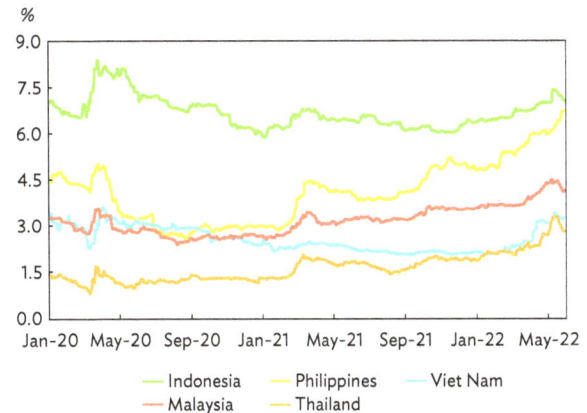

Note: Data coverage is from 1 January 2020 to 31 May 2022.
Source: Based on data from Bloomberg LP.

The economic outlook also remained cloudy for most markets in the region. Only Malaysia (5.0% versus 3.6%), the Philippines (8.3% versus 7.8%), and Thailand (2.2% versus 1.8%) posted faster y-o-y gains in Q1 2022 versus Q4 2021. Indonesia's y-o-y GDP growth was relatively stable at 5.0% in Q1 2022 and Q4 2021, but y-o-y growth moderated in the Republic of Korea (3.0% from 4.2%), Singapore (3.7% from 6.1%), and Viet Nam (5.0% from 5.2%). Meanwhile, GDP growth contracted in Hong Kong, China by 4.0% y-o-y in Q1 2022, following 4.7% y-o-y growth in Q4 2021.

While the growth outlook was initially positive in early 2022 due to the expectations that many markets would begin reopening, or had already reopened, the contraction in the US economy in Q1 2022, with GDP falling at an annualized rate of 1.5%, elevated global inflation, and shocks in global supply chains combined to lead to a softening in the growth outlook.

Despite the weaker growth outlook, supply-side pressures have largely pushed inflation upward in most markets. Thailand briefly had the region's highest inflation rate in March at 5.7% y-o-y before falling to 4.7% y-o-y in April (**Figure 15a**). Singapore registered the highest inflation rate in April at 5.4% y-o-y (**Figure 15b**). Only Malaysia showed a decline in inflation starting in November, while the inflation rate was roughly stable in the PRC.

As a result, despite a potentially weaker economic outlook, central banks in the region have begun to tighten, while other central banks that have not yet done so have raised expectations of tightening. The Bank of Korea was the first central bank in the region to raise policy rates in 2022, by 25 bps on 15 January, followed by MAS, which raised the rate of appreciation of the Singapore dollar nominal effective exchange rate in an off-cycle meeting on 25 January (**Table 5**). On 14 April and 26 May, the Bank of Korea raised policy rates by 25 bps each time. MAS likewise raised in April the rate of appreciation of the Singapore dollar nominal effective exchange rate and also recentered its midpoint. Bank Negara Malaysia raised policy rates on 11 May by 25 bps, and the BSP also raised its policy rate by 25 bps each on 19 May and 23 June. On 24 May, Bank Indonesia left unchanged its policy rate but raised the reserve requirement ratio to 9.0% from 6.5%, effective in September.

The BOT remains the only central bank to not have adjusted monetary policy, but expectations of an increase are rising. In addition, the PBOC so far has been the region's sole dovish central bank, as inflation in the PRC has been relatively tame in comparison to other economies in the region. After having reduced its 1-year medium-term lending facility rate by 10 bps on 16 January, the PBOC also reduced the reserve requirement ratio rate by 25 bps on 14 April. On 20 May, the PBOC reduced by 15 bps the 5-year loan prime rate.

Figure 13: Benchmark Yield Curves—Local Currency Government Bonds

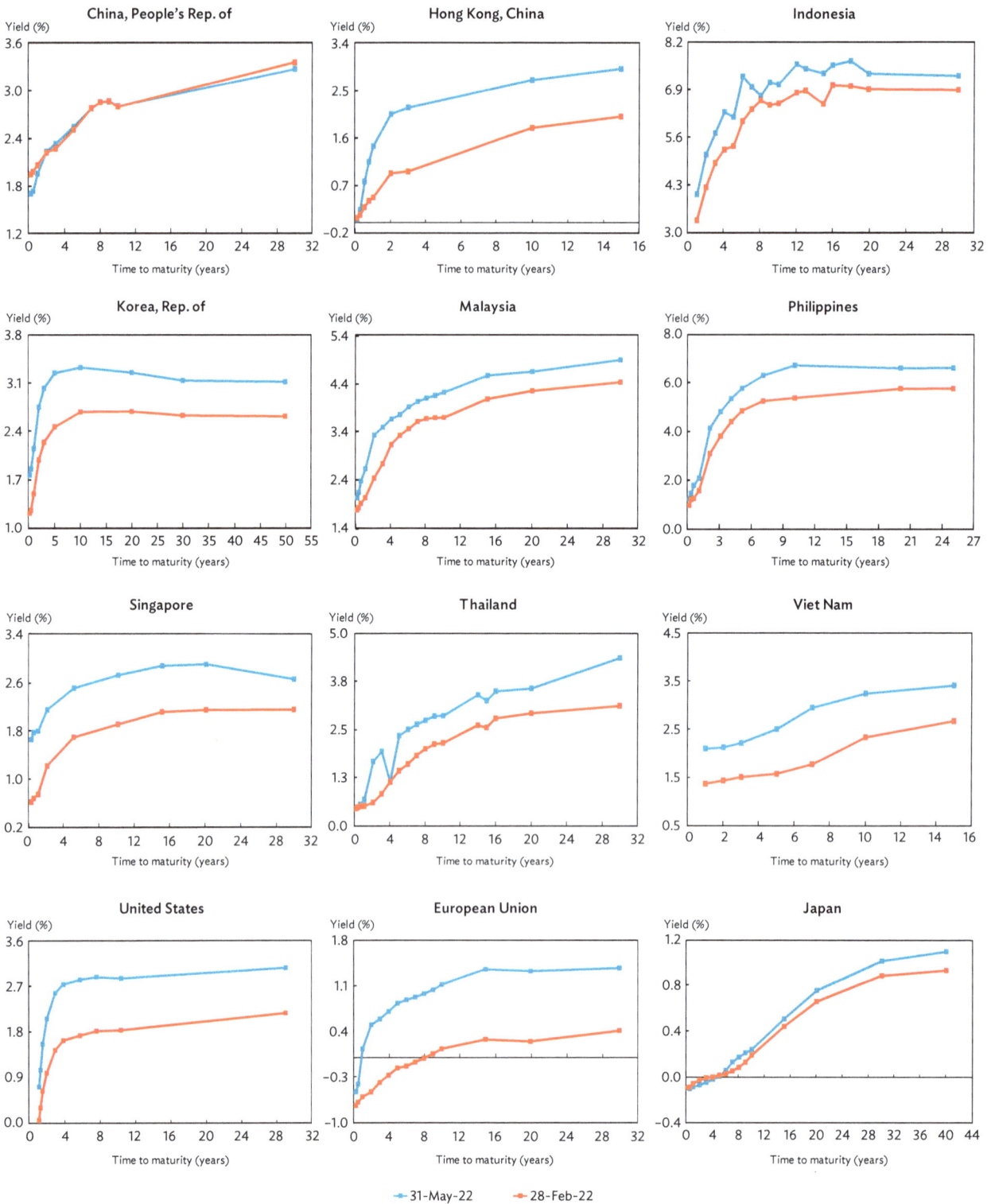

Sources: Based on data from Bloomberg LP and Thai Bond Market Association.

Figure 14: Yield Spreads between 2-Year and 10-Year Government Bonds

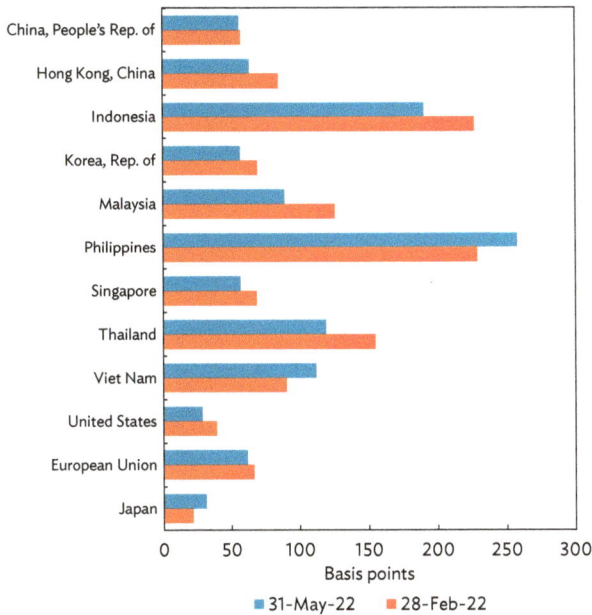

Source: *AsianBondsOnline* computations based on Bloomberg LP data.

Corporate spreads largely declined in the People's Republic of China and Malaysia.

The spread between AAA-rated yields and government yields fell in the PRC during the review period due to the monetary support being provided by the PBOC (**Figure 16a**). In addition, on 29 April, the Government of the PRC pledged that it would support the economy through measures that aid industries and small businesses and, on 23 May, the government announced a slew of support packages. The measures include tax rebates, cash subsidies, deferral on social insurance payments, and increased lending to small businesses. The corporate yield spread also fell in Malaysia and Thailand but rose in the Republic of Korea.

The spread between lower-rated bonds also fell in the PRC and Thailand during the review period, but rose in Malaysia and was unchanged in the Republic of Korea (**Figure 16b**).

Figure 15a: Headline Inflation Rates

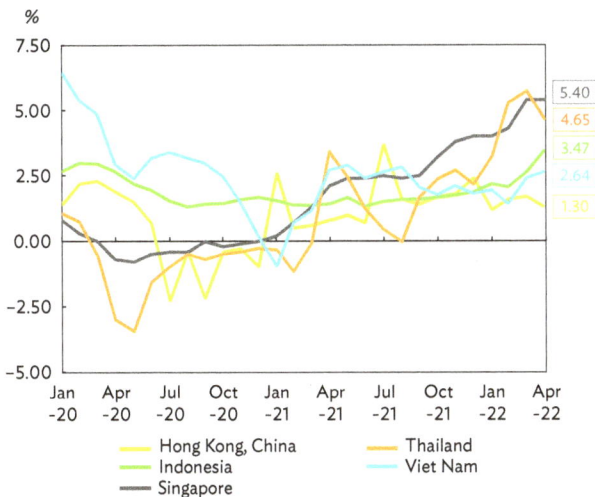

Note: Data coverage is from January 2020 to April 2022.
Source: Based on data from Bloomberg LP.

Figure 15b: Headline Inflation Rates

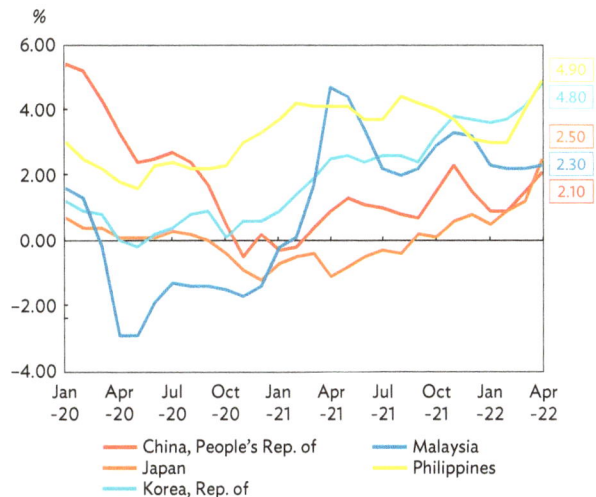

Note: Data coverage is from January 2020 to April 2022.
Source: Based on data from Bloomberg LP.

Table 5: Changes in Monetary Stances in Major Advanced Economies and Emerging East Asia

Economy	Policy Rate 30-Jun-2021 (%)	Jul- 2021	Aug- 2021	Sep- 2021	Oct- 2021	Nov- 2021	Dec- 2021	Jan- 2022	Feb- 2022	Mar- 2022	Apr- 2022	May- 2022	Jun- 2022	Policy Rate 9-Jun-2022 (%)	Change in Policy Rates (basis points)
United States	0.25									↑0.25		↑0.50		1.00	↑ 75
Euro Area	(0.50)													(0.50)	0
United Kingdom	0.10						↑0.15		↑0.25	↑0.25		↑0.25		1.00	↑ 90
Japan	(0.10)													(0.10)	0
China, People's Rep. of	2.95							↓0.10						2.85	↓ 10
Indonesia	3.50													3.50	0
Korea, Rep. of	0.50	↑0.25			↑0.25			↑0.25			↑0.25	↑0.25		1.75	↑ 125
Malaysia	1.75											↑0.25		2.00	↑ 25
Philippines	2.00											↑0.25		2.25	↑ 25
Singapore	–			↑				↑			↑			–	–
Thailand	0.50													0.50	0
Viet Nam	4.00													4.00	0

( ) = negative, – = not available.
Notes:
1. Data coverage is from 30 June 2021 to 9 June 2022.
2. For the People's Republic of China, data used in the chart are for the 1-year medium-term lending facility rate. While the 1-year benchmark lending rate is the official policy rate of the People's Bank of China, market players use the 1-year medium-term lending facility rate as a guide for the monetary policy direction of the People's Bank of China.
3. The up (down) arrow for Singapore signifies monetary policy tightening (loosening) by its central bank. The Monetary Authority of Singapore utilizes the exchange rate to guide its monetary policy.
Sources: Bloomberg LP and various central bank websites.

Figure 16a: Credit Spreads—Local Currency Corporates Rated AAA versus Government Bonds

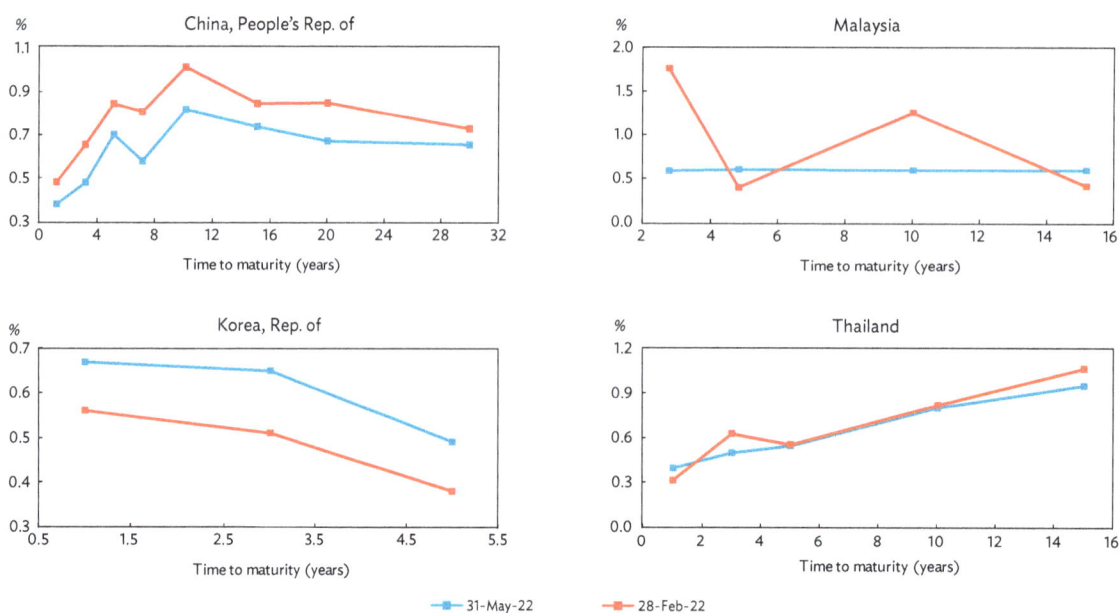

Note: Credit spreads are obtained by subtracting government yields from corporate indicative yields.
Sources: People's Republic of China (Bloomberg LP); Republic of Korea (KG Zeroin Corporation); Malaysia (Fully Automated System for Issuing/Tendering Bank Negara Malaysia); and Thailand (Bloomberg LP).

Figure 16b: Credit Spreads—Lower-Rated Local Currency Corporates versus AAA

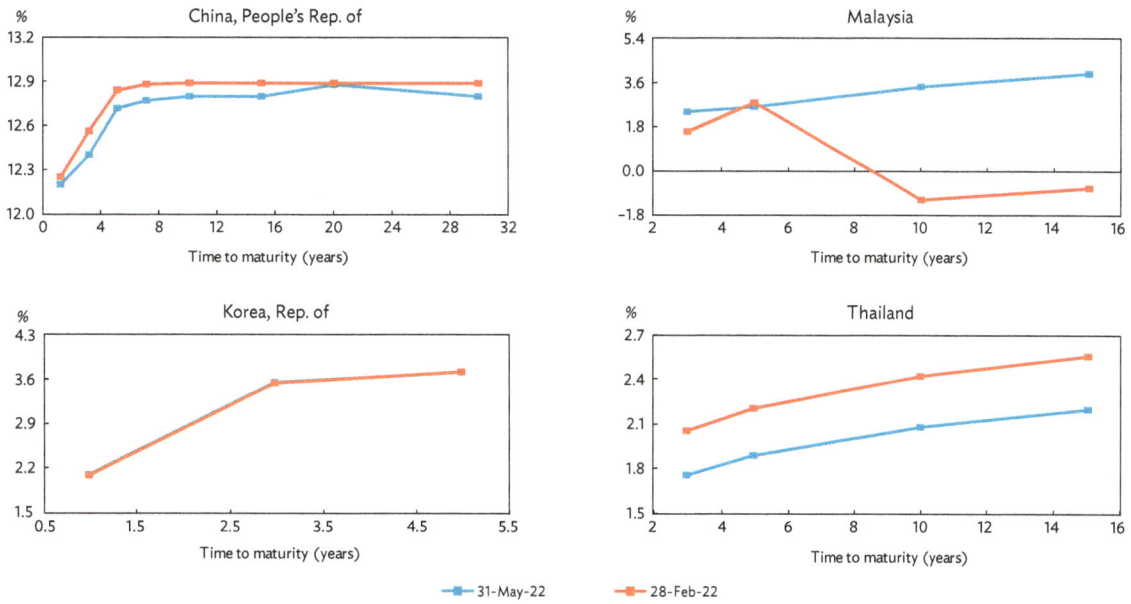

China, People's Rep. of

Malaysia

Korea, Rep. of

Thailand

— 31-May-22   — 28-Feb-22

Note: Credit spreads are obtained by subtracting government yields from corporate indicative yields.
Sources: People's Republic of China (Bloomberg LP); Republic of Korea (KG Zeroin Corporation); Malaysia (Fully Automated System for Issuing/Tendering Bank Negara Malaysia); and Thailand (Bloomberg LP).

Recent Developments in ASEAN+3 Sustainable Bond Markets

Sustainable bonds in ASEAN+3[7] markets continued to gain traction in the first quarter (Q1) of 2022, supported by robust issuance.[8] The amount of sustainable bonds outstanding in the region reached USD478.7 billion at the end of March, posting a year-on-year expansion of 51.3% and accelerating to growth of 9.7% quarter-on-quarter (q-o-q) in Q1 2022 from 5.6% q-o-q in the fourth quarter (Q4) of 2021 (**Figure 17**). ASEAN+3 accounts for 18.1% of global sustainable bonds outstanding, trailing only Europe as the second-largest regional market worldwide (**Figure 18**).

Outstanding green bonds reached USD333.6 billion at the end of Q1 2022, accounting for 69.7% of the regional sustainable bond stock. However, green bonds'

share of the region's total sustainable bond market has gradually slipped from 92.2% in Q1 2019 as the issuance of other types of sustainable bonds increased. The share of sustainability bonds and social bonds rose to 14.7% and 12.2%, respectively, at the end of Q1 2022. While the share of transition bonds (0.7%) remained low, ASEAN+3 does have the largest transition bond market globally, accounting for 54.1% of the global total at the end of March.

By individual economy, the People's Republic of China (PRC) is home to ASEAN+3's largest sustainable bond market, with 66.0% of the region's green bond stock, 66.8% of all sustainability-linked bonds, and 32.2% of the transition bond stock. At the end of

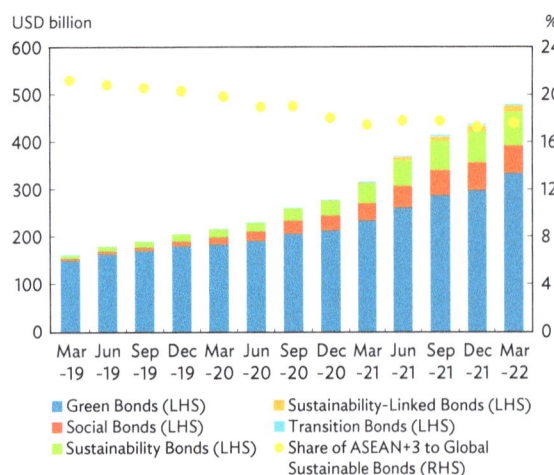

Figure 17: Sustainable Bonds Outstanding in ASEAN+3 Markets and Share of the Global Sustainable Bond Total

ASEAN = Association of Southeast Asian Nations, LHS = left-hand side, RHS = right-hand side, USD = United States dollar, y-o-y = year-on-year.
Notes:
1. ASEAN includes the markets of Indonesia, Malaysia, the Philippines, Singapore, Thailand, and Viet Nam.
2. ASEAN+3 includes ASEAN members plus the People's Republic of China; Hong Kong, China; Japan; and the Republic of Korea.
3. Data include both local currency and foreign currency issues.
Source: *AsianBondsOnline* computations based on Bloomberg LP data.

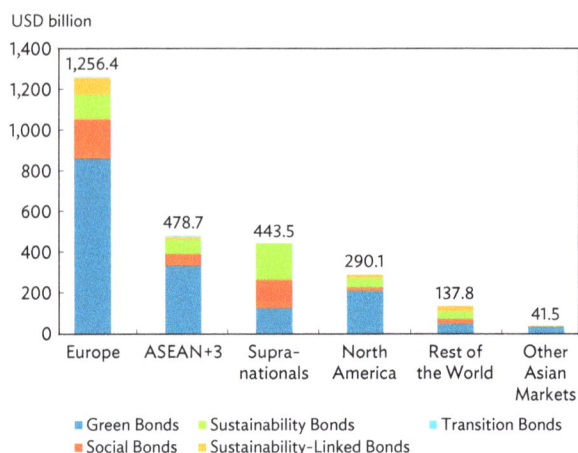

Figure 18: Sustainable Bonds Outstanding by Global Region

ASEAN = Association of Southeast Asian Nations, USD = United States dollar.
Notes:
1. ASEAN includes the markets of Indonesia, Malaysia, the Philippines, Singapore, Thailand, and Viet Nam.
2. ASEAN+3 includes ASEAN members plus the People's Republic of China; Hong Kong, China; Japan; and the Republic of Korea.
3. Data as of 31 March 2022 and include both foreign currency and local currency issues.
Source: *AsianBondsOnline* computations based on Bloomberg LP data.

---

[7] For the discussion on sustainable bonds, ASEAN+3 includes Association of Southeast Asian Nations (ASEAN) members Indonesia, Malaysia, the Philippines, Singapore, Thailand, and Viet Nam plus the People's Republic of China; Hong Kong, China; Japan; and the Republic of Korea.
[8] Sustainable bonds include green, social, sustainability, sustainability-linked, and transition bonds.

Q1 2022, the PRC had a total of USD238.8 billion worth of outstanding sustainable bonds, followed by the Republic of Korea (USD99.8 billion) and Japan (USD86.2 billion). The markets of ASEAN members had a combined USD34.3 billion worth of sustainable bonds outstanding. The region's social bond market is led by the Republic of Korea (59.6%) and Japan (38.6%). The Republic of Korea and Japan also dominate sustainability bonds outstanding, together accounting for 68.4% of the regional total. While ASEAN markets account for only 7.2% of ASEAN+3's total bond market stock, ASEAN members have a significant presence in the regional sustainability-linked (17.2%) and sustainability (18.4%) bond markets. ASEAN markets still have more scope for growth among the region's green (5.5%), social (1.4%), and transition (zero issuance) bond markets, particularly amid the global trend toward low-carbon transitions (**Figure 19**).

In Q1 2022, sustainable bond issuances in ASEAN+3 totaled USD59.2 billion, with green bond issuance reaching a record-high of USD47.7 billion and sustainability bond issuance rising 33.9% q-o-q to USD7.6 billion (**Figure 20**).

Private sector borrowers are major players in ASEAN+3 sustainable bond markets (**Figure 21**), with issuance

rising to 87.7% of total issuance in Q1 2022 from 83.7% in the previous quarter. In green bond markets, the private sector issuance share rose to 89.2% in Q1 2022 from 78.0% in Q4 2021. The financial sector has a significant stake in most types of sustainable bond issuances, accounting for 32.8% of total sustainable bond issuance in Q1 2022.

ASEAN+3 sustainable bond markets have a high concentration of short-tenor financing, with 76.3% of sustainable bonds outstanding having tenors of 5 years or less at the end of March (**Figure 22**). The region's average value-weighted tenor of sustainable bonds outstanding was 4.2 years in Q1 2022, down from 5.0 years in Q4 2021. Around 80% of outstanding green bonds in ASEAN+3 markets at the end of Q1 2022 carried maturities of 5 years or less, while this share was 78.1% for sustainability-linked bonds, 72.1% for social bonds, and 66.7% for sustainability bonds. At the end of March, 62.5% of ASEAN+3 sustainable bonds outstanding were issued in local currencies. Local currency bonds dominate most sustainable bond types, representing 82.1% of social bonds, 74.8% of sustainability-linked bonds, and 63.2% of green bonds. On the other hand, 57.8% of sustainability bonds and 70.4% of transition bonds were issued in foreign currencies, mainly denominated in United States dollars and euros.

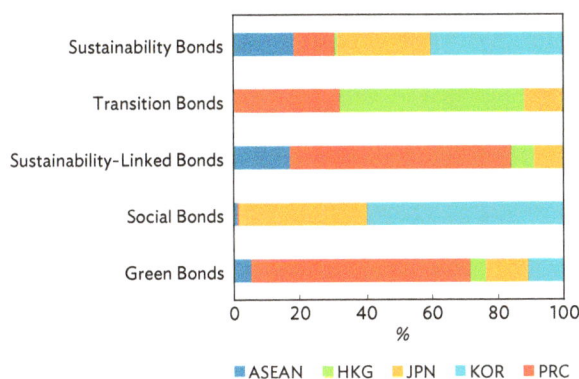

Figure 19: Sustainable Bonds Outstanding in ASEAN+3 by Economy Share

ASEAN = Association of Southeast Asian Nations; HKG = Hong Kong, China; JPN = Japan; KOR = Republic of Korea; PRC = People's Republic of China.
Notes:
1. ASEAN includes the markets of Indonesia, Malaysia, the Philippines, Singapore, Thailand, and Viet Nam.
2. ASEAN+3 includes ASEAN members plus the People's Republic of China; Hong Kong, China; Japan; and the Republic of Korea.
3. Data as of 31 March 2022 and include both foreign currency and local currency issues.
Source: *AsianBondsOnline* computations based on Bloomberg LP data.

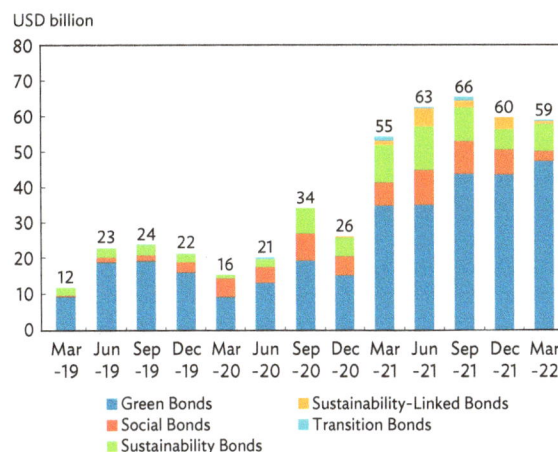

Figure 20: Quarterly Issuance Volumes of Sustainable Bonds in ASEAN+3

ASEAN = Association of Southeast Asian Nations, USD = United States dollar.
Notes:
1. ASEAN includes the markets of Indonesia, Malaysia, the Philippines, Singapore, Thailand, and Viet Nam.
2. ASEAN+3 includes ASEAN members plus the People's Republic of China; Hong Kong, China; Japan; and the Republic of Korea.
3. Data include both local currency and foreign currency issues.
Source: *AsianBondsOnline* computations based on Bloomberg LP data.

Figure 21: Issuance of Sustainable Bonds in ASEAN+3 by Sector in Q1 2022 (share of total)

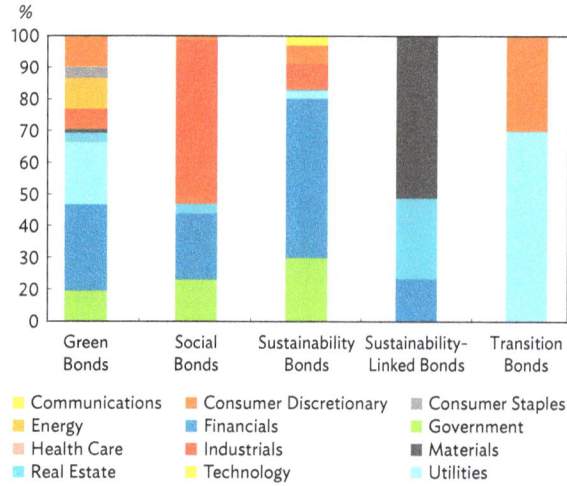

Communications, Consumer Discretionary, Consumer Staples, Energy, Financials, Government, Health Care, Industrials, Materials, Real Estate, Technology, Utilities

ASEAN = Association of Southeast Asian Nations, Q1 = first quarter.
Notes:
1. ASEAN includes the markets of Indonesia, Malaysia, the Philippines, Singapore, Thailand, and Viet Nam.
2. ASEAN+3 includes ASEAN members plus the People's Republic of China; Hong Kong, China; Japan; and the Republic of Korea.
3. Data include both foreign currency and local currency issues.
Source: AsianBondsOnline computations based on Bloomberg LP data.

Figure 22: Maturity and Currency Profiles of ASEAN+3 Sustainable Bonds Outstanding

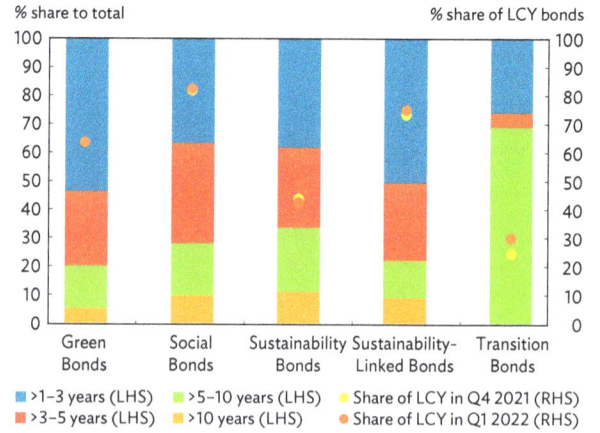

>1–3 years (LHS), >5–10 years (LHS), Share of LCY in Q4 2021 (RHS), >3–5 years (LHS), >10 years (LHS), Share of LCY in Q1 2022 (RHS)

ASEAN = Association of Southeast Asian Nations, LCY = local currency, LHS = left-hand side, Q1 = first quarter, Q4 = fourth quarter, RHS = right-hand side.
Notes:
1. ASEAN includes the markets of Indonesia, Malaysia, the Philippines, Singapore, Thailand, and Viet Nam.
2. ASEAN+3 includes ASEAN members plus the People's Republic of China; Hong Kong, China; Japan; and the Republic of Korea.
3. Data as of 31 March 2022 and includes both foreign currency and local currency issues
Source: AsianBondsOnline computations based on Bloomberg LP data.

Policy and Regulatory Developments

People's Republic of China

The People's Bank of China Allows Foreign Investors to Trade in the Exchange Market

In May, the People's Bank of China announced that foreign investors would be allowed to trade in its smaller exchange market, effective 30 June. The move was made to further attract capital flows into the bond market, following substantial capital outflows in February and March. In addition, financial institutions will be allowed to trade bonds and invest in derivatives and other financial instruments permitted by the People's Bank of China and the China Securities Regulatory Commission.

Hong Kong, China

Hong Kong Monetary Authority Maintains Countercyclical Capital Buffer Ratio at 1.0%

On 5 May, the Hong Kong Monetary Authority (HKMA) held the countercyclical capital buffer ratio (CCyB) steady at 1.0%. The HKMA noted that the latest economic data as of the fourth quarter of 2021 signaled a CCyB of 1.0%. Furthermore, economic activities slowed in the first quarter of 2022 and uncertainties regarding global and domestic conditions heightened. Thus, the HKMA decided to keep the CCyB unchanged at 1.0% and will continue to closely monitor developments. The CCyB is an integral part of the Basel III regulatory capital framework intended to improve the resilience of the banking sector.

Indonesia

Bank Indonesia to Accelerate Adjustments to Bank Reserve Requirement Ratios

On 24 May, Bank Indonesia announced that it would quicken the pace of reserve requirement ratio adjustments from its earlier announcement made in January. The move is part of the central bank's liquidity normalization policy. The first adjustment to the reserve requirement ratio proceeded as planned on 1 March. Subsequent adjustments will now take effect on 1 June, 1 July, and 1 September, bringing the rupiah reserve requirement ratio for conventional commercial banks to 6.0%, 7.5%, and 9.0%, respectively. The corresponding adjustments for Shariah banks and business units will be 4.5%, 6.0%, and 7.5%, respectively.

Republic of Korea

The Republic of Korea's National Assembly Passes the Second Supplementary Budget

On 29 May, the National Assembly passed the second supplementary budget of KRW62.0 trillion, which is to be largely allocated for programs involved in improving people's livelihoods. These include, among others, programs to compensate small business owners hit hard by the pandemic (KRW28.7 trillion) and policies intended to ensure proper pandemic control and the gradual transition to the general health-care system (KRW7.1 trillion). The government also announced that financing for the proposed supplementary budget would not entail the issuance of government bonds. The resulting 2022 budget is expected to generate a consolidated fiscal deficit equivalent to 3.3% of gross domestic product (GDP) and a government-debt-to-GDP ratio of 49.7%.

Malaysia

Bank Negara Malaysia Launches the Malaysia Islamic Overnight Rate

On 25 March, the Bank Negara Malaysia (BNM) announced the establishment of the Malaysia Islamic Overnight Rate (MYOR-i), which will be used as a reference rate for Shariah-compliant financial products. MYOR-i is expected to help develop the Islamic financial market of Malaysia, reinforcing best practices in the Shariah-compliant financial system. The BNM noted that MYOR-i is the first Islamic benchmark in the world that is transaction-based, and it will replace the Kuala Lumpur Islamic Reference Rate immediately. With this new Islamic benchmark, the BNM aims for better transparency and innovation in Islamic finance, leading to efficiency in pricing financial instruments and boosting the economy of Malaysia.

Philippines

Bureau of the Treasury Issues the Philippines' First Sustainability Samurai Bond

In April, the Bureau of the Treasury (BTr) issued the Philippines' first sustainability samurai bond in Japan. The issuance was part of the government's sustainability strategy to capture new accounts and mobilize capital from environmental, social, and governance-conscious investors, with the objective to transition to a more sustainable and climate-resilient economy. It also highlighted the government's commitment to climate change mitigation and adaptation and to deepening its domestic sustainable finance market. The JPY70.1 billion multi-tranche debt sale comprised 5-year bonds (JPY52.0 billion), 7-year bonds (JPY5.0 billion), 10-year bonds (JPY7.1 billion), and 20-year bonds (JPY6.0 billion).

Bureau of the Treasury Plans to Borrow PHP650.0 billion in the Second Quarter of 2022

The BTr is set to borrow PHP200.0 billion per month from the domestic debt market in April and May. The amount of monthly borrowing is lower compared to March (PHP250.0 billion). In June, the BTr is set to borrow PHP250.0 billion again as it has calibrated the volume based on domestic requirements and past rejections. In the months of April and May, the planned monthly Treasury bill offerings were PHP60.0 billion and Treasury bond offerings were PHP140.0 billion. In June, the Treasury bill and Treasury bond offerings were PHP75.0 billion and PHP175.0 billion, respectively.

Singapore

Singapore and Australia to Jointly Develop Financial Technology

On 13 April, Monetary Authority of Singapore and Australia Treasury signed an agreement committing both parties to strengthening their economies' financial technology network. Under the FinTech Bridge Agreement, the two governments agreed to improve multilateral cooperation on financial technology, expand business opportunities in each other's markets, work together with experts in both economies to generate new financial technology opportunities for Singaporeans and Australians, and share information on issues and market trends in financial technology.

Thailand

Thai Government Approves New Borrowing of THB1.4 Trillion for Fiscal Year 2022

On 12 April, the Government of Thailand approved new borrowing of THB1.40 trillion for fiscal year 2022, up from the previously planned amount of THB1.36 trillion. The new borrowing plan is projected to raise public debt to 62.8% of GDP at the end of the fiscal year, which is still below the government's 70.0% limit. The plan includes THB10.0 billion of borrowing for the state oil fund to stabilize domestic fuel prices, THB29.3 billion for restructuring government debt, and THB39.4 billion for investment projects. Public debt stood at 60.6% of GDP at the end of March.

Bank of Thailand Eases Foreign Exchange Regulations

As part of continuing efforts to develop Thailand's foreign exchange ecosystem, the Bank of Thailand announced a new set of regulatory changes on 18 April. Rules for cross-border currency transfer and payment transactions were relaxed to allow Thai residents greater flexibility in conducting foreign exchange transactions. Rules related to foreign exchange hedging were eased to help Thai companies manage their foreign exchange risks more efficiently. Documentary requirements for foreign exchange transactions were also simplified to reduce costs and facilitate foreign exchange activities through online channels. However, cross-border transfers of the Thai baht to pay for digital assets are still prohibited.

Viet Nam

Viet Nam Prime Minister Calls for Law Revision on Corporate Bonds

In April, Prime Minister Pham Minh Chinh issued Directive No. 304, which includes instructions for the Ministry of Finance to revise regulations on the corporate bond market in order to enhance efficiency in enforcing greater transparency and ensuring safety in the market. The directive stated that the focus should be placed on companies with a large amount of bond issuance, high-interest rates, and those having unfavorable business performance without sufficient guarantees. This follows the growing number of cases in Viet Nam of unlawful practices related to corporate bond issuance.

Special Topics on Bond Markets

Bond Market Development and Bank Diversification

Diversification is widely believed to enhance resilience and help reduce risks from concentrating in certain types of business activities.[9] For the banking industry, diversification in asset and liability portfolios, as well as income sources, helps reshape risk–return profiles and build greater resilience to shocks.

Existing banking literature has extensively studied the impact of diversification on banks' financial strength and resilience. For example, in the United States, greater diversification in income sources is found to improve banks' long-term performance and financial strength (Baele, De Jonghe, and Vander Vennet 2007; Shim 2019). In Italy, banks with greater income diversification witnessed higher risk-adjusted returns (Chiorazzo, Milani, and Salvini 2008). Similarly, bank diversification is found to be positively associated with better bank performance and financial stability in many emerging markets (Meslier, Tacneng, and Tarazi 2014; Moudud-Ul-Huq et al. 2018; Nguyen, Skully, and Perera 2012; Sanya and Wolfe 2011). Nevertheless, as diversification aims to reduce risks from concentrating in certain assets or income sources and to enhance stability and resilience, it does not necessarily improve bank performance and valuation in absolute terms. For example, the improvement of bank performance from diversification is limited in Germany (Hayden, Porath, and Westernhagen 2007), and in Italy, it depends on the risk level of banks (Acharya, Hasan, and Saunders 2006). Bank diversification is also found to reduce profits in the People's Republic of China (Berger, Hasan, and Zhou 2010). Laeven and Levine (2007) document a "diversification discount" in financial conglomerates' valuation when they engage in multiple activities, including both lending and nonlending financial services. However, the diversification discount for banks decreases over time and practically vanished after the global financial crisis, as shown in Guerry and Wallmeier (2017).

Bond market development is particularly relevant to bank operations. Banks are the major source of indirect debt financing, particularly for the private sector and households, while bond markets serve as the primary provider of direct debt financing to both the public and private sectors, including the banking industry. Bond markets provide more options for banks in terms of their asset and liability portfolios, but they also compete with banks for big corporate borrowers who can directly raise financing in the bond market and large-deposit clients such as government agencies, institutional investors, and wealthy individuals who prefer stable cash flows. Bond markets also offer banks more income sources beyond a traditional depositing and lending business, such as investment, brokerage, and underwriting. Bond market development is found to boost bank stability in emerging markets (Cagas, Park, and Tian 2021), and it also enhances banks' profit efficiency in Asia and the Pacific (Park, Tian, and Wu 2020). This study extends existing knowledge and investigates the implication of bond market development on banks' asset and income diversification.

Bond market development offers diversification opportunities to banks. Banks can diversify asset portfolios by holding multiple assets classes, including loans and securities, which can cover broader sectors and geographic locations. Banks can diversify liability portfolios by selling deposits as well as corporate bonds, commercial paper, and senior debentures to build a funding source with desired cost and maturity profiles. Bond markets offer income diversification potential via services, such as advisory and underwriting from bond issuances, as well as brokerage and investment from bond trading.

To investigate how bond market development empirically affects bank diversification in Asia and the Pacific, this study constructed a comprehensive sample consisting of 926 banks from 27 economies in the region over the period 2004–2017 (**Appendix Table**).

---

[9] This write-up was prepared by Qiongbing Wu (associate professor) in the School of Business at the Western Sydney University in Australia.

The data come from multiple sources including Fitch Connect, Bloomberg, the World Bank's World Development Indicators, the International Monetary Fund's World Economic Outlook Database, and the Heritage Foundation. Following existing literature (Curi, Lozano-Vivas, and Zelenyuk 2015; Meslier, Tacneng, and Tarazi 2014; Sanya and Wolfe 2011), this study utilizes the Herfindahl-Hirschman Index (HHI) that takes into account the distribution of asset types and income sources to measure a bank's asset (Asset_div) and income (Income_div) diversifications, as shown in equation (1):

$$Asset\_div = 1 - HHI = 1 - \left[\left(\frac{Net\ loans}{Total\ earning\ assets} \right)^2 + \left(\frac{Other\ earning\ assets}{Total\ earning\ assets} \right)^2 \right] \quad (1)$$

where other earning assets include securities and investments. Total earning assets is thus the sum of net loans and other earning assets. The values range between 0 and 0.5, and by subtracting HHI from 1, a higher value indicates a higher degree of asset diversification. Similarly, income diversification is measured in equation (2):

$$Income\_div = 1 - \left[\left(\frac{Interest\ income}{Total\ operating\ income} \right)^2 + \left(\frac{Other\ noninterest\ operating\ income}{Total\ operating\ income} \right)^2 \right] \quad (2)$$

where interest income includes interest income on loans and other interest income, and total operating income is the sum of interest income and noninterest operating income. The values again range between 0 and 0.5, with a higher value indicating greater income diversification.

In empirical models, the asset and income diversification measures are regressed on a vector of bond market development indicators—including total bond market size, government bond market size, and corporate bond market size—which are calculated as the value of outstanding bonds as a share of gross domestic product (GDP) in the same sample year. To control for other relevant factors that may influence banks' diversification strategy in terms of assets and income, bank-specific characteristics, banking sector characteristics, and country-specific characteristics, are included in the empirical model specification, as well as bank fixed-effects and time fixed-effects. The panel regression model is specified in equation (3):

$$Diversification_{i,t} = \alpha + \beta Bond_{i,t} + \gamma X_{i,t} + v_i + \theta_t + \epsilon_{i,t} \quad (3)$$

where i and t denote bank i and year t, respectively. $Diversification_{i,t}$ is the indicator of bank asset or income diversification. $Bond$ is the indicator of bond market development, which includes outstanding total bonds, government bonds, and corporate bonds as a share of GDP. $X_{i,t}$ is a vector of control variables, which include bank-specific characteristics such as bank size measured as the natural logarithm of total assets and capital as a share of total assets; market attributes such as real GDP growth, the natural logarithm of real GDP per capita, inflation rate, and investment freedom, following Luo, Tanna, and De Vita (2016); and banking sector characteristics such as bank activity restriction index, banking sector's asset concentration, asset diversification, foreign ownership, and government ownership, which are from Barth, Caprio, and Levine (2013) and based on World Bank surveys, following the literature (Doan, Lin, and Doong 2018; Meslier, Tacneng, and Tarazi 2014; Nguyen, Skully, and Perera 2012; Pennathur, Subrahmanyam, and Vishwasrao 2012; Saghi-Zedek 2016). v_i and θ_t represent bank and time fixed-effects, respectively. $\epsilon_{i,t}$ is the error term.

Results are presented in **Figure 23**, which shows that bond market development has a significant and positive impact on banks' asset and income diversification. When total bond market size as a share of the economy's GDP increases by 1%, the average bank's asset diversification increases by 0.018, which equals 4.5% of the sample mean of 0.396. This impact is much stronger for corporate bond markets than for government bond markets, with a 1% larger corporate bond market as a share of GDP associated with a 0.163 increase in banks asset diversification, which is 41.2% of the sample mean, while a 1% larger government bond market is associated with a 0.011 (2.8%) increase in banks' asset diversification. Turning to income diversification, a 1% increase in the overall bond market as a share of GDP is associated with an average of 0.007 greater income diversification of banks, which is 1.6% of the sample average of 0.426. This impact is largely driven by the corporate bond market. While the government bond market has a positive but insignificant impact on banks' income diversification, a 1% larger corporate bond market is associated with a 0.077 (18.1%) gain in income diversification on average.

Figure 23: Impact of Bond Market Development on Banks' Asset and Income Diversification

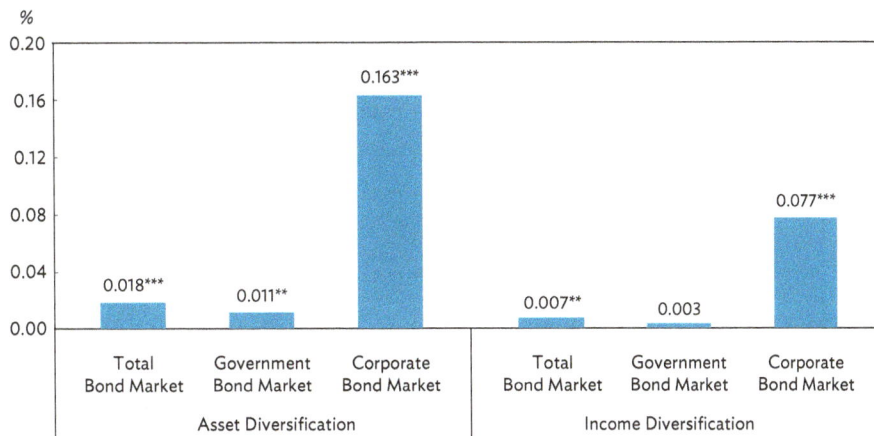

Note: *** and ** represent statistical significance at 1% and 5%, respectively.
Source: Author's calculation.

The results indicate that bond market development has a significant and positive effect on both bank asset diversification and income diversification, even when controlling for economy-, banking-industry-, and bank-specific factors. Both government bonds and corporate bonds are alternative investment assets for banks outside of their traditional lending business. Government bonds in a deep government bond market can store liquidity while generating yields. Corporate bonds offer similar features as loans but also provide diversification opportunities for more sectors and geographic locations. Thus, in an economy with a large bond market, banks are able to access more investments tools and income sources to diversify their assets and income from traditional lending business, which leads to a higher proportion of nonloan assets and noninterest income, on average, in banks' financial statements. This evidence is more pronounced for corporate bond markets, which points to the important role of corporate bonds in promoting bank asset and income diversification and reshaping banks' risk–return profile.

References

Acharya, Viral V., Iftekhar Hasan, and Anthony Saunders. 2006. "Should Banks Be Diversified? Evidence from Individual Bank Loan Portfolios." *The Journal of Business* 79 (3): 1355–412. doi: https://doi.org/10.1086/500679.

Baele, Lieven, Olivier De Jonghe, and Rudi Vander Vennet. 2007. "Does the Stock Market Value Bank Diversification?" *Journal of Banking and Finance* 31 (7): 1999–2023. doi: https://doi.org/10.1016/j.jbankfin.2006.08.003.

Barth, James, Gerard Caprio, and Ross Levine. 2013. "Bank Regulation and Supervision in 180 Countries from 1999 to 2011." *Journal of Financial Economic Policy* 5 (2): 111–219. doi: https://doi.org/10.1108/17576381311329661.

Berger, Allen N., Iftekhar Hasan, and Mingming Zhou. 2010. "The Effects of Focus versus Diversification on Bank Performance: Evidence from Chinese Banks." *Journal of Banking and Finance* 34 (7): 1417–35. doi: https://doi.org/10.1016/j.jbankfin.2010.01.010.

Cagas, Marie Anne, Donghyun Park, and Shu Tian. 2021. "Bond Market Development and Bank Stability: Evidence from Emerging Markets." *Research in International Business and Finance* 58 (C). doi: https://doi.org/10.1016/j.ribaf.2021.101498.

Chiorazzo, Vincenzo, Carlo Milani, and Francesca Salvini. 2008. "Income Diversification and Bank Performance: Evidence from Italian Banks." *Journal of Financial Services Research* 33 (3): 181–203. doi: https://doi.org/10.1007/s10693-008-0029-4.

Curi, Claudia, Ana Lozano-Vivas, and Valentin Zelenyuk. 2015. "Foreign Bank Diversification and Efficiency Prior to and during the Financial Crisis: Does One Business Model Fit All?" *Journal of Banking and Finance* 61 (2015): S22–S35. doi: https://doi.org/10.1016/j.jbankfin.2015.04.019.

Doan, Anh-Tuan, Kun-Li Lin, and Shuh-Chyi Doong. 2018. "What Drives Bank Efficiency? The Interaction of Bank Income Diversification and Ownership." *International Review of Economics and Finance* 55 (2018): 203–19. doi: https://doi.org/10.1016/j.iref.2017.07.019.

Guerry, Nicolas, and Martin Wallmeier. 2017. "Valuation of Diversified Banks: New Evidence." *Journal of Banking and Finance* 80 (2017): 203–14. doi: https://doi.org/10.1016/j.jbankfin.2017.04.004.

Hayden, Evelyn, Daniel Porath, and Natalja v. Westernhagen. 2007. "Does Diversification Improve the Performance of German Banks? Evidence from Individual Bank Loan Portfolios." *Journal of Financial Services Research* 32 (3): 123-140. doi: https://doi.org/10.1007/s10693-007-0017-0.

Laeven, Luc, and Ross Levine. 2007. "Is There a Diversification Discount in Financial Conglomerates?" *Journal of Financial Economics* 85 (2): 331–67. doi: https://doi.org/10.1016/j.jfineco.2005.06.001.

Luo, Yun, Sailesh Tanna, and Glauco De Vita. 2016. "Financial Openness, Risk and Bank Efficiency: Cross-Country Evidence." *Journal of Financial Stability* 24 (2016): 132–48. doi: https://doi.org/10.1016/j.jfs.2016.05.003.

Meslier, Céline, Ruth Tacneng, and Amine Tarazi. 2014. "Is Bank Income Diversification Beneficial? Evidence from an Emerging Economy." *Journal of International Financial Markets, Institutions and Money* 31 (2014): 97–126. doi: https://doi.org/10.1016/j.intfin.2014.03.007.

Moudud-Ul-Huq, Syed, Badar Nadeem Ashraf, Anupam Das Gupta, and Changjun Zheng. 2018. "Does Bank Diversification Heterogeneously Affect Performance and Risk-Taking in ASEAN Emerging Economies?" *Research in International Business and Finance* 46 (2018): 342–62. doi: https://doi.org/10.1016/j.ribaf.2018.04.007.

Nguyen, My, Michael Skully, and Shrimal Perera. 2012. "Market Power, Revenue Diversification, and Bank Stability: Evidence from Selected South Asian Countries." *Journal of International Financial Markets, Institutions and Money* 22 (4): 897–912. doi: https://doi.org/10.1016/j.intfin.2012.05.008.

Park, Donghyun, Shu Tian, and Qiongbing Wu. 2020. "Bank Efficiency and the Bond Markets: Evidence from the Asia and Pacific Region." ADB Economics Working Paper Series No. 612. doi: http://dx.doi.org/10.22617/WPS200104-2.

Pennathur, Anita K., Vijaya Subrahmanyam, and Sharmila Vishwasrao. 2012. "Income Diversification and Risk: Does Ownership Matter? An Empirical Examination of Indian Banks." *Journal of Banking and Finance* 36 (8): 2203–15. doi: https://doi.org/10.1016/j.jbankfin.2012.03.021.

Saghi-Zedek, Nadia. 2016. "Product Diversification and Bank Performance: Does Ownership Structure Matter?" *Journal of Banking and Finance* 71 (2016): 154–67. doi: https://doi.org/10.1016/j.jbankfin.2016.05.003.

Sanya, Sarah, and Simon Wolfe. 2011. "Can Banks in Emerging Economies Benefit from Revenue Diversification?" *Journal of Financial Services Research* 40 (1): 79–101. doi: https://doi.org/10.1007/s10693-010-0098-z.

Shim, Jeungbo. 2019. "Loan Portfolio Diversification, Market Structure and Bank Stability." *Journal of Banking and Finance* 104 (2019): 103–15. doi: https://doi.org/10.1016/j.jbankfin.2019.04.006.

Appendix Table: Sample Economies and the Number of Banks

Economy	No. of Banks	No. of Observations
China, People's Republic of	168	1,103
Japan	108	475
Indonesia	104	776
India	62	483
Viet Nam	49	257
Bangladesh	41	248
Malaysia	39	230
Philippines	36	298
Kazakhstan	32	281
Pakistan	28	168
Nepal	27	93
Cambodia	25	174
Australia	24	152
Thailand	24	241
Hong Kong, China	21	174
Sri Lanka	21	126
United Arab Emirates	20	177
Uzbekistan	19	142
Korea, Republic of	14	80
New Zealand	10	82
Lao People's Democratic Republic	10	51
Singapore	9	90
Bahrain	9	73
Mongolia	9	53
Myanmar	8	18
Tajikistan	6	34
Papua New Guinea	3	26
Total	**926**	**6,105**

Source: Author's compilation.

Risk and Return Spillover in ASEAN Bond Markets

Over the last 2 decades, the bond markets of emerging economies have attracted significant attention from the global investment community due to several factors.[10] First, emerging markets have grown and continue to grow rapidly. Second, since the 1990s, bond markets have become a major source of financing for businesses in emerging markets. Finally, the transparency and liquidity of emerging bond markets have improved significantly (Agur et al. 2019; Ahmad, Mishra, and Daly 2018; Hyun, Park, and Tian 2017). The rapid development of bond markets in emerging economies offers global investors higher yields in the global low-interest rate environment that has prevailed since the global financial crisis. They also provide alternative investment opportunities with diversification and risk management benefits.

Local currency (LCY) bonds outstanding in six Association of Southeast Asian Nations (ASEAN) economies expanded significantly from USD216.9 billion in 2000 to USD1,965.7 billion in 2021.[11] The average share of foreign holdings in these markets grew from 0.03% in 2003 to 15.2% in 2021. ASEAN economies are more connected with the rest of the world than ever before as their financial markets receive increasing attention from global investors. As such, it is interesting to know how closely ASEAN bond markets are linked with major Asian and global bond markets. However, such knowledge is limited in the literature. This paper adds to the literature by deriving a risk spillover measure based on the characteristics of static and dynamic spillover models. It empirically evaluates how the bond markets of Indonesia, Malaysia, the Philippines, and Thailand, which are collectively referred to as ASEAN-4, receive or send shocks among each other and with major Asian bond markets and global bond markets. By examining the strength and direction of return and risk spillovers between ASEAN-4 and major Asian and global advanced bond markets, this study provides new evidence on the level of integration of ASEAN-4 bond markets with regional and global bond markets.

Using the Diebold and Yilmaz (2014) spillover framework, this study constructs the return and conditional volatility (risk) network connectedness, between January 2012 and January 2022, among ASEAN-4 LCY bond markets and major Asian (the People's Republic of China [PRC], India, Japan, and the Republic of Korea) and major non-Asian advanced (the European Union [EU], the United Kingdom [UK], and the United States [US]) LCY bond markets. Panels A and B of **Figure 24** show the 10% strongest links for the return and conditional volatility (risk) network connectedness series during the sample period, respectively. There is strong inter-market connectedness among the underlying LCY bond markets. Specifically, major non-Asian advanced LCY bond markets (US, EU, and UK) exhibit strong interconnectedness with each other. Notably, the largest links are flowing from the US market for maturities of 7 years and 10 years. However, we do not observe significant collective return and volatility connectedness between ASEAN-4 bond markets and major Asian and global advanced bond markets, although some economy pair volatilities are exceptions. These include EU–Philippines, US–Indonesia, Republic of Korea–Philippines, PRC–Philippines, and Japan–Malaysia.

While there is some volatility connectedness among major Asian bond markets—particularly between the PRC, the Republic of Korea, and Japan—both return and volatility linkages within ASEAN-4 remain low. Moreover, major Asian bond markets—such as the PRC, India, Japan, and the Republic of Korea—do not exhibit close return and risk spillover effects with non-Asian advanced bond markets. This evidence indicates that ASEAN bond markets generally are not integrated with major regional and global advanced bond markets, while the bond market integration levels within broader Asia and between Asia and non-Asian advanced bond markets are also low. The lack of integration suggests that the exposure of ASEAN-4 and other Asian bond markets to global shocks may be limited. From an investment perspective, the low level of integration indicates that emerging Asian bond markets offer diversification potential as well as relatively higher yields for global investors.

---

[10] This write-up was prepared by Gazi Salah Uddin (professor) in the Department of Management and Engineering at the Linköping University in Sweden. The content is based on Uddin, Gazi Salah, Muhammad Yahya, Donghyun Park, Axel Hedström, and Shu Tian. 2022. "Bond Market Spillover Network During the Global Pandemic: What We Learn from ASEAN-4 Markets." SSRN Working Paper. https://papers.ssrn.com/sol3/papers.cfm?abstract_id=4113778.

[11] The six ASEAN economies include Indonesia, Malaysia, the Philippines, Singapore, Thailand, and Viet Nam.

Figure 24: Return and Volatility Connectedness Network among ASEAN-4, Major Asian, and Global Bond Markets, January 2012–January 2022

Panel A: 10% Strongest Return Links

Panel B: 10% Strongest Volatility Links

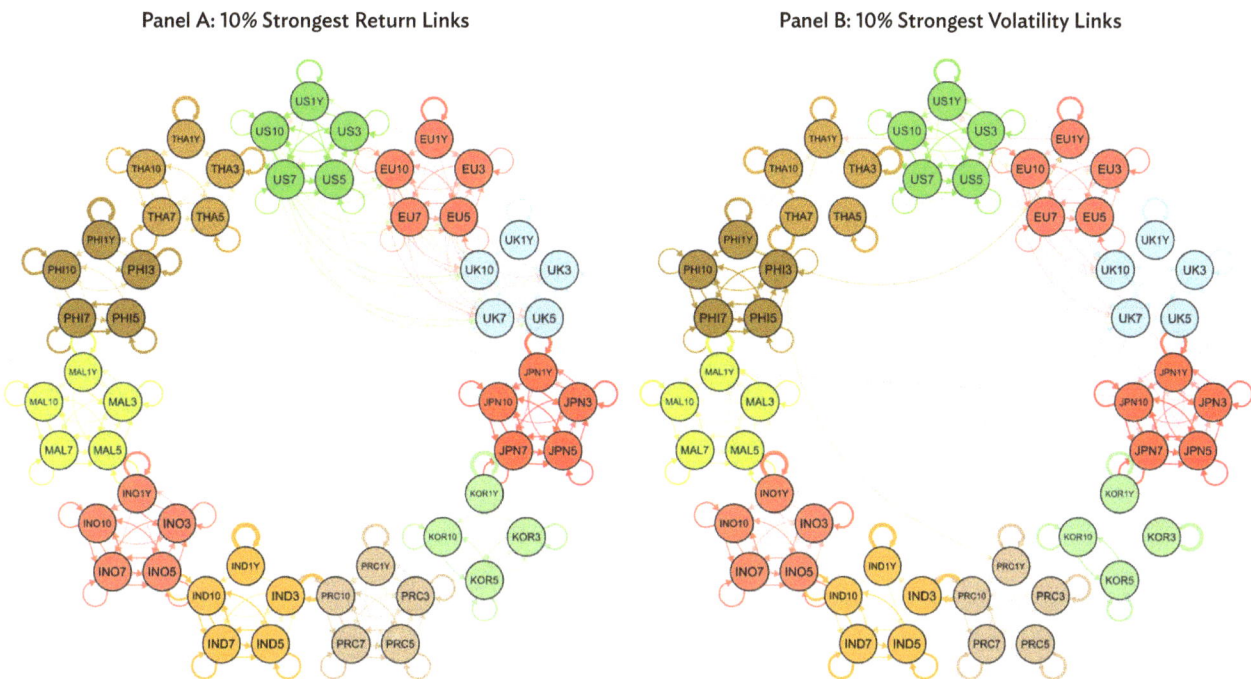

Notes: The total connectedness network is estimated using the Diebold and Yilmaz (2012, 2014) framework. THA, PHI, MAL, and INO refer to Thailand, the Philippines, Malaysia, and Indonesia, respectively. US, EU, UK, JPN, KOR, PRC, and the IND correspond to the United States, the European Union, the United Kingdom, Japan, the Republic of Korea, the People's Republic of China, and India, respectively. 1Y, 3Y, 5Y, 7Y, and 10Y refer to bond maturities at these years.
Source: Authors' estimations based on Bloomberg data and utilizing the Diebold and Yilmaz (2012, 2014) framework.

To further clarify whether ASEAN-4 bond markets serve as a good diversification option during crisis, this study focuses on the coronavirus disease (COVID-19) period—from January 2020 to January 2022—when global investment sentiment and liquidity conditions shifted rapidly. Panels A and B of **Figure 25** show the 10% strongest links for return and conditional volatility (risk) network connectedness during the COVID-19 period, respectively. During this period, volatility spillover was more strongly interconnected compared to the overall sample estimation. Especially, we see a stronger volatility spillover between Japan and the three global advanced bond markets (EU, UK, and US) and in some Asian market pairs such as US–Indonesia. But overall, spillover between developing Asian bond markets and the three global advanced bond markets remains limited. Risk spillover between Japan and Thailand, Japan and Indonesia, and the PRC and Thailand became stronger, as it did between the PRC, Japan, and the Republic of Korea. Overall, for global investors, developing Asia's bond

markets still presented diversification opportunities for risk management purposes during the COVID-19 period.

Meanwhile, descriptive statistics in general show that positive returns were observed during the COVID-19 period for longer maturity bonds in the Republic of Korea, Malaysia, the Philippines, and Thailand. Thus, the low level of interconnectedness between emerging Asian bond markets and major global advanced bond markets provides a portfolio diversification opportunity as well as a good risk–return profile, particularly for longer maturity bonds. This study shows global bond investors that a diversification strategy of mixing developed and emerging bond markets could be helpful in hedging risks during market turbulence. A potential implication for regulators is the importance of acting early against potential financial risk spillovers in the face of global shocks. An example of this can be seen in the US Federal Reserve currently tightening faster than major Asian central banks.

Figure 25: Return and Volatility Connectedness Network among ASEAN-4, Major Asian, and Global Bond Markets, January 2020–January 2022

Panel A: 10% Strongest Return Links

Panel B: 10% Strongest Volatility Links

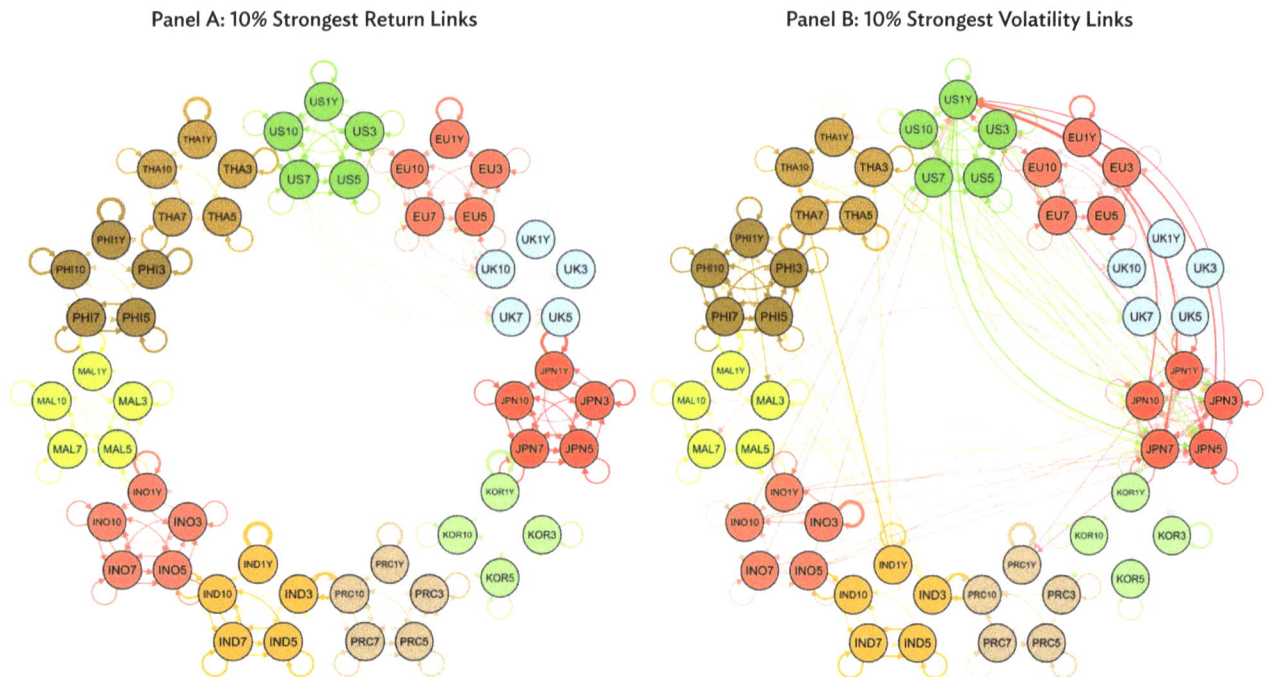

Notes: The total connectedness network is estimated using the Diebold and Yilmaz (2012, 2014) framework. THA, PHI, MAL, and INO refer to Thailand, the Philippines, Malaysia, and Indonesia, respectively. US, EU, UK, JPN, KOR, PRC, and the IND correspond to the United States, the European Union, the United Kingdom, Japan, the Republic of Korea, the People's Republic of China, and India, respectively. 1Y, 3Y, 5Y, 7Y, and 10Y refer to bond maturities at these years.
Source: Authors' estimations based on Bloomberg data and utilizing the Diebold and Yilmaz (2012, 2014) framework.

References

Agur, Itai, Melissa Chan, Mangal Goswami, and Sunil Sharma. 2019. "On International Integration of Emerging Sovereign Bond Markets." *Emerging Markets Review* 38 (2019). https://doi.org/10.1016/j.ememar.2018.11.006.

Ahmad, Wasim, Anil V. Mishra, and Kevin J. Daly. 2018. "Financial Connectedness of BRICS and Global Sovereign Bond Markets." *Emerging Markets Review* 37 (2018): 1-16. https://doi.org/10.1016/j.ememar.2018.02.006.

Diebold, Francis X., and Kamil Yilmaz. 2012. "Better to Give than to Receive: Predictive Directional Measurement of Volatility Spillovers." *International Journal of Forecasting* 28 (1): 57–66. https://doi.org/10.1016/j.ijforecast.2011.02.006.

———. 2014. "On the Network Topology of variance Decompositions: Measuring the Connectedness of Financial Firms." *Journal of Econometrics* 182 (1): 119–134. https://doi.org/10.1016/j.jeconom.2014.04.012.

Hyun, Suk, Donghyun Park, and Shu Tian. 2017. "Infrastructure Bond Markets Development in Asia: Challenges and Solutions." *Global Economic Review* 46 (4). https://doi.org/10.1080/1226508X.2017.1379910.

Rhee, Changyong, and Katsiaryna Svirydzenka. 2021. *Policy Advice to Asia in the COVID-19 Era.* Washington, DC: International Monetary Fund.

Market Summaries

People's Republic of China

Yield Movements

Between 28 February and 15 May, local currency (LCY) government bond yields in the People's Republic of China (PRC) were marginally changed (**Figure 1**). Bond yields fell for all maturities of 1 year or less, shedding an average of 11 basis points (bps), and for the 30-year tenor, which slipped by 1 bp. The largest decline in yields was seen for the 3-month maturity, which fell by 21 bps. In contrast, yields for maturities of 2 years through 10 years gained an average of 5 bps. The spread between the 2-year and 10-year tenors narrowed slightly to 56 bps on 15 May from 58 bps on 28 February.

Bucking the regional trend, the PRC was the sole market in emerging East Asia that saw only marginal upward movements for some maturities during the review period, with declines for some others. Yield divergence in the PRC was reflective of the overall weakness of its economic recovery. The lockdowns to contain the spread of the coronavirus disease (COVID-19) in several cities have resulted in supply chain disruptions that further exacerbate global inflationary pressure. The slowdown in the PRC economy is also contributing to the heightened uncertainty surrounding the global growth recovery.

To support the economy, the People's Bank of China (PBOC) has largely maintained an accommodative monetary stance. The PBOC was the sole central bank in the region to have reduced policy rates in 2022, a stark contrast to the tightening stances of some central banks in advanced economies and the region. On 16 January, the PBOC reduced by 10 bps the 1-year medium-term lending facility rate to 2.85%. The central bank also lowered the reserve requirement ratio by 25 bps in April and the 5-year loan prime rate by 15 bps in May. This largely influenced the decline in yields as well as capped gains across the yield curve.

Economic growth in the PRC rose to 4.8% year-on-year (y-o-y) in the first quarter (Q1) of 2022, up from 4.0% y-o-y in the fourth quarter (Q4) of 2021. Gross

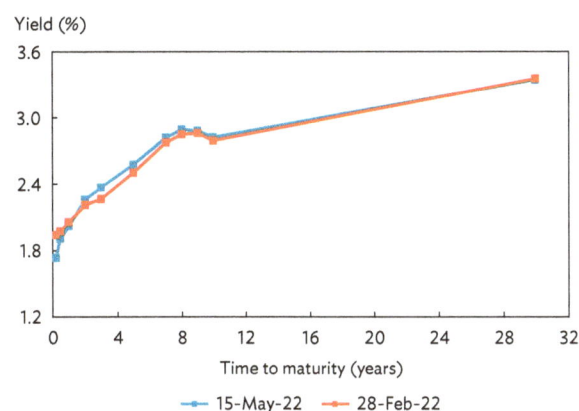

Figure 1: The People's Republic of China's Benchmark Yield Curve—Local Currency Government Bonds

Source: Based on data from Bloomberg LP.

domestic product growth, however, was lower compared to the 18.3% y-o-y growth recorded in Q1 2021. Other economic indicators also pointed to weaker growth, as unemployment in 31 major cities inched up to 6.0% in March from 5.4% in February. Consumer price inflation remained relatively low compared to global and other regional economies, recording a 2.1% y-o-y rise in May, the same rate as in April.

On 31 May, weaknesses in the domestic economy led the Government of the PRC to enact additional stimulus measures. Among these measures include tax rebates, expansion of Value Added Tax credits, deferral in social security premiums, and additional infrastructure spending and subsidies.

Size and Composition

The LCY bond market in the PRC continued to expand and reached a size of CNY118.9 trillion (USD18.8 trillion) at the end of March (**Table 1**). Overall growth moderated to 3.3% quarter on-quarter (q-o-q) in Q1 2022 from 3.9% q-o-q in Q4 2021. The slowing growth was largely influenced by weak issuance volume during the quarter.

Table 1: Size and Composition of the Local Currency Bond Market in the People's Republic of China

| | Outstanding Amount (billion) | | | | | | Growth Rates (%) | | | |
| | Q1 2021 | | Q4 2021 | | Q1 2022 | | Q1 2021 | | Q1 2022 | |
	CNY	USD	CNY	USD	CNY	USD	q-o-q	y-o-y	q-o-q	y-o-y
Total	103,528	15,799	115,154	18,117	118,908	18,755	2.1	17.3	3.3	14.9
Government	66,198	10,102	74,373	11,701	76,404	12,051	1.6	18.5	2.7	15.4
Treasury Bonds and Other Government Bonds	21,032	3,210	23,420	3,685	23,359	3,684	0.5	24.8	(0.3)	11.1
Central Bank Bonds	15	2	15	2	15	2	0.0	(18.9)	0.0	0.0
Policy Bank Bonds	18,382	2,805	19,681	3,096	20,107	3,171	1.9	15.0	2.2	9.4
Local Government Bonds	26,769	4,085	31,257	4,918	32,922	5,193	2.4	16.4	5.3	23.0
Corporate	37,329	5,697	40,781	6,416	42,504	6,704	2.9	15.2	4.2	13.9

CNY = Chinese yuan, q-o-q = quarter-on-quarter, Q1 = first quarter, Q4 = fourth quarter, USD = United States dollar, y-o-y = year-on-year.
Notes:
1. Treasury bonds include savings bonds and local government bonds.
2. Bloomberg LP end-of-period local currency–USD rates are used.
3. Growth rates are calculated from local currency base and do not include currency effects.
Sources: CEIC Data Company and Bloomberg LP.

On a y-o-y basis, however, bond market growth rose to 14.9% in Q1 2022. The PRC is home to the largest LCY bond market in emerging East Asia, accounting for nearly 80.0% of the region's aggregate bond stock at the end of March.

Government bonds. Government bonds accounted for 64.3% of the PRC's total bond stock at the end of March. Outstanding government bonds tallied CNY76.4 trillion (USD12.1 trillion) on growth of 2.7% q-o-q in Q1 2022, down from 4.5% q-o-q in Q4 2021. The tepid growth in government bonds stemmed from a slowdown in issuance of Treasury bonds during the quarter. The government's risk control policies resulted in a 0.3% q-o-q contraction in the stock of Treasury bonds at the end of March.

Growth in the government bond segment was largely driven by the 5.3% q-o-q growth in local government bonds, as the quota gets replenished at the start of the year. The special bond quota for 2022 was set at CNY3.7 trillion, the same volume as in 2021. Issuance of local government bonds swelled to 108.7% y-o-y as the government pushed local governments to tap this facility and frontload issuance to bolster economic recovery.

Policy bank bonds also contributed to the q-o-q growth but to a lesser extent. The stock of policy bank bonds grew 2.2% q-o-q to reach CNY20.1 trillion at the end of March.

Corporate bonds. The PRC's corporate bond market represented 76.4% of emerging East Asia's total corporate bond stock at the end of March. Corporate bond market growth picked up in Q1 2022, rising to 4.2% q-o-q

from 2.9% q-o-q in the prior quarter. The corporate bond market's size reached CNY42.5 trillion at the end of March.

Among the different categories of corporate bonds, listed corporate bonds accounted for the largest share, reaching CNY12.1 trillion at the end of March on growth of 2.8% q-o-q and 13.9% y-o-y (**Table 2**). Next were financial bonds at a size of CNY9.3 trillion on an expansion of 6.7% q-o-q and 19.8% y-o-y. The fastest growth, however, was seen in commercial paper, which expanded 19.9% q-o-q and 23.1% y-o-y on a softening interest rate outlook. In contrast, q-o-q contractions were recorded in the stocks of enterprise bonds and asset-backed securities at the end of March.

Amid the weakening growth outlook and COVID-19 lockdown measures, corporate bond issuance declined 11.0% q-o-q in Q1 2022. The issuance of financial bonds, listed corporate bonds, and asset-backed securities contracted in Q1 2022, falling 18.3% q-o-q, 20.0% q-o-q, and 56.6% q-o-q, respectively (**Figure 2**).

At the end of March, the top 30 issuers of corporate bonds in the PRC had an outstanding bond stock of CNY11.3 trillion, representing 26.6% of the corporate bond total (**Table 3**). State-owned China Railway continued to account for the largest amount of bonds outstanding at CNY3.0 trillion, representing 7.0% of the total corporate bond stock. Next was Industrial and Commercial Bank of China with bonds outstanding of CNY761.1 billion and a share of 1.8% of the corporate total. The top 30 list comprised 17 state-owned firms and 22 listed firms.

Table 2: Corporate Bonds Outstanding in Key Categories

| | Amount (CNY billion) | | | Growth Rate (%) | | | |
| | | | | Q1 2021 | | Q1 2022 | |
	Q1 2021	Q4 2021	Q1 2022	q-o-q	y-o-y	q-o-q	y-o-y
Financial Bonds	7,746	8,701	9,281	1.0	21.7	6.7	19.8
Enterprise Bonds	3,860	3,931	3,930	1.0	4.1	(0.02)	1.8
Listed Corporate Bonds	10,603	11,752	12,079	1.0	27.3	2.8	13.9
Commercial Paper	2,344	2,407	2,886	1.1	(12.2)	19.9	23.1
Medium-Term Notes	7,382	7,971	8,268	1.0	8.1	3.7	12.0
Asset-Backed Securities	2,942	3,487	3,441	1.0	23.2	(1.3)	17.0

( ) = negative, CNY = Chinese yuan, q-o-q = quarter-on-quarter, Q1 = first quarter, Q4 = fourth quarter, y-o-y = year-on-year.
Source: CEIC Data Company.

Figure 2: Corporate Bond Issuance in Key Sectors

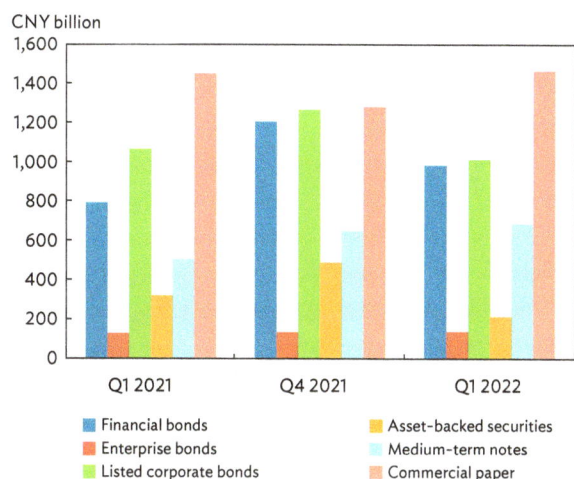

CNY billion

CNY = Chinese yuan, Q1 = first quarter, Q4 = fourth quarter.
Source: *ChinaBond*.

The largest corporate bond issuances in the PRC for Q1 2022 are presented in **Table 4**. The largest bond issuers during the quarter came from four banking institutions and state-owned China Railway. Banking firms continued to be major issuers of bonds as they beefed up their capital for lending activities, while China Railway issued bonds for infrastructure development. Among the issuances in the list, the shortest dated was a 3-year bond and the longest dated was a 30-year bond.

Investor Profile

Government bonds. At the end of March, banking institutions remained the largest investor group in the PRC's government bond market (**Figure 3**). The share of bank holdings in policy bank bonds, Treasury bonds, and local government bonds were 54.1%, 65.0%, and 86.4%, respectively, at the end of the review period. However, all of these shares slipped compared with year earlier.

Despite the capital outflows recorded in the PRC bond market in Q1 2022, the foreign holdings share was little changed versus its level in Q1 2021. The foreign holdings share of policy bank bonds dipped 5.0% in Q1 2022 from 5.4% in Q1 2021, while it rose for Treasury bonds to 11.6% from 10.9% over the same period. The foreign holdings share of local government bonds remained very small.

Policy, Institutional, and Regulatory Developments

The People's Bank of China Allows Foreign Investors to Trade in the Exchange Market

In May, the PBOC announced that foreign investors would be allowed to trade in its smaller exchange market, effective 30 June. The move was made to further attract capital flows into the bond market, following substantial capital outflows in February and March. In addition, financial institutions will be allowed to trade bonds and invest in derivatives and other financial instruments permitted by the PBOC and the China Securities Regulatory Commission.

Table 3: Top 30 Issuers of Local Currency Corporate Bonds in the People's Republic of China

	Issuers	Outstanding Amount		State-Owned	Listed Company	Type of Industry
		LCY Bonds (CNY billion)	LCY Bonds (USD billion)			
1.	China Railway	2,985.5	470.90	Yes	No	Transportation
2.	Industrial and Commercial Bank of China	761.1	120.05	Yes	Yes	Banking
3.	Bank of China	738.1	116.42	Yes	Yes	Banking
4.	Agricultural Bank of China	690.0	108.83	Yes	Yes	Banking
5.	Bank of Communications	519.2	81.90	Yes	Yes	Banking
6.	China Construction Bank	493.0	77.76	Yes	No	Asset Management
7.	Shanghai Pudong Development Bank	442.2	69.75	Yes	Yes	Banking
8.	Central Huijin Investment	387.0	61.04	No	Yes	Banking
9.	State Grid Corporation of China	353.0	55.68	No	Yes	Banking
10.	Industrial Bank	331.1	52.23	No	Yes	Banking
11.	China Citic Bank	315.0	49.68	No	Yes	Banking
12.	China Minsheng Bank	270.0	42.59	Yes	No	Energy
13.	China Merchants Bank	252.2	39.78	Yes	Yes	Banking
14.	State Power Investment	225.4	35.56	Yes	No	Power
15.	Huaxia Bank	220.0	34.70	No	Yes	Banking
16.	China Everbright Bank	215.9	34.05	No	Yes	Banking
17.	China National Petroleum	209.9	33.11	No	Yes	Banking
18.	Postal Savings Bank of China	190.0	29.97	Yes	Yes	Coal
19.	Ping An Bank	180.0	28.39	No	Yes	Banking
20.	CITIC Securities	166.1	26.20	Yes	No	Public Utilities
21.	China Southern Power Grid	164.6	25.96	No	Yes	Banking
22.	Huatai Securities	159.5	25.16	No	No	Brokerage
23.	Shaanxi Coal and Chemical Industry Group	148.0	23.34	No	Yes	Brokerage
24.	Guotai Junan Securities	134.7	21.24	No	Yes	Brokerage
25.	China Merchants Securities	133.4	21.04	Yes	Yes	Brokerage
26.	Tianjin Infrastructure Investment Group	131.9	20.81	Yes	Yes	Brokerage
27.	Bank of Beijing	127.9	20.17	No	Yes	Banking
28.	China Chengtong Holdings	120.6	19.02	Yes	No	Holding Company
29.	Shenwan Hongyuan Securities	141.5	22.32	Yes	No	Brokerage
30.	China Cinda Asset Management	117.0	18.45	Yes	Yes	Asset Management
	Total Top 30 LCY Corporate Issuers	**11,323.8**	**1,786.10**			
	Total LCY Corporate Bonds	**42,504.2**	**6,704.1**			
	Top 30 as % of Total LCY Corporate Bonds	**26.6%**	**26.6%**			

CNY = Chinese yuan, LCY = local currency, USD = United States dollar.
Notes:
1. Data as of 31 March 2022.
2. State-owned firms are defined as those in which the government has more than a 50% ownership stake.
Source: *AsianBondsOnline* calculations based on Bloomberg LP data.

Table 4: Notable Local Currency Corporate Bond Issuances in the First Quarter of 2022

Corporate Issuers	Coupon Rate (%)	Issued Amount (CNY billion)
Industrial Bank of China[a]		
3-year bond	3.00	10
3-year bond	2.96	25
9-year bond	3.45	30
Bank of China		
3-year bond	2.60	30
10-year bond	3.25	30
Shanghai Pudong Development Bank[a]		
3-year bond	2.78	30
3-year bond	2.69	25
China State Railway Group		
3-year bond	3.26	10
5-year bond	2.85	10
10-year bond	3.34	10
30-year bond	3.63	10
Postal Savings Bank		
10-year bond	3.54	35
15-year bond	3.74	5

CNY = Chinese yuan.
[a] Multiple issuance of the same tenor indicates issuance on different dates.
Source: Based on data from Bloomberg LP.

Figure 3: Local Currency Treasury Bonds and Policy Bank Bonds Investor Profile

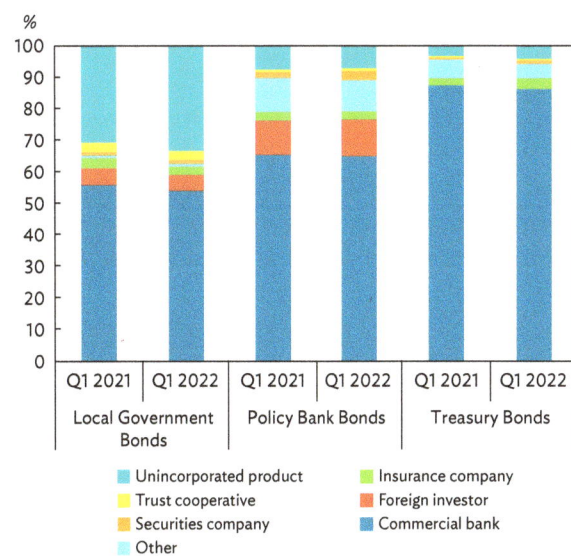

Q1 = first quarter.
Source: CEIC Data Company.

Hong Kong, China

Yield Movements

Between 28 February and 15 May, the local currency (LCY) government bond yield curve in Hong Kong, China shifted upward, with yields rising for all tenors except the 1-month tenor, which fell 5 basis points (bps) (**Figure 1**). On average, yields gained 96 bps across the curve. Yields for bonds with maturities of 1 year or less climbed an average of 63 bps, while yields for bonds with maturities longer than 1 year jumped 130 bps on average. The 3-year tenor showed the largest yield gain, jumping 160 bps. The 2-year yield soared 143 bps, while the 10-year jumped 109 bps. The spread between the 2-year and 10-year bond yields narrowed to 51 bps on 15 May from 85 bps on 28 February.

The rise in yields of Hong Kong, China's LCY bonds broadly tracked the jump in United States (US) Treasury yields during the review period as the Hong Kong dollar is pegged to the US dollar. US Treasury yields rose for all tenors, surging an average of 95 bps. The rise in US Treasury yields was largely driven by elevated inflation and the ensuing aggressive monetary policy tightening of the US Federal Reserve. Pandemic-driven supply chain disruptions, exacerbated by supply shocks caused by the Russian invasion of Ukraine as well as heightened domestic demand, triggered soaring prices. Consumer price inflation in the US climbed to 8.6% year-on-year (y-o-y) in May from 8.3% y-o-y in April. The US Federal Reserve adjusted upward the target for its policy rate by 25 bps to a range of 0.25%–0.50% in its 14–15 March meeting, and by an additional 50 bps to a range of 0.75%–1.00% in its 4–5 May meeting.

To maintain the Hong Kong dollar's peg to the US dollar, the Hong Kong Monetary Authority (HKMA) raised its base rate by 25 bps to 0.75% on 17 March and by another 50 bps to 1.25% on 5 May.[12] Despite the rise in the base rate, excess liquidity in the local banking system kept the Hong Kong Interbank Offered Rate low. The gap between US interest rates and the Hong Kong Interbank Offered Rate encouraged carry trades, pushing the Hong Kong dollar to the weak-side of its trading band against the US dollar in May. On 13 May, the HKMA

Figure 1: Hong Kong, China's Benchmark Yield Curve—Exchange Fund Bills and Notes

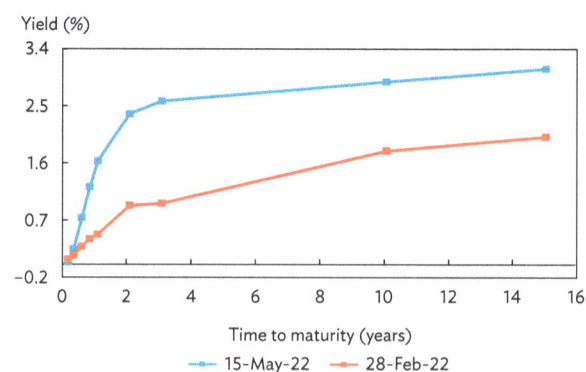

Source: Based on data from Bloomberg LP.

purchased HKD1.6 billion (USD202.0 million) to maintain the local currency's peg to the US dollar. The HKMA's intervention lowered the aggregate balance—an indicator of liquidity in the financial system—to HKD336.0 billion on 13 May from HKD377.5 billion at the beginning of the year.

Hong Kong, China's gross domestic product (GDP) contracted by 4.0% year-on-year (y-o-y) in the first quarter (Q1) of 2022, reversing the growth posted in the preceding 4 quarters. Merchandise exports fell 4.5% y-o-y as global demand declined and pandemic-induced, cross-border transportation bottlenecks curtailed the movement of goods. Private consumption contracted 5.5% y-o-y as restrictions imposed to curb a severe fifth wave of coronavirus disease (COVID-19) infections constrained economic activities. Investment expenditure fell 8.4% y-o-y as heightened local and global uncertainties worsened business sentiment. In May, the government revised its GDP growth forecast for full-year 2022 downward to 1.0%–2.0% from a forecast of 2.0%–3.5% previously announced in February.

Consumer price inflation in Hong Kong, China remained relatively mild compared to that of other economies in emerging East Asia. In May, consumer price inflation eased to 1.2% y-o-y from 1.3% y-o-y in April and 1.7% y-o-y in March. The underlying inflation, which

---

[12] The Hong Kong dollar is pegged to a narrow band of between 7.75 and 7.85 versus the US dollar. The base rate is set at either 50 bps above the lower end of the prevailing target range of the US Federal Reserve rate or the average of the 5-day moving averages of the overnight and 1-month Hong Kong Interbank Offered Rate, whichever is higher.

nets out the effects of the government's relief measures, inched up to 1.7% y-o-y in May from 1.6% y-o-y in April. While external price pressures are expected to persist, the government projects that domestic cost pressures will remain moderate. Government forecasts for full-year 2022 headline and underlying inflation are 2.1% and 2.0%, respectively.

Size and Composition

Hong Kong, China's LCY bond market reached a size of HKD2,546.2 billion (USD325.1 billion) at the end of March (**Table 1**). Overall growth dropped to 0.8% quarter-on-quarter (q-o-q) in Q1 2022 from 4.0% q-o-q in the fourth quarter (Q4) of 2021 due primarily to a contraction in the corporate bond segment. On a y-o-y basis, Hong Kong, China's LCY bond market expanded 4.1% in Q1 2022, down from 5.0% in Q4 2021. Government bonds comprised 53.4% of Hong Kong, China's LCY bond market at the end of March, up from 52.2% at the end of December.

Government bonds. Outstanding LCY government bonds amounted to HKD1,360.6 billion at the end of March on growth of 3.3% q-o-q and 14.6% y-o-y. The q-o-q growth in Q1 2021 was driven by increases in the outstanding stock of Exchange Fund Bills (EFBs) and Hong Kong Special Administrative Region (HKSAR) bonds. The stock of Exchange Fund Notes (EFNs) was steady between Q4 2021 and Q1 2022.

Issuance of new government bonds totaled HKD941.2 billion in Q1 2022 on growth of 2.5% q-o-q and 15.1% y-o-y. Issuance growth was primarily driven by increased issuance of EFBs, which the HKMA implemented from September 2021 to February 2022.

Exchange Fund Bills. EFBs outstanding reached HKD1,165.8 billion at the end of March on growth of 3.6% q-o-q and 11.7% y-o-y. EFBs comprised 85.7% of total LCY government bonds at the end of March. Issuance of EFBs totaled HKD936.7 billion in Q1 2022. Issuance growth eased to 3.0% q-o-q in Q1 2022 from 6.9% q-o-q in the previous quarter. To absorb excess liquidity in the financial system, the HKMA increased its issuance of 91-day EFBs by HKD5.0 billion in each of the regular tenders from September 2021 to February 2022. EFB issuance reverted to its previous level in March, hence the impact on issuance was greater in Q4 2021 than in Q1 2022.

Exchange Fund Notes. Outstanding EFNs totaled HKD23.4 billion at the end of March. Issuance of EFNs has been limited to 2-year tenors since 2015. In February, the HKMA issued HKD1.2 billion of 2-year EFNs. Due to maturities, the stock of outstanding EFNs remained the same between the end of December and the end of March. On a y-o-y basis, outstanding EFNs contracted 6.4% in Q1 2021, the same rate of decline recorded in the previous quarter. EFNs accounted for 1.7% of total LCY government bonds at the end of March.

Table 1: Size and Composition of the Local Currency Bond Market in Hong Kong, China

	Outstanding Amount (billion)						Growth Rate (%)			
	Q1 2021		Q4 2021		Q1 2022		Q1 2021		Q1 2022	
	HKD	USD	HKD	USD	HKD	USD	q-o-q	y-o-y	q-o-q	y-o-y
Total	2,446	315	2,525	324	2,546	325	1.7	8.4	0.8	4.1
Government	1,187	153	1,317	169	1,361	174	0.2	1.5	3.3	14.6
Exchange Fund Bills	1,043	134	1,125	144	1,166	149	0.02	(1.5)	3.6	11.7
Exchange Fund Notes	25	3	23	3	23	3	–	(6.0)	–	(6.4)
HKSAR Bonds	119	15	168	22	171	22	2.3	43.2	1.9	43.8
Corporate	1,258	162	1,208	155	1,186	151	3.1	15.9	(1.9)	(5.8)

( ) = negative, HKD = Hong Kong dollar, HKSAR = Hong Kong Special Administrative Region, q-o-q = quarter-on-quarter, Q1 = first quarter, Q4 = fourth quarter, USD = United States dollar, y-o-y = year-on-year.
Notes:
1. Bloomberg LP end-of-period local currency–USD rates are used.
2. Growth rates are calculated from local currency base and do not include currency effects.
Source: Hong Kong Monetary Authority.

HKSAR bonds. HKSAR bonds outstanding amounted to HKD171.4 billion at the end of March on growth of 1.9% q-o-q and 43.8% y-o-y. HKSAR bond issuance totaled HKD3.3 billion in Q1 2022. In January, the government issued HKD1.5 billion of 10-year government bonds through a reopening of an existing 15-year bond. In February, the HKMA issued HKD1.0 billion of 1-year floating-rate notes indexed to the Hong Kong Dollar Overnight Index Average. In March, the government issued HKD0.8 billion of 15-year bonds. HKSAR bonds comprised 12.6% of total LCY government bonds at the end of March.

Corporate bonds. Hong Kong, China's LCY corporate bond market reached a size of HKD1,185.6 billion at the end of March. The LCY corporate bond market contracted 1.9% q-o-q in Q1 2022, reversing the 2.7% q-o-q growth recorded in the previous quarter. The decline in the LCY corporate bond stock in Q1 2022 was primarily due to a relatively high volume of maturities, which outpaced the growth in issuance.

LCY bonds outstanding of the top 30 nonbank issuers in Hong Kong, China totaled HKD314.8 billion at the end of Q1 2022, accounting for 26.6% of the total corporate bond market (**Table 2**). Hong Kong Mortgage Corporation, Sun Hung Kai & Co., Hong Kong and China Gas Company, New World Development, and Hang Lung Properties were the top five nonbank issuers with outstanding bonds at the end of March of HKD80.7 billion, HKD20.6 billion, HKD17.8 billion, HKD15.8 billion, and HKD13.6 billion, respectively. The top 30 issuers were primarily finance and real estate firms. At the end of Q1 2022, finance firms collectively held a total of HKD144.5 billion of outstanding corporate bonds, comprising 12.2% of the LCY corporate bond market. Real estate companies had a total of HKD64.1 billion of outstanding corporate debt at the end of March, comprising 5.4% of the LCY corporate bond market.

Corporate debt issuance totaled HKD216.1 billion in Q1 2022 on an expansion of 5.5% q-o-q as corporates took advantage of relatively low interest rates to finance funding needs in anticipation of rising borrowing costs in the future as global central banks raise policy rates to temper inflation.

Table 3 shows notable issuers in Q1 2022. AIA Group, an insurance company, had the single-largest issuance of HKD6.5 billion for a 2-year bond. State-owned Hong Kong Mortgage Corporation remained the largest issuer after raising HKD15.3 billion from 39 issuances, including a 1-year bond worth HKD1.0 billion and a 5-year bond worth HKD0.5 billion. Haitong International issued a 92-day bond worth HKD0.9 billion and a 364-day bond worth 1.0 billion during the review period. Guotai Junan International raised a total of HKD1.9 billion from three issuances of short-term bonds. The longest tenor issued in Q1 2022 was Swire Pacific's 10-year bond worth HKD0.5 billion.

Ratings Update

On 7 April, Fitch Ratings affirmed Hong Kong, China's long-term foreign currency issuer default rating at AA– with a stable outlook. The rating affirmation was based on Hong Kong, China's large fiscal reserve, robust external finances, and high per capita income. Fitch Ratings forecast Hong Kong, China's GDP growth to ease to 1.0% in 2022 from 6.4% in 2021 due to the impacts of the latest wave of COVID-19 as well as potential spillovers of a slowdown in growth in the People's Republic of China. The rating agency also affirmed Hong Kong, China's long-term local currency issuer default rating at AA– with a stable outlook.

Policy, Institutional, and Regulatory Developments

Hong Kong Monetary Authority Maintains Countercyclical Capital Buffer Ratio at 1.0%

On 5 May, the HKMA held the countercyclical capital buffer ratio (CCyB) steady at 1.0%. The HKMA noted that the latest economic data as of Q4 2021 signaled a CCyB of 1.0%. Furthermore, economic activities slowed in Q1 2022 and uncertainties regarding global and domestic conditions heightened. Thus, the HKMA decided to keep the CCyB unchanged at 1.0% and will continue to closely monitor developments. The CCyB is an integral part of the Basel III regulatory capital framework intended to improve the resilience of the banking sector.

Table 2: Top 30 Nonbank Corporate Issuers of Local Currency Corporate Bonds in Hong Kong, China

	Issuers	Outstanding Amount		State-Owned	Listed Company	Type of Industry
		LCY Bonds (HKD billion)	LCY Bonds (USD billion)			
1.	Hong Kong Mortgage Corporation	80.7	10.3	Yes	No	Finance
2.	Sun Hung Kai & Co.	20.6	2.6	No	Yes	Finance
3.	The Hong Kong and China Gas Company	17.8	2.3	No	Yes	Utilities
4.	New World Development	15.8	2.0	No	Yes	Diversified
5.	Hang Lung Properties	13.6	1.7	No	Yes	Real Estate
6.	Link Holdings	13.1	1.7	No	Yes	Finance
7.	Henderson Land Development	12.9	1.6	No	Yes	Real Estate
8.	MTR	12.0	1.5	Yes	Yes	Transportation
9.	Hongkong Land	12.0	1.5	No	No	Real Estate
10.	CK Asset Holdings	10.0	1.3	No	Yes	Real Estate
11.	Swire Pacific	9.7	1.2	No	Yes	Diversified
12.	The Wharf Holdings	9.7	1.2	No	Yes	Finance
13.	Cathay Pacific	9.0	1.1	No	Yes	Transportation
14.	Airport Authority	8.9	1.1	Yes	No	Transportation
15.	AIA Group	8.9	1.1	No	Yes	Insurance
16.	Hongkong Electric	8.5	1.1	No	No	Utilities
17.	CLP Power Hong Kong Financing	7.4	0.9	No	No	Finance
18.	Swire Properties	7.3	0.9	No	Yes	Diversified
19.	Hysan Development Corporation	5.9	0.8	No	Yes	Real Estate
20.	Guotai Junan International Holdings	5.8	0.7	No	Yes	Finance
21.	Future Days	3.7	0.5	No	No	Transportation
22.	Wheelock and Company	3.3	0.4	No	Yes	Real Estate
23.	Lerthai Group	3.0	0.4	No	Yes	Real Estate
24.	Haitong International	3.0	0.4	No	Yes	Finance
25.	Farsail Goldman International	2.4	0.3	No	No	Finance
26.	Ev Dynamics Holdings	2.4	0.3	No	Yes	Diversified
27.	South Shore Holdings	2.2	0.3	No	Yes	Industrial
28.	IFC Development	2.0	0.3	No	No	Finance
29.	Nan Fung	1.8	0.2	No	No	Real Estate
30.	Champion REIT	1.7	0.2	No	Yes	Real Estate
	Total Top 30 Nonbank LCY Corporate Issuers	**314.8**	**40.2**			
	Total LCY Corporate Bonds	**1,185.6**	**151.4**			
	Top 30 as % of Total LCY Corporate Bonds	**26.6%**	**26.6%**			

HKD = Hong Kong dollar, LCY = local currency, REIT = real estate investment trust, USD = United States dollar.
Notes:
1. Data as of 31 March 2022.
2. State-owned firms are defined as those in which the government has more than a 50% ownership stake.
Source: *AsianBondsOnline* calculations based on Bloomberg LP data.

Table 3: Notable Local Currency Corporate Bond Issuances in the First Quarter of 2022

Corporate Issuers	Coupon Rate (%)	Issued Amount (HKD million)
AIA Group		
2-year bond	2.25	6,500
Hong Kong Mortgage Corporation		
1-year bond	0.61	1,000
2-year bond	1.43	1,000
3-year bond	1.66	450
5-year bond	1.90	500
Haitong International		
92-day bond	0.75	900
364-day bond	1.00	1,025
Guotai Junan International[a]		
181-day bond	0.80	1,200
181-day bond	0.83	460
182-day bond	0.00	240
Swire Pacific		
10-year bond	2.83	500

HKD = Hong Kong dollar.
[a] Multiple issuance of the same tenor indicates issuance on different dates.
Source: Bloomberg LP.

Indonesia

Yield Movements

Between 28 February and 15 May, the local currency (LCY) government bond yield curve in Indonesia shifted upward (**Figure 1**). Yields gained an average of 110 basis points (bps) across the curve, posting the steepest rise among all emerging East Asian markets. During the review period, bond yields gained the most for the 2-year maturity (197 bps) and the least for the 8-year maturity (13 bps). Yields rose much faster at the shorter-end of the curve than at the longer-end, leading to the narrowing of the spread between the 2-year and 10-year maturities from 227 bps on 28 February to 117 bps on 15 May.

Higher yields in advanced economies, due to persistent global inflationary pressure and the faster pace of monetary policy normalization by the United States (US) Federal Reserve, drove regional bond yields, including Indonesia's, to rise during the review period. The upward shift in Indonesia's yield curve also reflected rising domestic inflationary pressure, expectations of an earlier-than-planned policy rate hike, and the resulting capital outflows from the bond market due to the Federal Reserve's aggressive monetary tightening stance.

On the domestic front, consumer price inflation reached a 3-year high in April, rising to 3.5% year-on-year (y-o-y), and is approaching the upper-end of Bank Indonesia's target range of between 2.0% and 4.0% for full-year 2022. In May, consumer prices rose 3.6% y-o-y. Persistent inflation is expected to continue due to rising global commodity prices.

Further fueling the uptick in yields was the faster-than-expected pace of monetary normalization in advanced economies and some regional markets. With interest rates rising, Bank Indonesia is expected to raise rates earlier than previously expected to arrest the pull-back of foreign funds from its financial markets. In March and April, Indonesia recorded cumulative net foreign bond outflows of USD4.7 billion. This resulted in the further decline of the foreign holdings share to 17.0% at the end of April from 19.0% at the end of January.

Economic growth in the first quarter (Q1) of 2022 was marginally changed from the fourth quarter (Q4) of 2021 at 5.0% y-o-y. The sustained economic performance was fueled by the reopening of the economy and

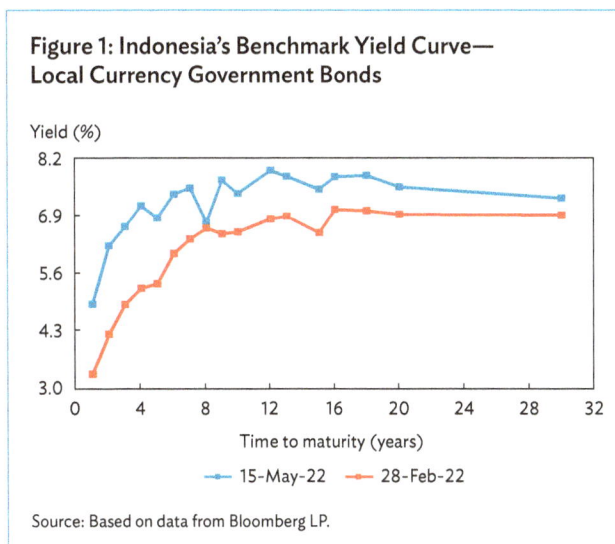

Figure 1: Indonesia's Benchmark Yield Curve—Local Currency Government Bonds

Source: Based on data from Bloomberg LP.

greater mobility as coronavirus disease (COVID-19) restrictions were gradually lifted. Growth in Q1 2022 was largely fueled by domestic consumption (4.3% y-o-y), investments (4.1% y-o-y), and exports (16.2% y-o-y).

However, the economic recovery remains fragile, dragged down by uncertainties over slowing global growth due to rising commodity prices and supply chain disruptions caused by the Russian invasion of Ukraine and COVID-19 lockdowns in the People's Republic of China. Amid expectations of weakening global growth and a slowdown in exports, Bank Indonesia slightly downgraded its gross domestic product (GDP) forecast for full-year 2022 to a range of 4.5%–5.3% in April, down from a 4.7%–5.5% projection at the start of the year.

To bolster economic recovery, Bank Indonesia continued to maintain an accommodative monetary stance. In its meeting held on 23–24 May, the Board of Governors of Bank Indonesia left unchanged the 7-day reverse repurchase rate at 3.50%, the deposit facility rate at 2.75%, and the lending facility rate at 4.25%. The decision was made to support economic growth amid uncertainties stemming from the Russian invasion of Ukraine and the quickening pace of monetary policy normalization from several central banks and monetary authorities globally. Meanwhile, Bank Indonesia opted to adjust the reserve requirement ratio at a much faster pace than previously announced in January (see Policy, Institutional, and Regulatory Developments section).

Size and Composition

The LCY bond market of Indonesia continued to post modest growth in Q1 2022, expanding to a size of IDR5,478.4 trillion (USD381.4 billion) at the end of March (**Table 1**). Growth, however, moderated to 3.1% quarter-on-quarter (q-o-q) in Q1 2022 from 4.4% q-o-q in the preceding quarter. Government bonds continued to drive growth, in particular Treasury bills and bonds, which comprised 88.1% of the total bond stock at the end of March. Also contributing to the overall growth were the central bank and corporate bond segments, both of which posted q-o-q expansions in Q1 2022. In contrast, the outstanding stock of nontradable bonds continued to decline at the end of March. On a y-o-y basis, Indonesia's LCY bond market grew 14.1% in Q1 2022, down from 17.7% in Q4 2021.

A majority of Indonesia's LCY bonds are structured as conventional bonds, which accounted for 82.5% of the total bond stock at the end of March. The share of Islamic bonds (*sukuk*) slipped to 17.5% of the outstanding bond total in the same period. Indonesia remains home to the second-largest *sukuk* market in emerging East Asia after Malaysia.

Government bonds. The total government bond stock rose to IDR5,028.8 trillion at the end of March from IDR4,884.2 trillion at the end of December 2021.

Growth in government bonds eased to 3.0% q-o-q in Q1 2022 from 4.6% q-o-q in Q4 2021. On a y-o-y basis, growth in the government bond segment moderated to 15.2% from 19.4% over the same period. Indonesia's LCY bond stock remained dominated by government bonds, which represented a share of 91.8% of the total bond size at the end of March. Indonesia has the largest share of government bonds to total bonds among its regional peers.

Central government bonds. The total stock of central government bonds, which comprise Treasury bills and bonds, climbed to IDR4,828.6 trillion at the end of March. The q-o-q growth eased to 3.2% in Q1 2022 from the 4.9% recorded in the preceding quarter. Despite a slowdown in issuance, the stock of central government bonds rose due to a lower volume of maturities during the quarter. Compared with the same period a year earlier, the growth in the stock of Treasury bills and bonds moderated to 16.2% y-o-y in Q1 2022 from 20.9% y-o-y in Q4 2021.

New issuance of central government bonds totaled IDR239.6 trillion in Q1 2022, down by 9.6% from IDR265.0 trillion in Q4 2021. The decline in issuance was due to the government's fiscal consolidation strategy for debt management. The government aims to bring the budget deficit below the estimate of 4.85% of GDP as set in the 2022 state budget, thus the need for less issuance

Table 1: Size and Composition of the Local Currency Bond Market in Indonesia

	Outstanding Amount (billion)						Growth Rate (%)			
	Q1 2021		Q4 2021		Q1 2022		Q1 2021		Q1 2022	
	IDR	USD	IDR	USD	IDR	USD	q-o-q	y-o-y	q-o-q	y-o-y
Total	4,799,432	330	5,314,547	373	5,478,441	381	6.2	36.0	3.1	14.1
Government	4,366,500	301	4,884,206	342	5,028,837	350	6.7	41.5	3.0	15.2
Central Govt. Bonds	4,155,596	286	4,678,977	328	4,828,648	336	7.4	46.7	3.2	16.2
of which: *Sukuk*	765,420	53	841,973	59	831,636	58	11.5	60.1	(1.2)	8.7
Nontradable Bonds	155,977	11	143,892	10	133,687	9	(5.7)	(23.5)	(7.1)	(14.3)
of which: *Sukuk*	35,684	2	31,666	2	26,324	2	(8.0)	(8.0)	(16.9)	(26.2)
Central Bank Bonds	54,927	4	61,337	4	66,501	5	(0.9)	13.4	8.4	21.1
of which: *Sukuk*	54,927	4	61,337	4	66,501	5	(0.9)	51.8	8.4	21.1
Corporate	432,931	30	430,341	30	449,604	31	1.7	(2.3)	4.5	3.9
of which: *Sukuk*	31,172	2	34,813	2	36,290	3	2.7	3.2	4.2	16.4

( ) = negative, IDR = Indonesian rupiah, q-o-q = quarter-on-quarter, Q1 = first quarter, Q4 = fourth quarter, USD = United States dollar, y-o-y = year-on-year.
Notes:
1.   Bloomberg LP end-of-period local currency–USD rates are used.
2.   Growth rates are calculated from local currency base and do not include currency effects.
3.   *Sukuk* refers to Islamic bonds.
Sources: Bank Indonesia; Directorate General of Budget Financing and Risk Management, Ministry of Finance; Indonesia Stock Exchange; and Bloomberg LP.

during the year. Aside from the regular weekly auctions of Treasury bills and Treasury bonds, the government also issued retail bonds in February amounting to IDR25.1 trillion.

Central bank bonds. At the end of March, the outstanding size of central bank bonds climbed to IDR66.5 trillion on growth of 8.4% q-o-q in Q1 2022. This was faster than the 1.0% q-o-q expansion recorded in Q4 2021. Issuance of Sukuk Bank Indonesia in Q1 2022 slowed to IDR379.4 trillion, down 4.8% q-o-q but up 120.3% y-o-y.

Corporate bonds. The stock of outstanding corporate bonds in Indonesia swelled to IDR449.6 trillion at the end of March, with growth rising to 4.5% q-o-q in Q1 2022 from 2.0% q-o-q in Q4 2021. The uptick in corporate bonds was due to a higher issuance volume that outpaced maturities during the quarter. Corporate bonds accounted for only 8.2% of Indonesia's LCY bond stock at the end of March, the smallest share in emerging East Asia.

The 30 largest corporate bond issuers in Indonesia had an aggregate bond stock of IDR315.6 trillion at the end of March (**Table 2**). Collectively, they represented a 70.2% share of the corporate bond total at the end of the review period. Out of the 30 firms on the list, 15 comprised firms from the banking and financial sector. All other corporate entities were from highly capitalized industries such as energy, telecommunications, construction, and manufacturing. The top 30 list included 17 state-owned firms and 18 Indonesia Stock Exchange-listed firms.

Energy firm Perusahaan Listrik Negara maintained the top spot, with bonds outstanding amounting to IDR34.5 trillion, representing 7.7% of the LCY corporate bond total, at the end of March. In the second spot was financing firm Indonesia Eximbank with outstanding bonds of IDR19.9 trillion and a 4.4% share of the corporate bond stock. Climbing to the third spot was Indah Kiat Pulp & Paper, which ranked sixth at the end of December, with bonds totaling IDR18.1 trillion and comprising a 4.0% share of the corporate total. Bank Rakyat maintained its hold of the fourth spot with bonds totaling IDR16.4 trillion and a 3.7% share. Dropping to the fifth spot (from the third sport at the end of December) was financing firm Sarana Multi Infrastruktur with bonds totaling IDR16.3 trillion and a share of 3.6% of the corporate bond stock at the end of March.

New corporate bonds issued reached IDR38.7 trillion in Q1 2022, rising 24.0% q-o-q after a decline of 4.4% q-o-q in Q4 2021. Several corporates took advantage of low borrowing costs ahead of expectations of an interest rate hike in the second half of the year. A total of 27 firms tapped the bond market in Q1 2022 versus 17 institutions in Q4 2021.

New corporate bonds issued during the quarter comprised 78 bond series including 16 series structured as *sukuk*. Of the 16 series of *sukuk*, 14 were structured as *sukuk mudharabah* (Islamic bonds backed by a profit-sharing scheme from a business venture or partnership), while 2 were structured as *sukuk ijarah* (Islamic bonds backed by lease agreements).

In terms of maturity, more than a third each of the corporate bonds issued during the quarter carried maturities of 3 years (28 series) and 5 years (24 series). The shortest-dated bond had a maturity of 367 days, which was issued by Merdeka Copper Gold, and the longest was 10 years, which was issued by Energi Mitra Investama and Chandra Asri Petrochemical.

Some of the largest corporate bond issuances in Q1 2022 are shown in **Table 3**. Paper manufacturing firm OKI Pulp & Paper Mills led the list with aggregate bond issuances of IDR3.5 trillion issued in three tranches in March. Next was another paper manufacturing firm, Indah Kiat Pulp & Paper, with new bond sales in February amounting to IDR3.2 trillion, of which three tranches were conventional bonds and three tranches were *sukuk mudharabah*. Financing firm Astra Sedaya Finance and mining firm Merdeka Copper Gold raised IDR3.0 trillion worth of bonds each in March, while state-owned construction firm Wijaya Karya issued IDR2.5 trillion of bonds in February.

Investor Profiles

Foreign selling from Indonesia's bond market continued in Q1 2022, albeit at a slower pace as net outflows totaled USD3.0 billion compared with USD4.9 billion recorded in Q4 2021. The faster-than-expected monetary policy tightening by the Federal Reserve led to a foreign sell-off, with outflows continuing into April that amounted to USD1.4 billion. This led the foreign holdings share in Indonesia's LCY government bond market to further decline to 17.6% at the end of March from 19.0%

Table 2: Top 30 Issuers of Local Currency Corporate Bonds in Indonesia

	Issuers	Outstanding Amount		State-Owned	Listed Company	Type of Industry
		LCY Bonds (IDR billion)	LCY Bonds (USD billion)			
1.	Perusahaan Listrik Negara	34,489	2.40	Yes	No	Energy
2.	Indonesia Eximbank	19,869	1.38	Yes	No	Finance
3.	Indah Kiat Pulp & Paper	18,074	1.26	No	Yes	Pulp and Paper
4.	Bank Rakyat Indonesia	16,426	1.14	Yes	Yes	Banking
5.	Sarana Multi Infrastruktur	16,255	1.13	Yes	No	Finance
6.	Bank Mandiri	12,900	0.90	Yes	Yes	Banking
7.	Bank Tabungan Negara	12,445	0.87	Yes	Yes	Banking
8.	Permodalan Nasional Madani	11,923	0.83	Yes	No	Finance
9.	Sarana Multigriya Finansial	11,865	0.83	Yes	No	Finance
10.	Astra Sedaya Finance	11,134	0.78	No	No	Finance
11.	Wijaya Karya	10,000	0.70	Yes	Yes	Building Construction
12.	Indosat	9,546	0.66	No	Yes	Telecommunications
13.	Hutama Karya	9,313	0.65	Yes	No	Nonbuilding Construction
14.	Pegadaian	9,049	0.63	Yes	No	Finance
15.	Pupuk Indonesia	9,046	0.63	Yes	No	Chemical Manufacturing
16.	Tower Bersama Infrastructure	8,633	0.60	No	Yes	Telecommunications Infrrastructure Provider
17.	Waskita Karya	8,604	0.60	Yes	Yes	Building Construction
18.	Bank Pan Indonesia	7,802	0.54	No	Yes	Banking
19.	Adira Dinamika Multi Finance	7,622	0.53	No	Yes	Finance
20.	OKI Pulp & Paper Mills	7,500	0.52	No	No	Pulp and Paper Manufacturing
21.	Chandra Asri Petrochemical	7,250	0.50	No	Yes	Petrochemicals
22.	Sinar Mas Agro Resources and Technology	7,203	0.50	No	Yes	Food
23.	Semen Indonesia	7,078	0.49	Yes	Yes	Cement Manufacturing
24.	Telkom Indonesia	7,000	0.49	Yes	Yes	Telecommunications
25.	Federal International Finance	6,938	0.48	No	No	Finance
26.	Merdeka Copper Gold	6,877	0.48	No	Yes	Mining
27.	Bank CIMB Niaga	5,606	0.39	No	Yes	Banking
28.	Bank Pembangunan Daerah Jawa Barat Dan Banten	5,413	0.38	Yes	Yes	Banking
29.	Adhi Karya	4,990	0.35	Yes	Yes	Building Construction
30.	Bussan Auto Finance	4,702	0.33	No	No	Finance
	Total Top 30 LCY Corporate Issuers	315,552	21.97			
	Total LCY Corporate Bonds	449,604	31.30			
	Top 30 as % of Total LCY Corporate Bonds	70.2%	70.2%			

IDR = Indonesian rupiah, LCY = local currency, USD = United States dollar.
Notes:
1. Data as of 31 March 2022.
2. State-owned firms are defined as those in which the government has more than a 50% ownership stake.
Source: *AsianBondsOnline* calculations based on Indonesia Stock Exchange data.

Table 3: Notable Local Currency Corporate Bond Issuances in the First Quarter of 2022

Corporate Issuers	Coupon Rate (%)	Issued Amount (IDR billion)
OKI Pulp & Paper Mills		
370-day bond	5.75	1,319
3-year bond	9.00	1,801
5-year bond	9.75	381
Indah Kiat Pulp & Paper		
370-day bond	6.00	708
370-day sukuk mudharabah	6.00	702
3-year bond	8.75	1,077
3-year sukuk mudharabah	8.75	451
5-year bond	9.25	204
5-year sukuk mudharabah	9.25	108
Astra Sedaya Finance		
370-day bond	3.50	1,028
3-year bond	5.70	1,972
Merdeka Copper Gold		
367-day bond	5.00	959
3-year bond	7.80	2,041
Wijaya Karya		
3-year bond	6.50	594
3-year sukuk mudharabah	6.50	413
5-year bond	7.75	425
5-year sukuk mudharabah	7.75	176
7-year bond	8.30	731
7-year sukuk mudharabah	8.30	161

IDR = Indonesian rupiah.
Note: *Sukuk mudharabah* are Islamic bonds backed by a profit-sharing scheme from a business venture or partnership.
Source: Indonesia Stock Exchange.

at the end of December and from 22.9% at the end of March 2021 (**Figure 2**). Total holdings by offshore investors declined 10.8% y-o-y to IDR848.3 trillion at the end of Q1 2022 from IDR951.4 trillion a year earlier.

A majority of bonds held by foreign investors carried maturities of over 5 years to 10 years, representing 36.9% of their total holdings at the end of March (**Figure 3**). The share of foreign holdings with maturities of over

Figure 3: Foreign Holdings of Local Currency Central Government Bonds by Maturity

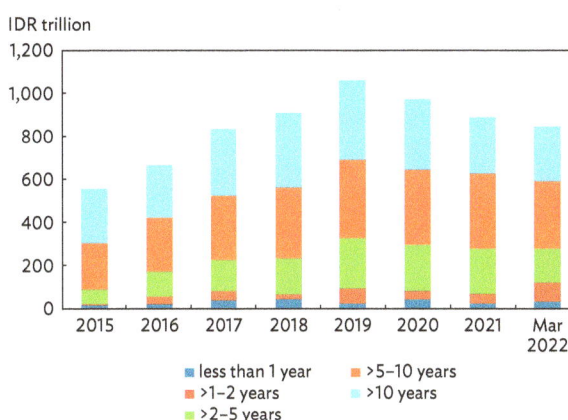

IDR = Indonesian rupiah.
Source: Directorate General of Budget Financing and Risk Management, Ministry of Finance.

Figure 2: Local Currency Central Government Bonds Investor Profile

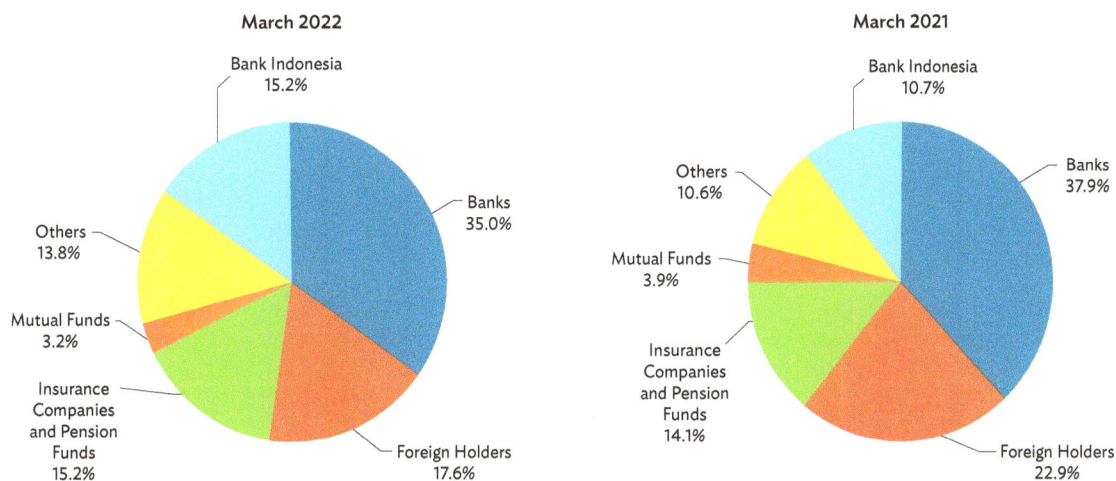

Source: Directorate General of Budget Financing and Risk Management, Ministry of Finance.

5 years to 10 years, however, fell from 39.0% at the end of December 2021. A similar declining trend was noted for bonds with maturities of more than 2 years to 5 years, which accounted for 18.7% of total offshore holdings at the end of March, down from 23.8% at the end of December. All other maturity buckets—less than 1 year, more than 1 year to 2 years, and over 10 years—experienced an increase in its respective share of the total in March compared with December.

Domestic investors picked up the slack in foreign investor holdings. Banking institutions accounted for the largest share of bond holdings at 35.0% at the end of March. This, however, represented a decline from a share of 37.9% in the same period a year earlier. Mutual fund holdings of LCY government bonds slipped to 3.2% from 3.9% over the same period.

At the end of March, bond holdings of Bank Indonesia gained the most among all domestic investors with its share rising to 15.2% from 10.7% a year earlier. Bank Indonesia remains committed to supporting the bond market in line with its burden-sharing agreement with the government. The central bank participates in the purchase of bonds through primary auctions, greenshoe options, and private placements. Year-to-date through 23 May, Bank Indonesia's government bond purchases totaled IDR30.2 trillion.

The other investors group, which includes individuals, also increased its holdings at the end of March, possibly a result of the issuance of retail Treasury bonds in February. The bond holdings of other investors inched up to a 13.8% share at the end of March from 10.6% a year earlier. Insurance and pension funds also increased their holdings of government bonds, accounting for a 15.2% share versus 14.1% over the same period.

Ratings Update

On 27 April, S&P Global Ratings (S&P) affirmed Indonesia's BBB investment grade sovereign rating, citing strong growth prospects and prudent policy dynamics. The outlook for the ratings was also revised to stable from negative on the back of improvements in its external position, fiscal consolidation measures, and growth prospects for the next 2 years. The rating agency estimates Indonesia's GDP growth will quicken to 5.1% in 2022 from 3.7% in 2021. Risks remain, however, including the ongoing impact of the Russian invasion of Ukraine, among others.

Policy, Institutional, and Regulatory Developments

Bank Indonesia to Accelerate Adjustments to Bank Reserve Requirement Ratios

On 24 May, Bank Indonesia announced that it would quicken the pace of reserve requirement ratio adjustments from its earlier announcement made in January. The move is part of the central bank's liquidity normalization policy. The first adjustment to the reserve requirement ratio proceeded as planned on 1 March. Subsequent adjustments will now take effect on 1 June, 1 July, and 1 September, bringing the rupiah reserve requirement ratio for conventional commercial banks to 6.0%, 7.5%, and 9.0%, respectively. The corresponding adjustments for Shariah banks and business units will be 4.5%, 6.0%, and 7.5%, respectively.

Republic of Korea

Yield Movements

The Republic of Korea's local currency (LCY) government bond yields rose for all tenors between 28 February and 15 May (**Figure 1**). Yields for the 3-month through 1-year tenors rose 33 basis points (bps) on average. Meanwhile, yields for the 2-year through 5-year tenors surged 68 bps on average, with the 2-year tenor posting the largest increase at 71 bps. Yields for tenors of between 10 years and 50 years rose 50 bps on average. The spread between the 2-year and 10-year tenors fell to 53 bps from 70 bps during the review period, causing a slight flattening of the yield curve.

Yields rose across the curve during the review period amid rising global and domestic inflation, and monetary policy normalization by both the United States (US) Federal Reserve and the Bank of Korea (BOK). In its 15–16 March and 3–4 May monetary policy meetings, the US Federal Reserve raised the federal funds rate target range by 75 bps in total to a range of between 0.75% and 1.00%. In addition, the Federal Reserve in May signaled that further and larger rate hikes would be forthcoming to address inflation, and it announced the reduction of its bond holdings starting in June.

To address market yield volatility and as part of its market stabilization efforts, the BOK purchased KRW2.0 trillion worth of state bonds on 5 April. This was the second bond purchase of the year, following a KRW2.0 trillion purchase in February. However, volatility in US Treasuries continued to weigh on the domestic bond market.

On the domestic front, the BOK raised its base rate by 25 bps to 1.50% at its 14 April monetary policy meeting, with market expectations of further rate hikes amid the sharp rise in inflation. Inflation peaked at 4.8% in April, the highest since October 2008, from an average of 3.8% in the first quarter (Q1) of the year due to rising energy prices and supply chain disruptions. Subsequently, on 26 May, the BOK raised the base rate by another 25 bps to 1.75%. In addition, the central bank announced that inflation would remain at around the 5.0% level for the rest of the year and raised its 2022 and 2023 inflation forecasts to 4.5% and 2.9%, respectively, from the February forecasts of 3.1% and 2.0%. Meanwhile, 2022 and 2023 economic growth forecasts were lowered

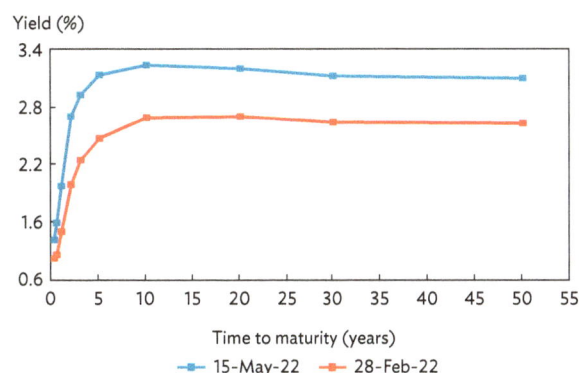

Figure 1: The Republic of Korea's Benchmark Yield Curve—Local Currency Government Bonds

Source: Based on data from Bloomberg LP.

to 2.7% and 2.4%, respectively, from the forecasts of 3.0% and 2.5% announced in February. Downside risks to the outlook include a prolonged Russian invasion of Ukraine, a slowdown in economic growth in the People's Republic of China, and faster-than-expected monetary policy normalization in the US.

Upward pressure on domestic yields also stemmed from bond oversupply concerns due to uncertainties on the fiscal policy of the newly elected government. However, concerns eased as the government announced in May that the financing of the proposed second supplementary budget of KRW59.4 trillion would not involve the additional issuance of government bonds. This led to a decline in yields after the announcement, slightly cushioning the surge in yields in March and April.

The Republic of Korea's economic growth slowed to 3.0% year-on-year (y-o-y) in Q1 2022 from 4.2% y-o-y in the fourth (Q4) of 2021, based on preliminary estimates by the BOK. The lower growth was primarily driven by the 3.5% y-o-y contraction in gross fixed capital formation, a reversal from the 1.4% y-o-y increase in the previous quarter. Both private and public consumption also posted lower annual increases in Q1 2022. Moreover, export growth slowed to 7.3% y-o-y from 7.9% y-o-y in the previous quarter. On a quarter-on-quarter (q-o-q) basis, domestic economic growth decelerated to 0.6% in Q1 2022 from 1.3% in Q4 2021.

Foreign demand for the Republic of Korea's LCY bonds remained strong in the first 2 months of the year, with the market recording net inflows of KRW3,673.0 billion and KRW3,950.0 billion, respectively. However, foreign inflows dropped to KRW279.0 billion in March and KRW36.0 billion in April due to the narrowing interest rate differential between US Treasuries and domestic government bonds and the continued depreciation of the Korean won. The Korean won was one of the weakest currencies in the region during the review period, depreciating 6.3% versus the US dollar to KRW1,283.8 per USD1.0 as of 15 May.

Size and Composition

The size of the Republic of Korea's LCY bond market reached KRW2,898.1 trillion (USD2.4 trillion) at the end of March (**Table 1**). Growth rose to 2.0% q-o-q in Q1 2022 from 1.5% q-o-q in the previous quarter, largely driven by the government sector as the corporate segment posted marginal growth. From the same period in 2021, the Republic of Korea's LCY bond market grew 7.5% y-o-y, slightly lower than the 7.9% y-o-y increase posted in Q4 2021.

Government bonds. Growth in the Republic of Korea's LCY government bond market accelerated to 3.4% q-o-q in Q1 2022 from 0.2% q-o-q in Q4 2021 to reach a size of KRW1,222.4 trillion at the end of March. The higher growth rate was solely driven by the 4.8% q-o-q rise in the stock of central government bonds, as both outstanding central bank bonds and other government bonds fell

during the quarter. Issuance of central government bonds surged 76.9% q-o-q in Q1 2022, in line with the government's frontloading policy program wherein 73% of the budget is allocated to be spent in the first half of the year. Meanwhile, Monetary Stabilization Bonds issued by the BOK declined 0.1% q-o-q as maturities exceeded issuance during the quarter, while outstanding bonds issued by other government-owned entities fell 0.3% q-o-q.

Corporate bonds. The Republic of Korea's LCY corporate bond market posted a marginal increase of 1.0% q-o-q to reach KRW1,675.7 trillion at the end of March. This was lower than the 2.4% q-o-q growth posted in the previous quarter. **Table 2** lists the top 30 LCY corporate bond issuers in the Republic of Korea at the end of March, which had aggregate outstanding bonds of KRW997.8 trillion and accounted for 59.5% of the total LCY corporate bond market. Companies from the financial sector continued to dominate the list with a share of 65.2% of the top 30's outstanding bonds. Korea Housing Finance Corporation remained the largest corporate issuer in the market with total bonds outstanding of KRW150.5 trillion at the end of Q1 2022. The Industrial Bank of Korea and Korea Investment and Securities were the next largest issuers at KRW78.6 trillion and KRW54.1 trillion, respectively.

The marginal growth in the Republic of Korea's corporate bond market in Q1 2022 was due to the 21.1% q-o-q decline in issuance to KRW135.5 billion from KRW171.8 billion in Q4 2021. Fewer companies issued

Table 1: Size and Composition of the Local Currency Bond Market in the Republic of Korea

| | Outstanding Amount (billion) | | | | | | Growth Rate (%) | | | |
| | Q1 2021 | | Q4 2021 | | Q1 2022 | | Q1 2021 | | Q1 2022 | |
	KRW	USD	KRW	USD	KRW	USD	q-o-q	y-o-y	q-o-q	y-o-y
Total	2,695,546	2,382	2,841,873	2,388	2,898,057	2,391	2.4	8.9	2.0	7.5
Government	1,122,368	992	1,182,573	994	1,222,359	1,009	4.0	13.1	3.4	8.9
Central Government Bonds	769,339	680	843,660	709	884,103	730	5.9	19.1	4.8	14.9
Central Bank Bonds	157,230	139	140,320	118	140,190	116	(1.3)	(5.1)	(0.1)	(10.8)
Others	195,799	173	198,592	167	198,065	163	1.5	8.4	(0.3)	1.2
Corporate	1,573,178	1,390	1,659,300	1,395	1,675,698	1,383	1.2	6.0	1.0	6.5

( ) = negative, KRW = Korean won, q-o-q = quarter-on-quarter, Q1 = first quarter, Q4 = fourth quarter, USD = United States dollar, y-o-y = year-on-year.
Notes:
1. Bloomberg LP end-of-period local currency–USD rates are used.
2. Growth rates are calculated from local currency base and do not include currency effects.
3. "Others" comprise Korea Development Bank Bonds, National Housing Bonds, and Seoul Metro Bonds.
4. Corporate bonds include equity-linked securities and derivatives-linked securities.
Sources: The Bank of Korea and KG Zeroin Corporation.

Table 2: Top 30 Issuers of Local Currency Corporate Bonds in the Republic of Korea

	Issuers	Outstanding Amount		State-Owned	Listed on		Type of Industry
		LCY Bonds (KRW billion)	LCY Bonds (USD billion)		KOSPI	KOSDAQ	
1.	Korea Housing Finance Corporation	150,503	124.2	Yes	No	No	Housing Finance
2.	Industrial Bank of Korea	78,620	64.9	Yes	Yes	No	Banking
3.	Korea Investment and Securities	54,058	44.6	No	No	No	Securities
4.	Mirae Asset Securities Co.	51,710	42.7	No	Yes	No	Securities
5.	Hana Financial Investment	50,820	41.9	No	No	No	Securities
6.	KB Securities	49,351	40.7	No	No	No	Securities
7.	Shinhan Investment Corporation	46,172	38.1	No	No	No	Securities
8.	Meritz Securities Co.	44,264	36.5	No	Yes	No	Securities
9.	Korea Electric Power Corporation	39,600	32.7	Yes	Yes	No	Electricity, Energy, and Power
10.	NH Investment & Securities	34,865	28.8	Yes	Yes	No	Securities
11.	Korea Land & Housing Corporation	32,014	26.4	Yes	No	No	Real Estate
12.	Shinhan Bank	29,392	24.3	No	No	No	Banking
13.	Samsung Securities	29,022	23.9	No	Yes	No	Securities
14.	Korea Expressway	26,990	22.3	Yes	No	No	Transport Infrastructure
15.	The Export-Import Bank of Korea	26,670	22.0	Yes	No	No	Banking
16.	Woori Bank	23,690	19.5	Yes	Yes	No	Banking
17.	KEB Hana Bank	22,575	18.6	No	No	No	Banking
18.	NongHyup Bank	20,220	16.7	Yes	No	No	Banking
19.	Korea SMEs and Startups Agency	20,018	16.5	Yes	No	No	SME Development
20.	Kookmin Bank	19,894	16.4	No	No	No	Banking
21.	Korea National Railway	19,380	16.0	Yes	No	No	Transport Infrastructure
22.	Shinhan Card	17,175	14.2	No	No	No	Credit Card
23.	Shinyoung Securities	16,779	13.8	No	Yes	No	Securities
24.	Hanwha Investment and Securities	15,283	12.6	No	No	No	Securities
25.	Hyundai Capital Services	14,955	12.3	No	No	No	Consumer Finance
26.	KB Kookmin Bank Card	14,695	12.1	No	No	No	Consumer Finance
27.	Standard Chartered Bank Korea	13,130	10.8	No	No	No	Banking
28.	NongHyup	12,830	10.6	Yes	No	No	Banking
29.	Samsung Card Co.	11,958	9.9	No	Yes	No	Credit Card
30.	Shinhan Financial Group	11,205	9.2	No	Yes	No	Banking
	Total Top 30 LCY Corporate Issuers	**997,838**	**823.3**				
	Total LCY Corporate Bonds	**1,675,698**	**1,382.7**				
	Top 30 as % of Total LCY Corporate Bonds	**59.5%**	**59.5%**				

KOSDAQ = Korean Securities Dealers Automated Quotations, KOSPI = Korea Composite Stock Price Index, KRW = Korean won, LCY = local currency, SMEs = small and medium-sized enterprises, USD = United States dollar.
Notes:
1. Data as of 31 March 2022.
2. State-owned firms are defined as those in which the government has more than a 50% ownership stake.
3. Corporate bonds include equity-linked securities and derivatives-linked securities.
Sources: *AsianBondsOnline* calculations based on Bloomberg LP and KG Zeroin Corporation data.

in Q1 2022 due to high borrowing costs and increased market volatility. **Table 3** lists the notable corporate bond issuances in Q1 2022. Financial firms such as the Industrial Bank of Korea and the Export–Import Bank of Korea had the largest aggregate issuances for the quarter. Meanwhile, NongHyup Life Insurance had the single-largest issuance for the quarter.

Investor Profile

Government bonds. Insurance companies and pension funds continued to be the largest investor group in the Republic of Korea's LCY government bond market at the end of December 2021 (**Figure 2**). However, its share declined to 34.3% from 35.7% in the same period in 2020.

Table 3: Notable Local Currency Corporate Bond Issuances in the First Quarter of 2022

Corporate Issuers	Coupon Rate (%)	Issued Amount (KRW billion)	Corporate Issuers	Coupon Rate (%)	Issued Amount (KRW billion)
Industrial Bank of Korea[a]			Korea Electric Power[a]		
6-month bond	–	570	2-year bond	2.73	200
6-month bond	–	340	3-year bond	2.50	270
9-month bond	–	400	3-year bond	2.89	210
1-year bond	–	330	3-year bond	2.89	200
1-year bond	1.53	310	5-year bond	3.03	300
1-year bond	1.72	300	5-year bond	2.69	280
10-year bond	3.41	400	5-year bond	2.53	200
Export–Import Bank of Korea[a]			7-year bond	2.83	200
6-month bond	–	440	7-year bond	2.75	200
6-month bond	–	300	NongHyup Life Insurance		
1-year bond	1.71	420	10-year bond	4.35	600
1-year bond	1.44	360			
1-year bond	–	300			
1.5-year bond	2.12	330			
1.7-year bond	–	310			

– = not available, KRW = Korean won.
[a] Multiple issuance of the same tenor indicates issuance on different dates.
Source: Based on data from Bloomberg LP.

Figure 2: Local Currency Government Bonds Investor Profile

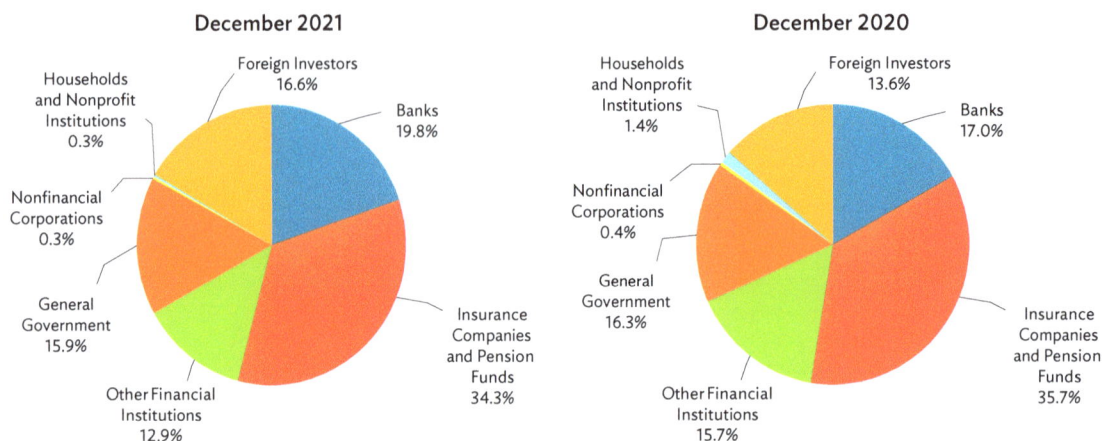

December 2021

- Households and Nonprofit Institutions 0.3%
- Foreign Investors 16.6%
- Banks 19.8%
- Insurance Companies and Pension Funds 34.3%
- Other Financial Institutions 12.9%
- General Government 15.9%
- Nonfinancial Corporations 0.3%

December 2020

- Households and Nonprofit Institutions 1.4%
- Foreign Investors 13.6%
- Banks 17.0%
- Insurance Companies and Pension Funds 35.7%
- Other Financial Institutions 15.7%
- General Government 16.3%
- Nonfinancial Corporations 0.4%

Source: *AsianBondsOnline* and The Bank of Korea.

Banks were the second-largest investor group with a share of 19.8% at the end of December, up from 17.0% in Q4 2020. Foreign investors surpassed both general government and other financial institutions as the third-largest group at the end of December. Foreign holdings rose to 16.6% in Q4 2021 from 13.6% in Q4 2020, as the domestic bond market registered high levels of foreign inflows in 2021.

Corporate bonds. Other financial institutions held the largest investor group share of the Republic of Korea's LCY corporate bonds at the end of December with its share rising to 40.9% from 36.8% a year earlier (**Figure 3**). Meanwhile, the share of insurance companies and pension funds fell to 35.3% from 37.1%. The share of the general government was almost unchanged at 13.3% during the same period, while the share of foreign holders remained negligible.

Foreign fund flows. In January and February, the Republic of Korea's LCY bond market posted net inflows of KRW3,673.0 billion and KRW3,950.0 billion, respectively (**Figure 4**). Foreign demand at the start of the year was driven by the relatively high interest rate differential of LCY bonds over US Treasuries and the stable Korean won. However, the rate hike by the Federal Reserve in March and expectations of faster-than-expected monetary policy normalization led to a sharper rise in US Treasury yields, narrowing the interest rate gap. The Korean won also depreciated versus the US dollar, reaching a low of KRW1,272.5 per

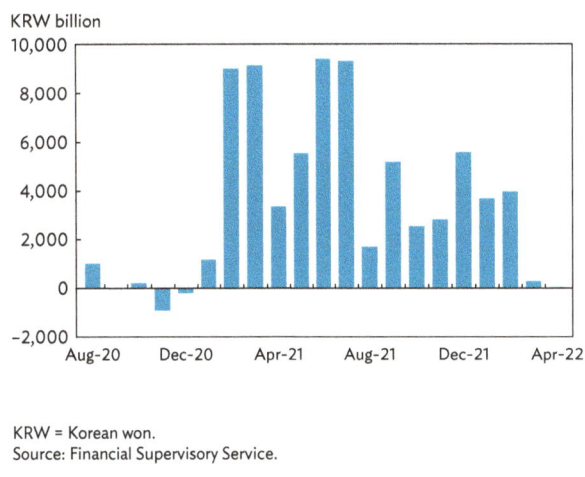

Figure 4: Net Foreign Investment in Local Currency Bonds in the Republic of Korea

KRW = Korean won.
Source: Financial Supervisory Service.

USD1.0 on 28 April. This resulted in a drop of foreign flows to KRW279.0 billion in March and further down to KRW36.0 billion in April. The foreign sell-off was most significant in bonds with remaining maturities of less than 1 year (**Figure 5**).

Ratings Update

On 26 April, S&P Global Ratings affirmed the Republic of Korea's sovereign credit ratings at AA with a stable outlook. The rating agency cited prudent policy decisions, solid fiscal conditions, and high monetary flexibility as the

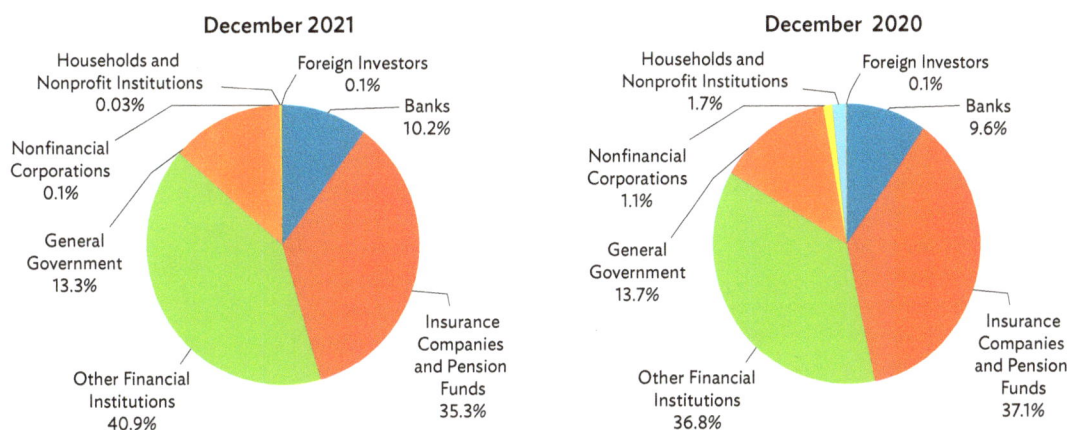

Figure 3: Local Currency Corporate Bonds Investor Profile

December 2021

Households and Nonprofit Institutions 0.03%
Foreign Investors 0.1%
Banks 10.2%
Nonfinancial Corporations 0.1%
General Government 13.3%
Other Financial Institutions 40.9%
Insurance Companies and Pension Funds 35.3%

December 2020

Households and Nonprofit Institutions 1.7%
Foreign Investors 0.1%
Banks 9.6%
Nonfinancial Corporations 1.1%
General Government 13.7%
Other Financial Institutions 36.8%
Insurance Companies and Pension Funds 37.1%

Source: *AsianBondsOnline* and The Bank of Korea.

Figure 5: Net Foreign Investment in Local Currency Bonds in the Republic of Korea by Remaining Maturity

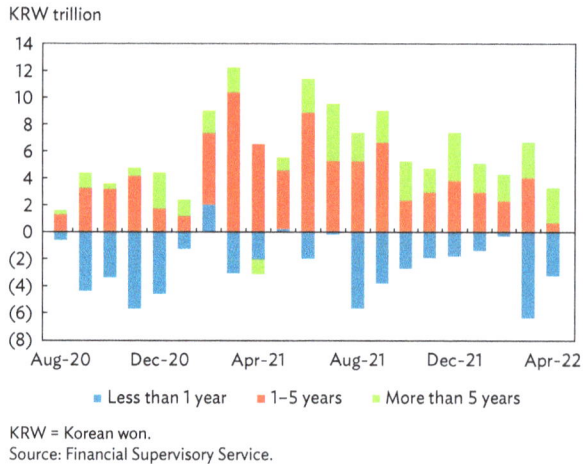

KRW = Korean won.
Source: Financial Supervisory Service.

reasons behind the rating affirmation. The rating agency forecast 2022 gross domestic product (GDP) growth to be 2.5%, supported by exports and improved private spending. Downside risks to the growth outlook include continued high inflation from rising energy prices and high levels of household debt that may dampen consumption. Meanwhile, the fiscal deficit is expected to be 3.3% of GDP in 2022, with the government balance to return to surplus by 2024.

Policy, Institutional, and Regulatory Developments

The Republic of Korea's National Assembly Passes the Second Supplementary Budget

On 29 May, the National Assembly passed the second supplementary budget of KRW62.0 trillion, which is to be largely allocated for programs involved in improving people's livelihoods. These include, among others, programs to compensate small business owners hit hard by the pandemic (KRW28.7 trillion) and policies intended to ensure proper pandemic control and the gradual transition to the general health-care system (KRW7.1 trillion). The government also announced that financing for the proposed supplementary budget would not entail the issuance of government bonds. The resulting 2022 budget is expected to generate a consolidated fiscal deficit equivalent to 3.3% of GDP and a government-debt-to-GDP ratio of 49.7%.

Malaysia

Yield Movements

Yields on Malaysia's local currency (LCY) government bonds jumped for all tenors between 28 February and 15 May (**Figure 1**). An average increase of 28 basis points (bps) was logged for the yields of short-term tenors (1–6 months). Meanwhile, the yields of longer tenors (4–30 years) ascended an average of 79 bps. The smallest increase in yields was recorded for the 1-month tenor at 23 bps. Among all tenors, the 2-year yield soared the most with a 120 bps gain. A contraction in the 2-year and 10-year government bond yield spread was recorded, from 126 bps to 82 bps, during the review period.

The upward movement of the yield curve was due to Bank Negara Malaysia's (BNM) decision to raise its overnight policy rate in May, following the global trend whereby central banks around the world have been raising interest rates to combat inflationary pressure.

On 11 May, the Monetary Policy Committee of the BNM hiked its policy rate to 2.00% from 1.75%. The central bank deemed it necessary to increase interest rates as a precautionary measure against rising inflation caused by the growing cost of commodities and global supply chain concerns exacerbated by the Russian invasion of Ukraine.

The increase in prices of basic goods and services in Malaysia was largely unchanged during the first quarter (Q1) of 2022. Coming from a high of 3.3% year-on-year (y-o-y) in November 2021, consumer price inflation continued to decelerate each month during the quarter, recording inflation of 2.3% y-o-y in January and 2.2% y-o-y in both February and March. In April, inflation increased marginally to 2.3% y-o-y. The BNM expects inflation for full-year 2022 of between 2.2% and 3.2%.

The Malaysian economy recorded an expansion of 5.0% y-o-y in Q1 2022, up from 3.6% y-o-y in the previous quarter, buoyed by faster growth in the services sector as containment measures in response to the coronavirus disease (COVID-19) continued to ease. The BNM expects the annual growth rate of Malaysia for full-year 2022 to be in the 5.3%–6.3% range.

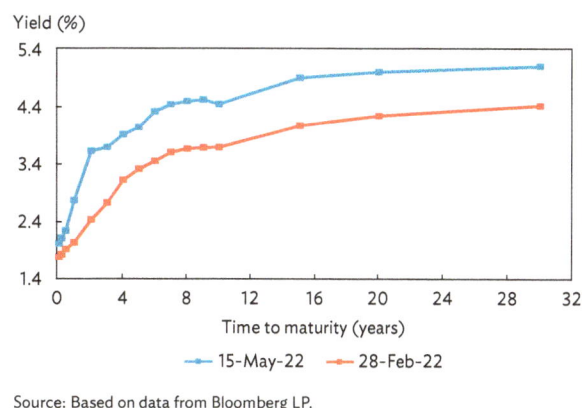

Figure 1: Malaysia's Benchmark Yield Curve— Local Currency Government Bonds

Source: Based on data from Bloomberg LP.

Size and Composition

The LCY bond market of Malaysia expanded 1.7% quarter-on-quarter (q-o-q) in Q1 2022, reaching a size of MYR1,764.9 billion (USD419.8 billion) at the end of March, up from MYR1,736.2 billion at the end of the fourth quarter (Q4) of 2021 (**Table 1**). This growth was faster than the 1.0% q-o-q increase registered in the prior quarter. On an annual basis, Malaysia's LCY bond market expanded 7.0% y-o-y, decelerating from the growth of 8.2% y-o-y posted in Q4 2021. The growth of the bond market was due to expansions in both LCY government and corporate bonds outstanding, which accounted for 55.3% and 44.7%, respectively, of total outstanding LCY bonds at the end of the review period. Total outstanding *sukuk* (Islamic bonds) hit MYR1,122.5 billion at the end of Q1 2022, growing 1.8% q-o-q. This jump was supported by increased stocks of government and corporate *sukuk*.

Issuances of LCY bonds in Q1 2022 fell 8.6% q-o-q to MYR81.4 billion from MYR89.0 billion in the prior quarter due to a decline in issuance of corporate bonds.

Government bonds. At the end of March, Malaysia's LCY government bond market grew 2.8% q-o-q to MYR975.9 billion from MYR949.4 billion at the end of Q4 2021. This is an acceleration from the growth of 1.2% q-o-q logged in the prior quarter. Growth in the LCY government bond market was driven by a 2.8% q-o-q

Table 1: Size and Composition of the Local Currency Bond Market in Malaysia

| | Outstanding Amount (billion) | | | | | | Growth Rate (%) | | | |
| | Q1 2021 | | Q4 2021 | | Q1 2022 | | Q1 2021 | | Q1 2022 | |
	MYR	USD	MYR	USD	MYR	USD	q-o-q	y-o-y	q-o-q	y-o-y
Total	1,649	398	1,736	417	1,765	420	2.8	7.9	1.7	7.0
Government	890	215	949	228	976	232	4.3	10.7	2.8	9.7
Central Government Bonds	865	209	931	224	958	228	4.6	12.8	2.8	10.8
of which: *Sukuk*	403	97	441	106	455	108	5.1	11.5	3.2	12.9
Central Bank Bills	1	0	0	0	0	0	(50.0)	(90.0)	–	(100.0)
of which: *Sukuk*	0	0	0	0	0	0	–	(100.0)	–	–
Sukuk Perumahan Kerajaan	24	6	18	4	18	4	0.0	(10.1)	0.0	(24.9)
Corporate	759	183	787	189	789	188	1.0	4.8	0.3	3.9
of which: *Sukuk*	614	148	643	154	649	154	0.9	6.5	0.9	5.7

( ) = negative, – = not applicable, MYR = Malaysian ringgit, q-o-q = quarter-on-quarter, Q1 = first quarter, Q4 = fourth quarter, USD = United States dollar, y-o-y = year-on-year.
Notes:
1. Bloomberg LP end-of-period local currency–USD rates are used.
2. Growth rates are calculated from local currency base and do not include currency effects.
3. *Sukuk* refers to Islamic bonds.
4. Sukuk Perumahan Kerajaan are Islamic bonds issued by the Government of Malaysia to refinance funding for housing loans to government employees and to extend new housing loans.
Sources: Bank Negara Malaysia Fully Automated System for Issuing/Tendering and Bloomberg LP.

expansion of outstanding central government bonds, which accounted for 98.1% of total LCY government bonds outstanding at the end of Q1 2022. There were no central bank bills outstanding at the end of the review period, while the amount of Sukuk Perumahan Kerajaan outstanding at the end of March was unchanged from the previous quarter.

LCY government bonds issued in Q1 2022 increased 4.5% q-o-q to MYR50.0 billion from MYR47.9 billion in Q4 2021. The growth was spurred by an increase in issuances of Treasury bills. Issuance of Malaysian Government Securities (conventional bonds) decreased, while Government Investment Issues (Islamic bonds) increased in Q1 2022 compared to the prior quarter.

Corporate bonds. The amount of outstanding LCY corporate bonds grew 0.3% q-o-q to MYR789.0 billion in Q1 2022 from MYR786.8 billion at the end of the previous quarter. This was a deceleration from the 0.8% q-o-q growth logged in Q4 2021. Outstanding corporate *sukuk* expanded 0.9% q-o-q to MYR649.1 billion at the end of March from MYR643.5 billion at the end of December. The growth rate in Q1 2022 was the same as in the prior quarter.

Malaysia's top 30 corporate bond issuers had a combined MYR468.5 billion worth of outstanding LCY corporate bonds at the end of Q1 2022, a share of 59.4% of the total LCY corporate bond market (**Table 2**). State-owned

DanaInfra Nasional had the largest amount of outstanding LCY corporate bonds during the review period, totaling MYR79.9 billion. Among all sectors in the top 30 list, the biggest share comprised financial institutions (51.4%) with MYR240.9 billion worth of LCY corporate bonds outstanding at the end of Q1 2022.

LCY corporate bonds issued during the review period fell 23.7% q-o-q to MYR31.4 billion from MYR41.2 billion in Q4 2021 due to rising interest rates that made it more expensive for companies to raise funds. The contraction was a reversal from the growth of 7.6% q-o-q logged in the prior quarter.

In January and March, Cagamas issued several Islamic medium-term notes (MTNs) (**Table 3**). It also issued conventional MTNs in February and March. The MTNs had tenors from 1 year to 3 years and coupon rates from 2.47% to 3.31%. In March, Kuala Lumpur Kepong, a palm oil producer, issued a dual-tranche *sukuk* totaling MYR2.0 billion. The tenors of the tranches were 10 years and 15 years, and the periodic distribution rates were 4.17% and 4.55%, respectively. Proceeds from the issuance will be used for the company's general corporate purposes, which are Shariah-compliant. Toward the end of Q1 2022, Perbadanan Tabung Pendidikan Tinggi Nasional raised MYR1.5 billion through a four-tranche *sukuk* issuance with tenors from 5 years to 15 years and coupon rates from 3.49% to 4.31%. The funds raised will be used for Shariah-compliant education financing.

Table 2: Top 30 Issuers of Local Currency Corporate Bonds in Malaysia

	Issuers	Outstanding Amount		State-Owned	Listed Company	Type of Industry
		LCY Bonds (MYR billion)	LCY Bonds (USD billion)			
1.	DanaInfra Nasional	79.9	19.0	Yes	No	Finance
2.	Prasarana	39.7	9.4	Yes	No	Transport, Storage, and Communications
3.	Lembaga Pembiayaan Perumahan Sektor Awam	37.6	8.9	Yes	No	Property and Real Estate
4.	Cagamas	31.2	7.4	Yes	No	Finance
5.	Project Lebuhraya Usahasama	28.2	6.7	No	No	Transport, Storage, and Communications
6.	Urusharta Jamaah	27.3	6.5	Yes	No	Finance
7.	Perbadanan Tabung Pendidikan Tinggi Nasional	24.6	5.9	Yes	No	Finance
8.	Pengurusan Air	18.7	4.5	Yes	No	Energy, Gas, and Water
9.	CIMB Group Holdings	14.3	3.4	Yes	No	Finance
10.	Maybank Islamic	13.0	3.1	No	Yes	Banking
11.	Malayan Banking	12.5	3.0	No	Yes	Banking
12.	Khazanah	11.9	2.8	Yes	No	Finance
13.	Tenaga Nasional	11.6	2.8	No	Yes	Energy, Gas, and Water
14.	CIMB Bank	11.6	2.7	Yes	No	Finance
15.	Sarawak Energy	10.8	2.6	Yes	No	Energy, Gas, and Water
16.	Danga Capital	10.0	2.4	Yes	No	Finance
17.	Jimah East Power	8.8	2.1	Yes	No	Energy, Gas, and Water
18.	Danum Capital	8.0	1.9	No	No	Finance
19.	Public Bank	6.9	1.6	No	No	Banking
20.	Kuala Lumpur Kepong	6.6	1.6	No	Yes	Energy, Gas, and Water
21.	Sapura TMC	6.4	1.5	No	No	Finance
22.	Malaysia Rail Link	6.2	1.5	Yes	No	Construction
23.	YTL Power International	5.8	1.4	No	Yes	Energy, Gas, and Water
24.	Infracap Resources	5.8	1.4	Yes	No	Finance
25.	Bakun Hydro Power Generation	5.5	1.3	No	No	Energy, Gas, and Water
26.	Bank Pembangunan Malaysia	5.5	1.3	Yes	No	Banking
27.	Turus Pesawat	5.3	1.3	Yes	No	Transport, Storage, and Communications
28.	GOVCO Holdings	5.1	1.2	Yes	No	Finance
29.	1Malaysia Development	5.0	1.2	Yes	No	Finance
30.	EDRA Energy	5.0	1.2	No	Yes	Energy, Gas, and Water
	Total Top 30 LCY Corporate Issuers	**468.5**	**111.4**			
	Total LCY Corporate Bonds	**789.0**	**187.7**			
	Top 30 as % of Total LCY Corporate Bonds	**59.4%**	**59.4%**			

LCY = local currency, MYR = Malaysian ringgit, USD = United States dollar.
Notes:
1. Data as of 31 March 2022.
2. State-owned firms are defined as those in which the government has more than a 50% ownership stake.
Source: *AsianBondsOnline* calculations based on Bank Negara Malaysia Fully Automated System for Issuing/Tendering data.

Table 3: Notable Local Currency Corporate Bond Issuances in the First Quarter of 2022

Corporate Issuers	Coupon Rate (%)	Issued Amount (MYR million)
Cagamas[a]		
1-year Islamic MTN	2.47	100.0
2-year MTN	2.93	400.0
2-year MTN	2.95	330.0
2-year Islamic MTN	2.95	200.0
2-year MTN	2.86	150.0
3-year Islamic MTN	3.31	930.0
3-year Islamic MTN	3.10	200.0
Kuala Lumpur Kepong		
10-year Islamic MTN	4.17	1,500.0
15-year Islamic MTN	4.55	500.0
Perbadanan Tabung Pendidikan Tinggi Nasional		
5-year Islamic MTN	3.49	400.0
7-year Islamic MTN	3.73	600.0
13-year Islamic MTN	4.11	150.0
15-year Islamic MTN	4.31	350.0

MTN = medium-term note, MYR = Malaysian ringgit.
[a] Multiple issuance of the same tenor indicates issuance on different dates.
Source: Bank Negara Malaysia Bond Info Hub.

Figure 2: Foreign Holdings and Capital Flows in the Malaysian Local Currency Government Bond Market

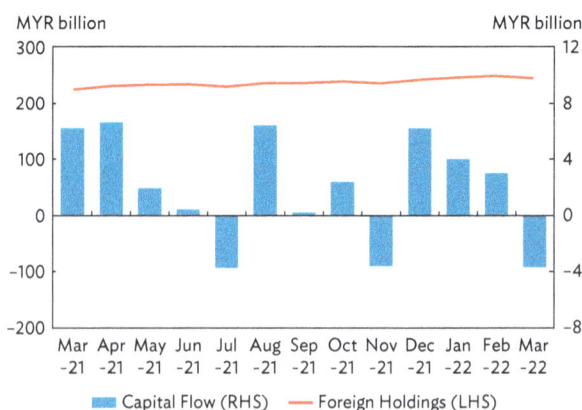

LHS = left-hand side, MYR = Malaysian ringgit, RHS = right-hand side.
Notes:
1. Figures exclude foreign holdings of Bank Negara Malaysia bills.
2. Month-on-month changes in foreign holdings of local currency government bonds were used as a proxy for bond flows.
Source: Bank Negara Malaysia Monthly Statistical Bulletin.

Investor Profile

Foreign holdings of LCY government bonds in Malaysia increased in February, with holdings of foreign investors amounting to MYR248.9 billion worth of LCY government bonds, up from MYR245.9 billion in January (**Figure 2**). In March, foreign holdings were closer to their January level again at MYR245.2 billion. Net capital outflows from the bond market were recorded in March totaling MYR3.7 billion, somewhat offsetting the inflows of MYR4.0 billion and MYR3.0 billion in the preceding

2 months. The sell-off in March followed a global trend in bond markets worldwide spurred by the monetary policy tightening of the United States Federal Reserve. Foreign holdings as a share of LCY government bonds declined from 26.1% at the end of January to 26.0% at the end of February and to 25.6% at the end of March.

At the end of Q4 2021, financial institutions and social security institutions were the largest investors in LCY government bonds, holding 33.6% and 27.5% of total bonds outstanding, respectively (**Figure 3**). Financial

Figure 3: Local Currency Government Bonds Investor Profile

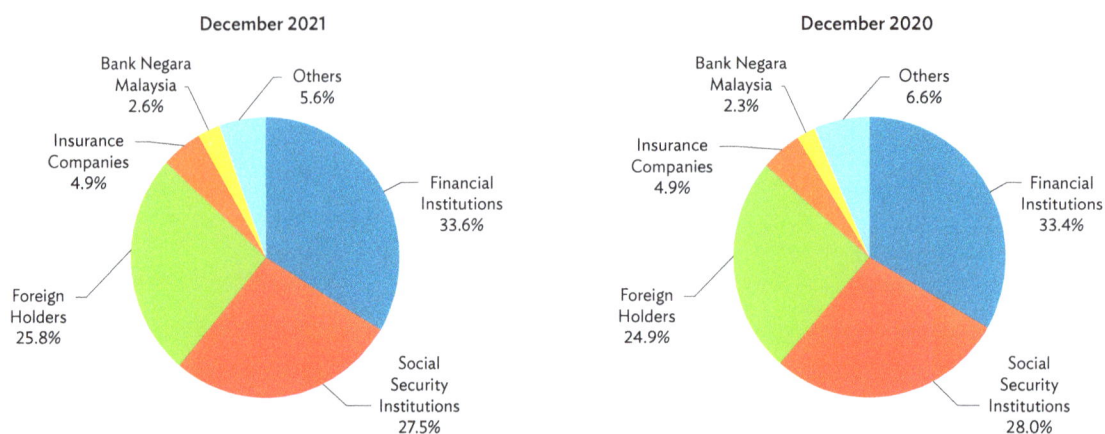

December 2021

December 2020

Note: "Others" include statutory bodies, nominees and trustee companies, and cooperatives and unclassified items.
Source: Bank Negara Malaysia.

institutions' holdings increased compared to the same period in 2020. On the other hand, the share of social security institutions declined. Foreign holders' share of the pie grew to 25.8% from 24.9% in the previous year during the review period. The share of insurance companies was steady at 4.9%, while that of the BNM grew to 2.6% from 2.3% between December 2020 and December 2021.

Policy, Institutional, and Regulatory Developments

Bank Negara Malaysia Launches the Malaysia Islamic Overnight Rate

On 25 March, the BNM announced the establishment of the Malaysia Islamic Overnight Rate (MYOR-i), which will be used as a reference rate for Shariah-compliant financial products. MYOR-i is expected to help develop the Islamic financial market of Malaysia, reinforcing best practices in the Shariah-compliant financial system. The BNM noted that MYOR-i is the first Islamic benchmark in the world that is transaction-based, and it will replace the Kuala Lumpur Islamic Reference Rate immediately. With this new Islamic benchmark, the BNM aims for better transparency and innovation in Islamic finance, leading to efficiency in pricing financial instruments and boosting the economy of Malaysia.

Philippines

Yield Movements

The Philippines' local currency (LCY) government bond yields increased across all tenors between 28 February and 15 May (**Figure 1**). On average, yields surged 61 basis points (bps) for all maturities. The yields on 3-year to 10-year bonds had the largest increases, ranging from 74 bps to 88 bps. Smaller yield increases were seen at the shorter-end of the curve (1-month to 1-year maturities), averaging 32 bps. Yield increases on bonds with 2-year, 20-year, and 25-year maturities averaged 63 bps. The movements caused the yield spread between the 2-year and 10-year tenors to widen during the review period from 229 bps to 253 bps.

The large yield increases reflect the defensive stance of investors toward government securities prompted by surging inflationary risks, the impending monetary tightening of the Bangko Sentral ng Pilipinas (BSP) during the review period, and policy uncertainty induced by the recently concluded national elections. On the international front, aggressive monetary policy normalization by the United States (US) Federal Reserve and the heightened global uncertainty caused by the Russian invasion of Ukraine also contributed to the yield hikes.

Yields on the shorter-end of the curve had relatively smaller increases as investor preferences were skewed toward these tenors because they serve as a vehicle for investors to park money while waiting for more clarity on the direction of the market. On the other hand, larger yield increases for bonds with longer maturities were due to investors seeking a higher risk premium amid expectations of continued high inflation and multiple interest rate hikes by the BSP and the Federal Reserve in coming months.

On 19 May, the BSP raised the benchmark policy rate by 25 bps to 2.25% after having kept the interest rate at a record low of 2.00% since November 2020. The decision was made to ease rising inflationary pressures and help prevent further second-round effects. The better-than-expected economic expansion in the first quarter (Q1) of 2022, which signaled the that the economic recovery is gaining traction, provided scope for the BSP to increase

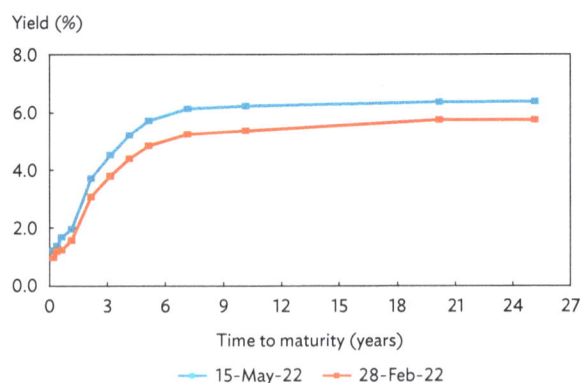

Figure 1: Philippines' Benchmark Yield Curve—Local Currency Government Bonds

Source: Based on data from Bloomberg LP.

the rate and proceed with plans to gradually withdraw its extraordinary liquidity interventions and start the normalization of monetary policy settings. The central bank also stated that it would reconfigure its government securities purchasing window from a crisis intervention measure into a regular liquidity facility.

Consumer price inflation in the Philippines surged to a 42-month high of 5.4% year-on-year (y-o-y) in May from 4.9% y-o-y in April. The elevated inflation rate was mainly due to faster price increases for food and nonalcoholic beverages and transport as consequence of the Russian invasion of Ukraine and supply chain disruptions, which kept global commodity prices high. The year-to-date average inflation of 4.1% breached the government's annual target of 2.0%–4.0% for 2022. Along with the rate hike, the BSP raised its full-year 2022 inflation forecast to 4.6% from 4.3% due to expected sustained pressure from higher oil and commodity prices. The BSP forecasts inflation to decelerate to 3.9% in 2023, which is up from an earlier forecast of 3.6%.

The Philippine economy grew better than expected in Q1 2022 with gross domestic product (GDP) increasing 8.3% y-o-y, marking the fourth consecutive quarter of expansion. The growth was faster than the revised 7.8% y-o-y uptick in the fourth quarter (Q4) of 2021 and a strong reversal from the 3.8% y-o-y contraction in Q1 2021. On the expenditure side, all components posted growth, with household consumption, which accounts for about 75% of GDP, increasing 10.1% y-o-y. On the production side, major economic sectors—primary, industry, and services—all posted positive growth rates. The broad-based expansion in Q1 2022 was underpinned by the policy shift to fully open the economy that allowed businesses to operate at full capacity. The government is targeting strong full-year economic growth of 7%–8% in 2022.

The Philippine peso weakened 2.9% from the start of the year through 15 May, when it traded at PHP52.5 per USD1.0. The Philippine peso lost ground against the US dollar as the BSP kept the benchmark rate at a record low during the review period, while developed economies such as the US were increasing the pace of monetary tightening and some emerging Asian economies began raising their policy rates. The widening trade deficit and uncertainty over the policies of the president-elect on key issues also contributed to downward pressure on the local currency.

Size and Composition

The Philippines' LCY bonds outstanding amounted to PHP10,426.7 billion (USD201.5 billion) in Q1 2022 on an expansion of 6.5% quarter-on-quarter (q-o-q), up from marginal growth of 0.3% q-o-q in Q4 2021. Both the government and corporate segments posted strong

increases during the quarter (**Table 1**). On an annual basis, the LCY bond market expanded 14.3% y-o-y, which was almost unchanged from Q4 2021. Government bonds accounted for 85.5% of the total bond market at the end of March, while corporate bonds accounted for 14.5%.

Government bonds. Total outstanding LCY government bonds increased 6.5% q-o-q to PHP8,911.5 billion in Q1 2022, which was quicker than the growth of 0.5% q-o-q recorded in Q4 2021. The expansion was driven by Treasury bonds and the rebound in BSP bill issuance.

Treasury bonds outstanding expanded 7.4% q-o-q to reach PHP7,803.2 billion in Q1 2022, accelerating from 5.6% q-o-q growth in the previous quarter. The faster growth was due to the large sale of Retail Treasury Bonds (RTBs) during the quarter. On the other hand, Treasury bills outstanding amounted to PHP656.6 billion in Q1 2022 on a decline of 17.5% q-o-q, which followed a drop of 15.5% in Q4 2021.

BSP bills outstanding rebounded to expand 57.7% q-o-q in Q1 2022 from a decline of 40.9% q-o-q in the previous quarter. BSP bills outstanding reached PHP410.0 billion, adding to the size of the government bond market. Outstanding debt from government-related entities was unchanged during the quarter at PHP41.7 billion.

Table 1: Size and Composition of the Local Currency Bond Market in the Philippines

	Outstanding Amount (billion)						Growth Rate (%)			
	Q1 2021		Q4 2021		Q1 2022		Q1 2021		Q1 2022	
	PHP	USD	PHP	USD	PHP	USD	q-o-q	y-o-y	q-o-q	y-o-y
Total	9,122	188	9,787	192	10,427	201	6.5	28.4	6.5	14.3
Government	7,543	155	8,365	164	8,911	172	8.4	36.5	6.5	18.1
Treasury Bills	1,049	22	796	16	657	13	10.5	88.5	(17.5)	(37.4)
Treasury Bonds	6,130	126	7,267	143	7,803	151	7.2	24.3	7.4	27.3
Central Bank Securities	297	6	260	5	410	8	35.2	–	57.7	37.8
Others	66	1	42	1	42	0.8	(0.01)	65.2	(0.01)	(36.7)
Corporate	1,579	33	1,421	28	1,515	29	(2.0)	0.01	6.6	(4.1)

( ) = negative, – = not applicable, PHP = Philippine peso, q-o-q = quarter-on-quarter, Q1 = first quarter, Q4 = fourth quarter, USD = United States dollar, y-o-y = year-on-year.
Notes:
1. Bloomberg end-of-period local currency–USD rates are used.
2. Growth rates are calculated from local currency base and do not include currency effects.
3. "Others" comprise bonds issued by government agencies, entities, and corporations for which repayment is guaranteed by the Government of the Philippines. This includes bonds issued by Power Sector Assets and Liabilities Management and the National Food Authority, among others.
4. Peso Global Bonds (PHP-denominated bonds payable in USD) are not included.
Sources: Bloomberg LP and Bureau of the Treasury.

Total government issuance in Q1 2022 increased 14.5% q-o-q to PHP2,221.4 billion, driven by the issuance of Treasury bonds and BSP bills. The issuance of Treasury bonds in Q1 2022 amounted to PHP688.7 billion on growth of 37.8% q-o-q, mainly driven by the issuance of RTBs, which is a 10-year debt with a coupon rate of 4.88%. During the quarter, the Bureau of the Treasury's (BTr) bond issuance was below the level of planned sales, as three auctions had partial awards and two auctions had rejected bids due to higher rates being demanded by investors.

Treasury bill issuance amounted to PHP213.0 billion in Q1 2022, which was 11.2% lower compared to the issuance amount in Q4 2021. Even though planned issuance in Q1 2022 was higher than in Q4 2021, the unsuccessful auctions led to a decline in debt sales.

The unsuccessful auctions implied that investors were cautious about building major positions in the bond market on the back of elevated inflation and expectations of a rate hike by the BSP. The issuance of the PHP457.8 billion worth of RTBs and debt exchange in March more than offset the unsuccessful auctions, with the proceeds securing sufficient funding for the BTr. The RTB sales resulted in an overall increase in Treasury debt sales during the quarter.

The BSP issued PHP1,319.8 billion of 28-day bills in Q1 2022, climbing 10.0% q-o-q. The central bank increased its volume offer versus the previous quarter and all auctions were successful except for one where sales were below the offer amount. Nonetheless, strong demand for the securities reflected sustained high liquidity in the market. Government-related entities had no debt sales during Q1 2022.

The government returned to the international bond market in March, successfully raising a total of USD2.25 billion in USD-denominated debt even with a volatile market caused by the unwinding of expansionary monetary tools, particularly in the US, and the ongoing Russian invasion of Ukraine. The triple-tranche issuance comprised USD0.5 billion in 5-year bonds, USD0.75 billion in 10.5-year bonds, and USD1.0 billion in 25-year green bonds. The green bond was the maiden sustainability issuance from the Philippines, with proceeds to be used for the government's sustainable finance framework program. The triple issuance was the first and largest international sovereign bond offering in Southeast Asia in 2022.

The government plans to borrow PHP2.2 trillion in 2022, with PHP1.7 trillion to be sourced domestically and rest from foreign investors. The bulk of the financing requirements is preferred to be sourced locally to alleviate foreign exchange risks at a time when domestic market liquidity is high. In Q1 2022, the Philippines' debt reached a record high of PHP12.7 trillion, equivalent to 63.5% of GDP, exceeding the 60.0% threshold considered by multilateral lenders to be manageable for developing economies.

Corporate bonds. Outstanding corporate debt increased 6.6% q-o-q in Q1 2022 to PHP1,515.2 billion after dropping 1.3% q-o-q in Q4 2021. The reversal was underpinned by high debt sales from the corporate sector during the quarter.

The largest share of corporate bonds outstanding belonged to the banking sector with 40.9% at the end of March (**Figure 2**). However, this share was lower compared to 41.7% at the end of March 2021. The property sector, which ranked second, had a share of 23.5%, down slightly from 23.8% a year earlier. Holding firms overtook the utilities sector for third place at the end of March, with shares of 16.7% and 14.3%, respectively. The rankings of the transport, telecommunications, and "other" sectors were all unchanged, but the shares of the transport and telecommunications sectors were down, while that of the "other" sector was up, in March 2022 versus a year earlier.

The top 30 corporate issuers had aggregate bonds outstanding of PHP1,377.3 billion at the end of March, comprising 90.9% of the total corporate bond market (**Table 2**). The banking sector had outstanding bonds amounting to PHP598.0 billion (43.4%); followed by holdings firms with PHP334.8 billion (24.3%); property firms with PHP210.6 billion (15.3%); and electricity, energy, and power with PHP178.8 billion (13.0%). The remaining sectors comprised 4.0% of the total. BDO Unibank and San Miguel were the largest issuers at the end of March with outstanding debt of PHP162.6 billion and PHP113.3 billion, respectively.

Figure 2: Local Currency Corporate Bonds Outstanding by Sector

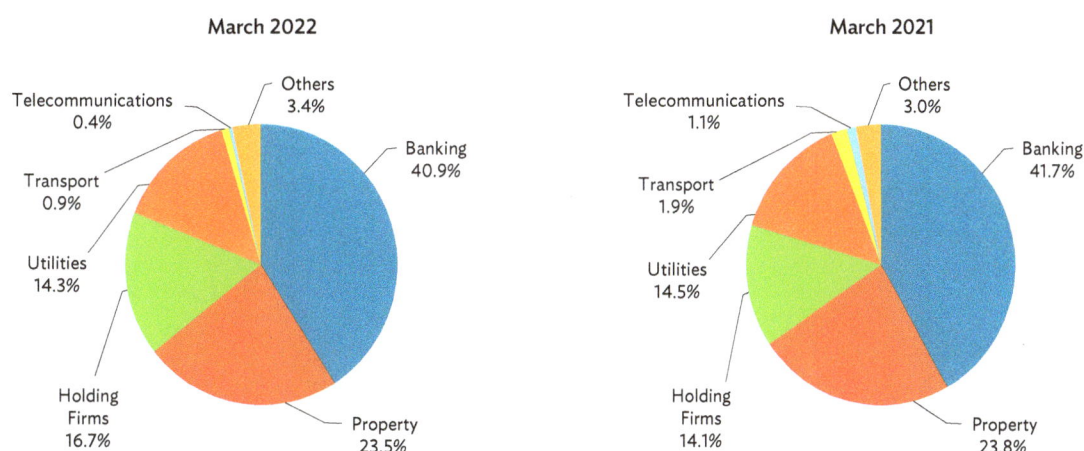

March 2022

- Others 3.4%
- Telecommunications 0.4%
- Transport 0.9%
- Utilities 14.3%
- Banking 40.9%
- Holding Firms 16.7%
- Property 23.5%

March 2021

- Others 3.0%
- Telecommunications 1.1%
- Transport 1.9%
- Utilities 14.5%
- Banking 41.7%
- Holding Firms 14.1%
- Property 23.8%

Source: Based on data from Bloomberg LP.

Corporate bond issuance was strong in Q1 2022 as the economy reopened amid declining coronavirus disease (COVID-19) cases. Debt sales during the quarter increased almost three-fold to PHP152.5 billion from PHP58.5 billion in Q4 2021. Firms issued bonds to fund their operations amid growing demand and, to an extent, to secure lower interest rates as the BSP and other central banks were expected to aggressively unwind their accommodative monetary policy stances to combat inflation. BDO Unibank had the single-largest bond issuance in Q1 2022 amounting to PHP52.7 billion, followed by Bank of the Philippine Islands with a PHP27.0 billion debt sale (**Table 3**).

Investor Profile

Banks and investment houses, and contractual savings and tax-exempt institutions were the largest investor groups in Philippine LCY government bonds at the end of March (**Figure 3**). The market share of banks and investment houses climbed to 43.6% from 37.5% in March 2021, while that of contractual savings and tax-exempt institutions declined to 33.5% from 35.7% over the same period. The "others" investors group (8.1%) was the third-largest investor group at the end of March, overtaking brokers, custodians, and depositories (7.5%), and BTr-managed funds (7.3%). Government-owned or -controlled corporations and local government units

remained the investor group with the smallest holdings of government bonds at 0.1%. Among all investor groups, only the share of banks and investment houses posted an increase between March 2021 and March 2022, while the share of the rest declined during the review period.

Ratings Update

On 17 February, Fitch Ratings (Fitch) affirmed the Philippines' sovereign credit rating at BBB with a negative outlook. Fitch cited the balance of strong external buffers against lagging per capita income and governance indicators as the basis for maintaining the credit rating. However, Fitch's decision to also keep the negative outlook was due to uncertainty about medium-term growth prospects and challenges ahead for the government in unwinding its policy response to the COVID-19 crisis and bringing government debt onto a firm downward path.

On 18 April, Rating and Investment Information, Inc. affirmed the Philippines' sovereign credit rating at BBB with a stable outlook as the economy continued to post strong growth despite a new wave of COVID-19 infections. The rating agency also cited the economy's strong external position and stable banking sector as grounds for the keeping the credit rating.

Table 2: Top 30 Issuers of Local Currency Corporate Bonds in the Philippines

	Issuers	Outstanding Amount		State-Owned	Listed Company	Type of Industry
		LCY Bonds (PHP billion)	LCY Bonds (USD billion)			
1.	BDO Unibank	162.6	3.1	No	Yes	Banking
2.	San Miguel	113.3	2.2	No	Yes	Holding Firms
3.	SM Prime Holdings	99.6	1.9	No	Yes	Holding Firms
4.	Ayala Land	95.9	1.9	No	Yes	Property
5.	Metropolitan Bank	93.8	1.8	No	Yes	Banking
6.	SMC Global Power	73.8	1.4	No	No	Electricity, Energy, and Power
7.	Bank of the Philippine Islands	73.5	1.4	No	Yes	Banking
8.	Rizal Commercial Banking Corporation	69.9	1.4	No	Yes	Banking
9.	China Bank	61.2	1.2	No	Yes	Banking
10.	Aboitiz Power	60.0	1.2	No	Yes	Electricity, Energy, and Power
11.	Security Bank	48.3	0.9	No	Yes	Banking
12.	Petron	45.0	0.9	No	Yes	Electricity, Energy, and Power
13.	Vista Land	42.7	0.8	No	Yes	Property
14.	Ayala Corporation	40.0	0.8	No	Yes	Holding Firms
15.	SM Investments	32.7	0.6	No	Yes	Holding Firms
16.	Philippine National Bank	31.8	0.6	No	Yes	Banking
17.	Filinvest Land	30.5	0.6	No	Yes	Property
18.	Aboitiz Equity Ventures	27.6	0.5	No	Yes	Holding Firms
19.	Union Bank of the Philippines	24.6	0.5	No	Yes	Banking
20.	Maynilad	18.5	0.4	No	No	Water
21.	East West Banking	16.2	0.3	No	Yes	Banking
22.	Philippine Savings Bank	16.1	0.3	No	Yes	Banking
23.	Doubledragon	15.0	0.3	No	Yes	Property
24.	San Miguel Food and Beverage	15.0	0.3	No	Yes	Food and Beverage
25.	Robinsons Land	14.6	0.3	No	Yes	Property
26.	Megaworld	12.0	0.2	No	Yes	Property
27.	Puregold	12.0	0.2	No	Yes	Whole and Retail Trading
28.	Metro Pacific Investments	11.4	0.2	No	Yes	Holding Firms
29.	GT Capital	10.1	0.2	No	Yes	Holding Firms
30.	San Miguel Brewery	9.5	0.2	No	No	Brewery
	Total Top 30 LCY Corporate Issuers	**1,377.3**	**26.6**			
	Total LCY Corporate Bonds	**1,515.2**	**29.3**			
	Top 30 as % of Total LCY Corporate Bonds	**90.9%**	**90.9%**			

LCY = local currency, PHP = Philippine peso, USD = United States dollar.
Notes:
1. Data as of 31 March 2022.
2. State-owned firms are defined as those in which the government has more than a 50% ownership stake.
Source: *AsianBondsOnline* calculations based on Bloomberg LP data.

Table 3: Notable Local Currency Corporate Bond Issuances in the First Quarter of 2022

Corporate Issuers	Coupon Rate (%)	Issued Amount (PHP billion)
BDO Unibank		
2-year bond	2.90	52.70
Bank of the Philippine Islands		
2-year bond	2.81	27.00
San Miguel Corporation		
5-year bond	5.27	17.44
7-year bond	5.84	12.56
Rizal Commercial Banking Corporation		
2-year bond	3.00	14.76
SM Investments		
3-year bond	3.59	7.50
5-year bond	4.77	7.50
Aboitiz Power		
5-year bond	5.31	3.00
7-year bond	5.74	7.00
Century Properties		
5-year bond	5.75	3.00

PHP = Philippine peso.
Source: Based on data from Bloomberg LP.

Policy, Institutional, and Regulatory Developments

Bureau of the Treasury Issues the Philippines' First Sustainability Samurai Bond

In April, the BTr issued the Philippines' first sustainability samurai bond in Japan. The issuance was part of the government's sustainability strategy to capture new accounts and mobilize capital from environmental, social, and governance-conscious investors, with the objective to transition to a more sustainable and climate-resilient economy. It also highlighted the government's commitment to climate change mitigation and adaptation and to deepening its domestic sustainable finance market. The JPY70.1 billion multi-tranche debt sale comprised 5-year bonds (JPY52.0 billion), 7-year bonds (JPY5.0 billion), 10-year bonds (JPY7.1 billion), and 20-year bonds (JPY6.0 billion).

Figure 3: Local Currency Government Bonds Investor Profile

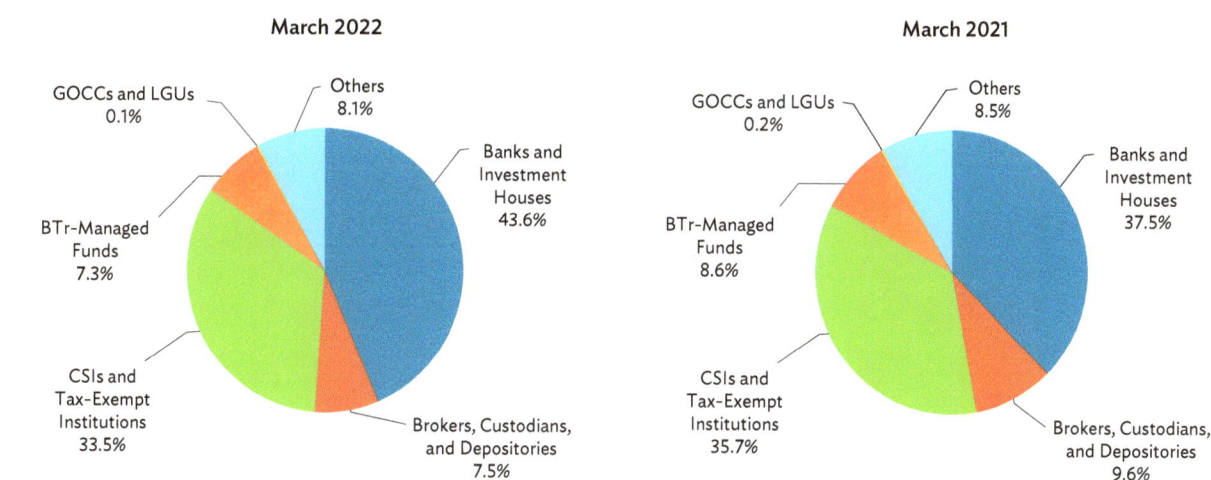

BTr = Bureau of the Treasury, CSI = contractual savings institution, GOCC = government-owned or -controlled corporation, LGU = local government unit.
Source: Bureau of the Treasury.

Bureau of the Treasury Plans to Borrow PHP650.0 billion in Q2 2022

The BTr is set to borrow PHP200.0 billion per month from the domestic debt market in April and May. The amount of monthly borrowing is lower compared to March (PHP250.0 billion). In June, the BTr is set to borrow PHP250.0 billion again as it has calibrated the volume based on domestic requirements and past rejections. In the months of April and May, the planned monthly Treasury bill offerings were PHP60.0 billion and Treasury bond offerings were PHP140.0 billion. In June, the Treasury bill and Treasury bond offerings were PHP75.0 billion and PHP175.0 billion, respectively.

Singapore

Yield Movements

Singapore's local currency (LCY) government bond yield curve increased for all tenors between 28 February and 15 May (**Figure 1**). An average jump of 96 basis points (bps) was recorded for tenors from 6 months to 2 years, while an average increase of 84 bps was reported for longer-term tenors (from 5 years to 20 years). During the review period, the 30-year yield recorded the smallest gain, increasing 60 bps. Meanwhile, the 6-month yield surged the most at 97 bps. A contraction from 69 bps to 61 bps was observed in the yield spread between 2-year and 10-year government bonds during the review period.

The yield curve's rise was mainly due to Monetary Authority of Singapore (MAS) tightening its monetary policy in April, following a global trend that saw economies around the world raise interest rates to combat inflationary pressures.

On 14 April, MAS decided to increase the slope and move the center of its Singapore dollar nominal effective exchange rate policy band. The tightening measure was meant to temper inflationary pressure as the Russian invasion of Ukraine and the ongoing pandemic led to supply chain disruptions and increased commodity prices.

Prices of basic goods and services in Singapore jumped 5.4% year-on-year (y-o-y) in April, the same level as in March, continuing the trend of elevated consumer price inflation that started in October 2021. Singapore's inflation rate averaged 4.8% year-to-date through the end of April. MAS expects full-year 2022 inflation to fall between 4.5% and 5.5%, higher than the central bank's previous forecast of between 2.5% and 3.5%.

Singapore's economy grew 3.7% y-o-y in the first quarter (Q1) of 2022, moderating from the 6.1% y-o-y growth recorded in the fourth quarter (Q4) of 2021. The slower expansion was due to slower growth in the performance of the manufacturing, construction, and services industries. In Q1 2022, Singapore's economy expanded 0.7% on a quarter-on-quarter (q-o-q) basis, following 2.3% q-o-q growth logged in the prior quarter. For full-year 2022, MAS expects Singapore's annual economic growth to be in the 3.0%–5.0% range.

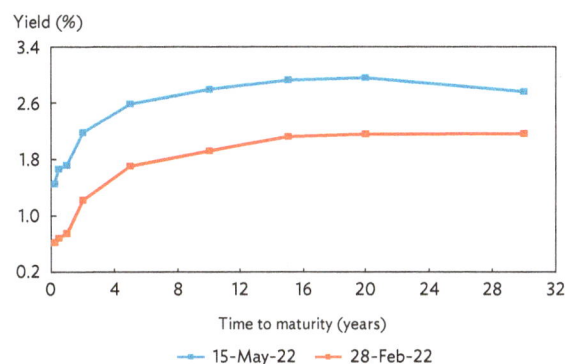

Figure 1: Singapore's Benchmark Yield Curve—Local Currency Government Bonds

Source: Based on data from Bloomberg LP.

Size and Composition

The LCY bond market of Singapore expanded 3.1% q-o-q in Q1 2022, growing to a size of SGD625.0 billion (USD461.5 billion) from SGD606.3 billion in Q4 2021 (**Table 1**). The bond market's growth decelerated from 3.8% q-o-q in the prior quarter. The LCY bond market expanded 20.9% y-o-y in Q1 2022, slower than the 21.9% y-o-y growth recorded at the end of December 2021. Singapore's LCY bond market growth was spurred by growth in its LCY government bonds outstanding, which accounted for 68.8% of total outstanding LCY bonds at the end of the review period.

LCY bond issuance in Q1 2022 declined 11.7% q-o-q to SGD290.6 billion from SGD329.1 billion in the prior quarter due to contractions in both government and corporate bond issuances. The decline in issuance was a reversal of the expansion of 18.0% q-o-q logged in Q4 2021.

Government bonds. Outstanding LCY government bonds grew 4.5% q-o-q during the review period to SGD430.2 billion from SGD411.5 billion in the previous quarter. This growth was an acceleration from the 4.1% q-o-q expansion recorded in Q4 2021. Singapore Government Securities bills and bonds outstanding, which comprised 51.6% of total outstanding LCY government bonds at the end of the review period, jumped 3.5% q-o-q. The other 48.4%, which consisted entirely of MAS bills, grew 5.6% q-o-q.

Table 1: Size and Composition of the Local Currency Bond Market in Singapore

	Outstanding Amount (billion)						Growth Rate (%)			
	Q1 2021		Q4 2021		Q1 2022		Q1 2021		Q1 2022	
	SGD	USD	SGD	USD	SGD	USD	q-o-q	y-o-y	q-o-q	y-o-y
Total	517	384	606	449	625	461	3.9	12.7	3.1	20.9
Government	349	260	412	305	430	318	6.0	19.3	4.5	23.2
SGS Bills and Bonds	203	151	214	159	222	164	3.5	8.3	3.5	9.2
MAS Bills	146	109	197	146	208	154	9.6	38.9	5.6	42.7
Corporate	168	125	195	144	195	144	(0.3)	1.1	(0.003)	16.3

( ) = negative, MAS = Monetary Authority of Singapore, q-o-q = quarter-on-quarter, Q1 = first quarter, Q4 = fourth quarter, SGD = Singapore dollar, SGS = Singapore Government Securities, USD = United States dollar, y-o-y = year-on-year.
Notes:
1. Corporate bonds are based on *AsianBondsOnline* estimates.
2. SGS bills and bonds do not include the special issue of SGS held by the Singapore Central Provident Fund.
3. Bloomberg LP end-of-period local currency–USD rates are used.
4. Growth rates are calculated from local currency base and do not include currency effects.
Sources: Bloomberg LP, Monetary Authority of Singapore, and Singapore Government Securities.

Issuance of LCY government bonds declined 10.8% q-o-q in Q1 2022. Central bank bills issued during the quarter decreased 10.6% q-o-q due to reduced issuance of MAS bills and MAS floating-rate notes. Similarly, issuance of Treasury securities declined 12.3% q-o-q on less issuance of Singapore Government Securities bills and bonds.

Corporate bonds. Outstanding LCY corporate bonds marginally declined to SGD194.8 billion in Q1 2022, essentially unchanged from the prior quarter. The slight decline was a reversal of the 3.3% q-o-q gain logged in the previous quarter.

At the end of Q1 2022, Singapore's top 30 LCY corporate bond issuers had combined outstanding bonds totaling SGD106.0 billion, or 54.4% of the LCY corporate bond market (**Table 2**). The largest issuer during the review period was the government's Housing & Development Board with LCY corporate bonds outstanding amounting to SGD26.9 billion. The largest sectoral share among the top issuers of LCY corporate bonds belonged to real estate companies (41.5%) with SGD43.9 billion of total LCY corporate bonds outstanding at the end of Q1 2022.

LCY corporate bond issuance fell during Q1 2022 to SGD2.4 billion, contracting 58.5% q-o-q from SGD5.9 billion in the prior quarter, due to lower volumes of fundraising activities in each month of the quarter compared to previous months. LCY corporate bond issuances have been declining since the third quarter of 2021.

Singapore's Housing & Development Board issued a total of SGD2.0 billion in Q1 2022 (**Table 3**). The state-owned company raised SGD1.0 billion and SGD950.0 million from a 5-year green bond and 7-year bond, respectively. Proceeds from the green bond will be used for projects that fall under the company's Green Finance Framework. Port and harbor operator PSA Treasury issued a SGD150.0 million 15-year bond in March, the longest tenor issued during the quarter. In January, Maxi-Cash Financial Services issued a 3-year bond worth SGD60.0 million, drawn from its multi-currency medium-term note program. The proceeds will be used for general corporate purposes. The issuance had the highest coupon during the quarter with a periodic distribution rate of 6.05%.

Policy, Institutional, and Regulatory Developments

Singapore and Australia to Jointly Develop Financial Technology

On 13 April, MAS and Australia Treasury signed an agreement committing both parties to strengthening their economies' financial technology network. Under the FinTech Bridge Agreement, the two governments agreed to improve multilateral cooperation on financial technology, expand business opportunities in each other's markets, work together with experts in both economies to generate new financial technology opportunities for Singaporeans and Australians, and share information on issues and market trends in financial technology.

Table 2: Top 30 Issuers of Local Currency Corporate Bonds in Singapore

	Issuers	Outstanding Amount		State-Owned	Listed Company	Type of Industry
		LCY Bonds (SGD billion)	LCY Bonds (USD billion)			
1.	Housing & Development Board	26.9	19.9	Yes	No	Real Estate
2.	Singapore Airlines	14.7	10.9	Yes	Yes	Transportation
3.	Land Transport Authority	9.5	7.0	Yes	No	Transportation
4.	CapitaLand	5.6	4.1	Yes	Yes	Real Estate
5.	Temasek Financial	5.1	3.8	Yes	No	Finance
6.	United Overseas Bank	4.0	3.0	No	Yes	Banking
7.	Frasers Property	3.8	2.8	No	Yes	Real Estate
8.	Sembcorp Industries	3.8	2.8	No	Yes	Diversified
9.	Mapletree Treasury Services	3.3	2.4	No	No	Finance
10.	DBS Bank	2.9	2.1	No	Yes	Banking
11.	Keppel Corporation	2.2	1.6	No	Yes	Diversified
12.	City Developments Limited	2.1	1.5	No	Yes	Real Estate
13.	CapitaLand Mall Trust	2.0	1.5	No	No	Finance
14.	Oversea-Chinese Banking Corporation	1.7	1.3	No	Yes	Banking
15.	Singapore Technologies Telemedia	1.7	1.2	Yes	No	Utilities
16.	National Environment Agency	1.7	1.2	Yes	No	Environmental Services
17.	Shangri-La Hotel	1.5	1.1	No	Yes	Real Estate
18.	NTUC Income	1.4	1.0	No	No	Finance
19.	Ascendas Real Estate Investment Trust	1.3	0.9	No	Yes	Finance
20.	Singtel Group Treasury	1.3	0.9	No	No	Finance
21.	Suntec Real Estate Investment Trust	1.1	0.8	No	Yes	Real Estate
22.	Olam International	1.1	0.8	No	Yes	Consumer Goods
23.	GuocoLand Limited IHT	1.1	0.8	No	No	Real Estate
24.	Public Utilities Board	1.0	0.7	Yes	No	Utilities
25.	Ascott Residence	1.0	0.7	No	Yes	Real Estate
26.	Singapore Press Holdings	1.0	0.7	No	Yes	Communications
27.	StarHub	0.9	0.7	No	Yes	Diversified
28.	Keppel Land International	0.9	0.7	No	No	Real Estate
29.	Olam Group	0.9	0.7	No	Yes	Consumer Goods
30.	Hyflux	0.9	0.7	No	Yes	Utilities
	Total Top 30 LCY Corporate Issuers	**106.0**	**78.2**			
	Total LCY Corporate Bonds	**194.8**	**143.8**			
	Top 30 as % of Total LCY Corporate Bonds	**54.4%**	**54.4%**			

LCY = local currency, SGD = Singapore dollar, USD = United States dollar.
Notes:
1. Data as of 31 March 2022.
2. State-owned firms are defined as those in which the government has more than a 50% ownership stake.
Source: *AsianBondsOnline* calculations based on Bloomberg LP data.

Table 3: Notable Local Currency Corporate Bond Issuances in the First Quarter of 2022

Corporate Issuers	Coupon Rate (%)	Issued Amount (SGD million)
Housing & Development Board		
5-year bond	1.845	1,000.0
7-year bond	1.971	950.0
PSA Treasury		
15-year bond	2.675	150.0
Maxi-Cash Financial Services		
3-year bond	6.050	60.0
Standard Chartered		
3-year bond	1.000	2.0

SGD = Singapore dollar.
Source: Bloomberg LP.

Thailand

Yield Movements

Between 28 February and 15 May, Thailand's local currency (LCY) government bond yield curve steepened, with yields soaring an average of 96 basis points (bps) (**Figure 1**). Apart from the 4-year tenor, whose yield was unchanged, all other tenors saw a jump in yields. The yields on bonds with maturities of less than 1 year gained an average of 6 bps, while those with maturities between 1 and 5 years jumped 84 bps. Bond yields for tenors between 6 years and 10 years soared 121 bps, on average, while yields for bonds with maturities longer than 10 years surged an average of 137 bps. The 30-year bond recorded the largest gain in its yield at 152 bps. The yield on 2-year bonds rose 140 bps, while the yield on 10-year bonds gained 115 bps. As a result, the spread between the 2-year and 10-year yields narrowed from 155 bps on 28 February to 130 bps on 15 May.

Thai LCY government bond yields rose in tandem with other regional bond yields in response to global inflationary pressure and monetary policy tightening by the United States (US) Federal Reserve. To curb mounting inflation, the US Federal Reserve adjusted upward the target range for its policy rate by 25 bps to a range of 0.25%–0.50% in March and by 50 bps to a range of 0.75%–1.00% in May.

The Federal Reserve's aggressive monetary policy tightening, combined with heightened global uncertainties due to Russia's invasion of Ukraine, led foreign investors to reduce exposure to emerging market bonds, including Thai bonds. The Thai LCY bond market saw net outflows of foreign funds amounting to THB67.0 billion in March.

The surge in Thai bond yields also reflected rising domestic inflation. Thailand's consumer price inflation surged to 7.1% year-on-year (y-o-y) in May from 4.7% y-o-y in April and 5.7% y-o-y in March. Inflationary pressure stemmed from elevated energy and fresh food prices as well as rising production costs due to global supply chain disruptions and the Russian invasion of Ukraine.

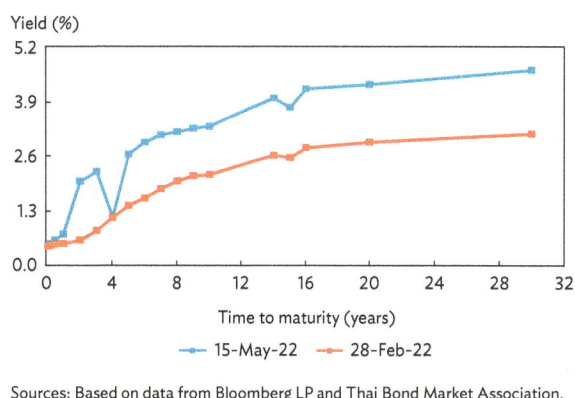

Figure 1: Thailand's Benchmark Yield Curve—Local Currency Government Bonds

Sources: Based on data from Bloomberg LP and Thai Bond Market Association.

Improved economic conditions created additional upward pressure on bond yields. The Thai economy continued to recover, with gross domestic product (GDP) growth accelerating to 2.2% y-o-y in the first quarter (Q1) of 2022 from 1.8% y-o-y in the fourth quarter (Q4) of 2021. Private consumption rose 3.9% y-o-y in Q1 2022, as business and tourism activities started to normalize with the reopening of the economy. Investment recovered, rising 0.8% y-o-y in Q1 2022 from a contraction of 0.2% y-o-y in the previous quarter, as business sentiment improved. Government consumption rose 4.6% y-o-y, while exports expanded 12.0% y-o-y. The National Economic and Social Development Council expects the economy to expand 2.5%–3.5% in 2022, supported by continued improvements in domestic demand and exports, as well a recovery in tourism.

The Bank of Thailand (BOT) has kept its policy rate accommodative amid monetary policy tightening of the Federal Reserve and several regional central banks. On 8 June, the BOT left its policy rate unchanged at 0.50% for a 16th straight meeting but signaled that it would soon start monetary policy normalization. The BOT expects the Thai economy to grow 3.3% in 2022 and 4.2% in 2023, and headline inflation to reach 6.2% in 2022 before easing to 2.5% in 2023. The BOT thus foresees that accommodative monetary policy will be less necessary going forward, given robust economic recovery and elevated inflation.

Size and Composition

Thailand's LCY bond market continued to expand, reaching a size of THB14,998.4 billion (USD450.7 billion) at the end of March (**Table 1**). Overall growth rose to 1.8% quarter-on-quarter (q-o-q) in Q1 2022 from 1.1% q-o-q in Q4 2021, driven by stronger growth in both the government and corporate bond segments. Annual growth also accelerated, rising to 8.4% y-o-y in Q1 2022 from 5.8% y-o-y in the previous quarter. Government bonds continued to dominate Thailand's LCY bond market, comprising 72.9% of the total bond stock at the end of March.

Government bonds. LCY government bonds outstanding totaled THB10,937.4 billion at the end of March. Growth in the stock of government bonds picked up, rising to 2.1% q-o-q in Q1 2022 from 1.6% q-o-q in Q4 2021. The faster expansion stemmed primarily from stronger growth in government bonds and Treasury bills, combined with a rebound in state-owned enterprise and other bonds. Growth in government bonds and Treasury bills outstanding accelerated to 4.1% q-o-q in Q1 2022 from 3.0% q-o-q in the preceding quarter. Outstanding state-owned enterprise and other bonds rose 1.8% q-o-q in Q1 2022, reversing the 0.7% q-o-q drop in the previous quarter. Meanwhile, the stock of BOT bonds continued to contract due to maturities, falling 2.6% q-o-q in Q1 2022 after a 1.0% q-o-q drop in Q4 2021. On a y-o-y basis, Thailand's LCY government bond market expanded 7.7% in Q1 2022, up from 4.7% in Q4 2021.

At the end of March, outstanding government and Treasury bills totaled THB7,162.7 billion, comprising the largest share of total LCY government bonds at 65.5%. Outstanding BOT bonds (THB2,822.0 billion) and state-owned enterprise and other bonds (THB952.7 billion) accounted for 25.8% and 8.7%, respectively, of total LCY government bonds.

Issuance of new LCY government bonds reached THB1,670.2 billion in Q1 2022. Issuance fell 0.4% q-o-q in Q1 2022, following a 10.1% q-o-q decline in the previous quarter. Contractions in issuance of government bonds and Treasury bills (12.7% q-o-q) and state-owned enterprise and other bonds (35.2% q-o-q) outpaced the growth in issuance of BOT bonds (8.0% q-o-q), leading to an overall decline in government bond issuance. On a y-o-y basis, issuance of Thai LCY government bonds continued to contract, falling 1.0% in Q1 2022 after a 14.1% drop in the previous quarter, as the government tapered borrowing to manage fiscal sustainability. The share of public debt to GDP stood at 60.6% at the end of March, up from 58.4% at the end of fiscal year 2021 and 49.5% at the end of fiscal year 2020.

Corporate bonds. LCY corporate bonds outstanding totaled THB4,061.0 billion at the end of March. Growth accelerated to 1.2% q-o-q in Q1 2022 from marginal growth in the previous quarter, driven primarily by robust issuance. On a y-o-y basis, the Thai corporate bond market expanded 10.1% in Q1 2022, following a rise of 8.6% in Q4 2021.

Table 1: Size and Composition of the Local Currency Bond Market in Thailand

| | Outstanding Amount (billion) | | | | | | Growth Rate (%) | | | |
| | Q1 2021 | | Q4 2021 | | Q1 2022 | | Q1 2021 | | Q1 2022 | |
	THB	USD	THB	USD	THB	USD	q-o-q	y-o-y	q-o-q	y-o-y
Total	13,842	443	14,728	443	14,998	451	(0.6)	5.1	1.8	8.4
Government	10,152	325	10,716	323	10,937	329	(0.8)	8.5	2.1	7.7
Government Bonds and Treasury Bills	6,349	203	6,883	207	7,163	215	5.5	25.0	4.1	12.8
Central Bank Bonds	2,911	93	2,898	87	2,822	85	(13.5)	(16.6)	(2.6)	(3.1)
State-Owned Enterprise and Other Bonds	892	29	936	28	953	29	5.5	14.1	1.8	6.8
Corporate	3,690	118	4,011	121	4,061	122	(0.1)	(3.3)	1.2	10.1

( ) = negative, q-o-q = quarter-on-quarter, Q1 = first quarter, Q4 = fourth quarter, THB = Thai baht, USD = United States dollar, y-o-y = year-on-year.
Notes:
1. Bloomberg LP end-of-period local currency–USD rates are used.
2. Growth rates are calculated from local currency base and do not include currency effects.
Source: Bank of Thailand.

At the end of March, the LCY bonds outstanding of Thailand's top 30 corporate issuers amounted to THB2,370.8 billion, comprising 58.4% of the Thai corporate bond market (**Table 2**). The top 30 issuers were dominated by companies in the commerce, energy and utilities, food and beverage, and communication sectors, which collectively held 33.1% of the total LCY corporate bond market. Only three of the top 30 were government-owned and the majority were listed on the Stock Exchange of Thailand. CP ALL, True Corporation,

Table 2: Top 30 Issuers of Local Currency Corporate Bonds in Thailand

	Issuers	Outstanding Amount		State-Owned	Listed Company	Type of Industry
		LCY Bonds (THB billion)	LCY Bonds (USD billion)			
1.	CP ALL	247.5	7.4	No	Yes	Commerce
2.	True Corporation	179.4	5.4	No	Yes	Communications
3.	Siam Cement	165.0	5.0	Yes	Yes	Construction Material
4.	Charoen Pokphand Foods	131.2	3.9	No	Yes	Food and Beverage
5.	Thai Beverage	129.2	3.9	No	No	Food and Beverage
6.	PTT	120.4	3.6	Yes	Yes	Energy and Utilities
7.	Berli Jucker	104.1	3.1	No	Yes	Commerce
8.	Bank of Ayudhya	94.9	2.9	No	Yes	Banking
9.	True Move H Universal Communication	88.1	2.6	No	No	Communications
10.	CPF Thailand	79.1	2.4	No	No	Food and Beverage
11.	Indorama Ventures	73.0	2.2	No	Yes	Petrochemicals and Chemicals
12.	Gulf Energy Development	69.5	2.1	No	Yes	Energy and Utilities
13.	Banpu	69.3	2.1	No	Yes	Energy and Utilities
14.	Minor International	67.1	2.0	No	Yes	Hospitality and Leisure
15.	Bangkok Commercial Asset Management	62.2	1.9	No	Yes	Finance and Securities
16.	Toyota Leasing Thailand	61.8	1.9	No	No	Finance and Securities
17.	PTT Global Chemical	61.7	1.9	No	Yes	Petrochemicals and Chemicals
18.	Frasers Property Thailand	51.0	1.5	No	Yes	Property and Construction
19.	Muangthai Capital	51.0	1.5	No	Yes	Finance and Securities
20.	Krungthai Card	45.5	1.4	No	Yes	Banking
21.	BTS Group Holdings	45.1	1.4	No	Yes	Diversified
22.	Krung Thai Bank	44.0	1.3	Yes	Yes	Banking
23.	TPI Polene	43.9	1.3	No	Yes	Property and Construction
24.	dtac TriNet	43.5	1.3	No	Yes	Communications
25.	Global Power Synergy	41.5	1.2	No	Yes	Energy and Utilities
26.	Sansiri	40.9	1.2	No	Yes	Property and Construction
27.	ICBC Thai Leasing	40.6	1.2	No	No	Finance and Securities
28.	Bangchak	40.5	1.2	No	Yes	Energy and Utilities
29.	Land & Houses	40.1	1.2	No	Yes	Property and Construction
30.	Bangkok Expressway & Metro	40.1	1.2	No	Yes	Transportation and Logistics
Total Top 30 LCY Corporate Issuers		**2,370.8**	**71.2**			
Total LCY Corporate Bonds		**4,061.0**	**122.0**			
Top 30 as % of Total LCY Corporate Bonds		**58.4%**	**58.4%**			

LCY = local currency, THB = Thai baht, USD = United States dollar.
Notes:
1. Data as of 31 March 2022.
2. State-owned firms are defined as those in which the government has more than a 50% ownership stake.
Source: *AsianBondsOnline* calculations based on Bloomberg LP data.

and Siam Cement were the top three corporate issuers, with outstanding bond stocks of THB247.5 billion, THB179.4 billion, and THB165.0 billion, respectively. The next largest issuers were Charoen Pokphand Foods, Thai Beverage, PTT, and Berli Jucker, all with outstanding LCY bonds of more than THB100.0 billion each.

Corporate bond issuance totaled THB438.1 billion in Q1 2022, up from THB366.7 billion in Q4 2021. Issuance of corporate debt rebounded in Q1 2022, jumping 19.5% q-o-q after a 22.1% q-o-q contraction in the previous quarter, as corporates took advantage of prevailing rates in anticipation of increased borrowing costs in succeeding quarters when the BOT starts tightening its monetary policy alongside other regional central banks. On an annual basis, corporate debt issuance continued to expand, rising 48.6% y-o-y in Q1 2022 after a 32.4% y-o-y jump in the previous quarter.

Table 3 lists the notable corporate debt issuances in Q1 2022. True Corporation, a communications company, was the top issuer, raising a total of THB35.3 billion

Table 3: Notable Local Currency Corporate Bond Issuances in the First Quarter of 2022

Corporate Issuers	Coupon Rate (%)	Issued Amount (THB billion)
True Corporation[a]		
1-year bond	2.32	0.3
1.2-year bond	2.39	4.5
3-year bond	3.20	5.6
3-year bond	3.20	5.0
4-year bond	3.60	2.9
4-year bond	3.55	2.4
5-year bond	4.00	3.7
5.8-year bond	4.25	5.1
5.8-year bond	4.25	5.9
PTT Global Chemical		
5-year bond	2.13	14.0
7-year bond	2.65	2.0
10-year bond	3.05	2.0
12-year bond	3.29	12.0
Gulf Energy		
3-year bond	2.02	10.0
5-year bond	2.97	8.0
7-year bond	3.21	1.0
10-year bond	3.70	5.0
Charoen Pokphand Foods		
Perpetual bond	4.50	15.0

THB = Thai baht.
[a] Multiple issuance of the same tenor indicates issuance on different dates.
Source: Bloomberg LP.

from bonds with tenors ranging from 1 year to 5.8 years. PTT Global Chemical was the next largest issuer, raising a total of THB30.0 billion from bonds with tenors of 5–12 years. Gulf Energy was the third-largest issuer, raising a total of THB24.0 billion from a quadruple-tranche issuance of bonds with tenors of 3–10 years. Charoen Pokphand Foods had the single-largest debt issuance during the quarter, raising THB15.0 billion from a perpetual bond carrying a coupon of 4.5%.

Investor Profiles

Central government bonds. The four largest holders of Thai government bonds at the end of March were financial corporations, other depository corporations, central government, and nonresidents (**Figure 2**). Financial corporations continued to be the primary holder of government bonds, although their collective share decreased to 36.8% in March 2022 from 39.1% in March 2021. Other depository corporations, which include commercial banks and finance companies, remained the second-largest holder of government bonds with a share of 23.6% at the end of March, up from 21.9% a year earlier. The central government, including state-owned nonprofit enterprises and the Social Security Office, had a 14.4% share, down from 15.4% in March 2021. Nonresidents' holdings of Thai government bonds inched up to 13.7% at the end of March from 12.9% a year earlier. The BOT's holdings of government bonds rose to 4.2% in March 2022 from 3.8% in March 2021.

Central bank bonds. Other depository corporations and financial corporations were the two largest holders of BOT bonds, with combined shares comprising 73.8% of total BOT bonds at the end of March (**Figure 3**). The share of other depository corporations increased to 42.1% in March 2022 from 38.3% in March 2021, while financial corporations' holdings slipped to 31.7% from 33.3% during the same period. The BOT's holdings of its own LCY bonds declined to 12.0% at the end of March from 14.2% a year earlier. The central government's share was little changed from 9.8% in March 2021 to 10.0% in March 2022. Nonresidents' holdings of BOT bonds remained negligible but rose slightly to 2.1% at the end of March from 0.9% a year earlier.

Net inflows from foreign investors to the Thai LCY bond market dropped to THB85.6 billion in Q1 2022

Figure 2: Local Currency Government Bonds Investor Profile

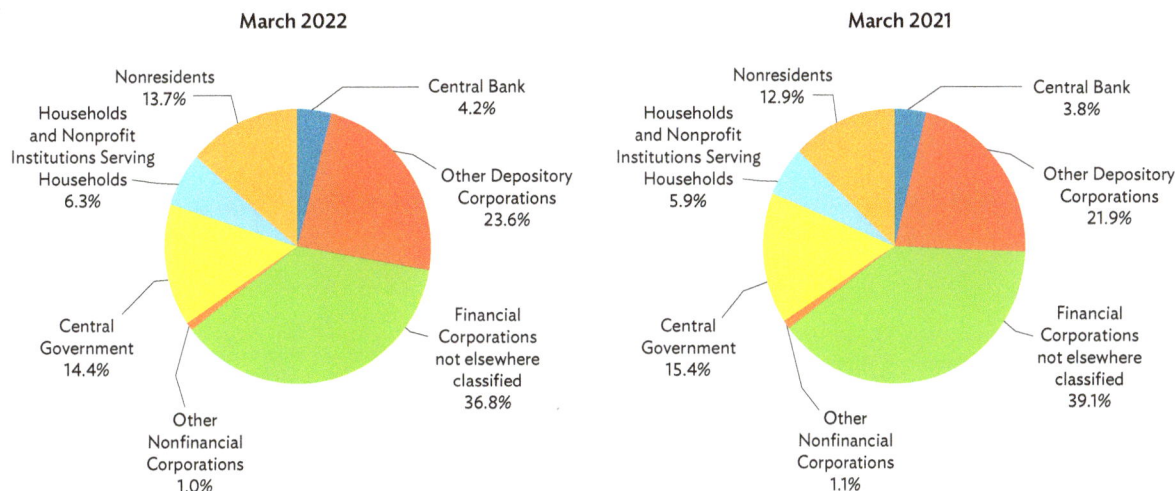

March 2022

March 2021

Note: Government bonds include Treasury bills and bonds.
Source: *AsianBondsOnline* and Bank of Thailand.

Figure 3: Local Currency Central Bank Securities Investor Profile

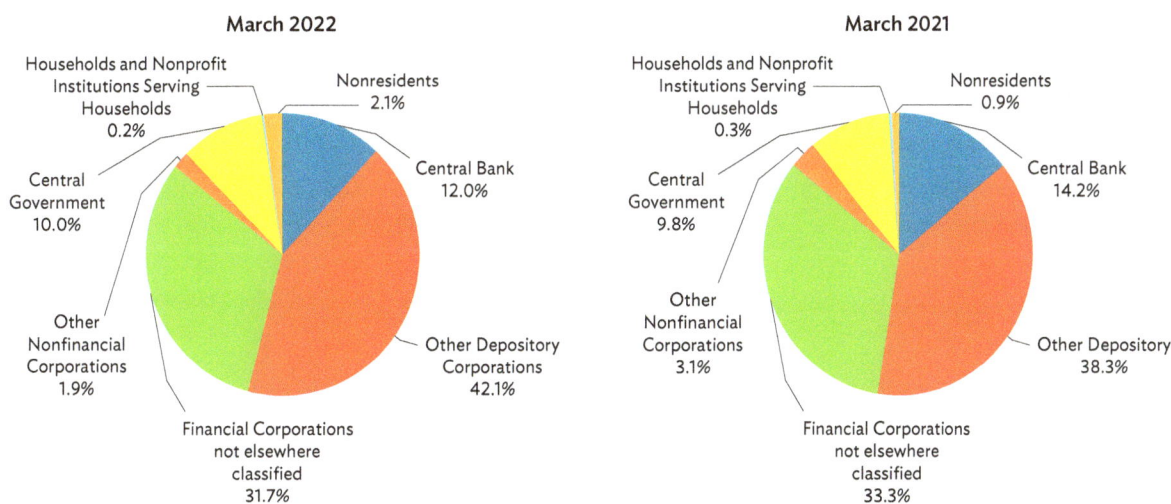

March 2022

March 2021

Source: Bank of Thailand.

from THB111.3 billion in the previous quarter (**Figure 4**). In January and February, the Thai LCY bond market saw net inflows of THB80.7 billion and THB71.9 billion, respectively, on improved market sentiment as the Thai economy reopened. However, the Federal Reserve's monetary tightening in March and elevated risks due to the quickening pace of inflation led global investors to reduce their emerging market bond exposure. The Thai LCY bond market recorded net outflows of THB67.0 billion in March, the second-highest monthly outflows since the onset of the pandemic. The global search for yields led to a return of some foreign investors to the Thai bond market in April, resulting in monthly net inflows of THB7.7 billion.

Figure 4: Foreign Investor Net Trading of Local Currency Bonds in Thailand

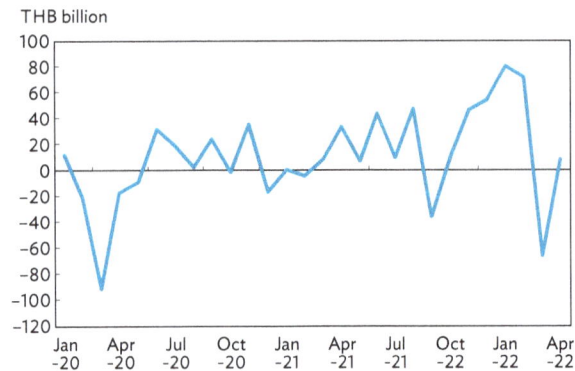

THB = Thai baht.
Source: Thai Bond Market Association.

Policy, Institutional, and Regulatory Developments

Thai Government Approves New Borrowing of THB1.4 Trillion for Fiscal Year 2022

On 12 April, the Government of Thailand approved new borrowing of THB1.40 trillion for fiscal year 2022, up from the previously planned amount of THB1.36 trillion. The new borrowing plan is projected to raise public debt to 62.8% of GDP at the end of the fiscal year, which is still below the government's 70.0% limit. The plan includes THB10.0 billion of borrowing for the state oil fund to stabilize domestic fuel prices, THB29.3 billion for restructuring government debt, and THB39.4 billion for investment projects. Public debt stood at 60.6% of GDP at the end of March.

Bank of Thailand Eases Foreign Exchange Regulations

As part of continuing efforts to develop Thailand's foreign exchange ecosystem, BOT announced a new set of regulatory changes on 18 April. Rules for cross-border currency transfer and payment transactions were relaxed to allow Thai residents greater flexibility in conducting foreign exchange transactions. Rules related to foreign exchange hedging were eased to help Thai companies manage their foreign exchange risks more efficiently. Documentary requirements for foreign exchange transactions were also simplified to reduce costs and facilitate foreign exchange activities through online channels. However, cross-border transfers of the Thai baht to pay for digital assets are still prohibited.

Viet Nam

Yield Movements

The yield curve for Viet Nam's local currency (LCY) government bonds shifted upward as yields in all maturities increased between 28 February and 15 May (**Figure 1**). Yields rose 98 basis points (bps) on average across the curve. Notably large yield jumps were seen on bonds with 5-year to 10-year tenors, averaging 115 bps. Yield increases on all remaining tenors averaged 85 bps. The shift in the yield curve resulted in the yield spread between the 2-year and 10-year tenors widening from 91 bps to 111 bps during the review period.

The upward yield movements were largely due to the combined effects of increasing domestic inflationary pressures and the hawkish stance of the United States (US) Federal Reserve in unwinding its accommodative monetary policy position. Reduced optimism about global economic growth, which could possibly spillover to the domestic economy through various channels, added to the uncertainty. Such risks would lead investors to continue demanding a higher risk premium on government securities. On the other hand, the persistence of the accommodative monetary policy of the State Bank of Vietnam (SBV) may have capped upward pressure on bond yields.

The SBV is not expected to increase its benchmark rate in the near future, as it will continue to prioritize supporting domestic demand and a full economic recovery from the coronavirus disease (COVID-19) pandemic.[13] While inflationary pressure is rising due to adverse global developments, Viet Nam's inflation rate remained well below the government's cap of 4.0% for 2022.

In May, consumer price inflation rose to 2.9% year-on-year (y-o-y) from 2.6% y-o-y in April. Transportation costs were the largest driver of inflation, jumping 18.4% y-o-y amid rising fuel prices. All other commodity groups posted higher prices except for postal and communication services and education. Inflation in January through May was 2.3% y-o-y. High inflation

Figure 1: Viet Nam's Benchmark Yield Curve— Local Currency Government Bonds

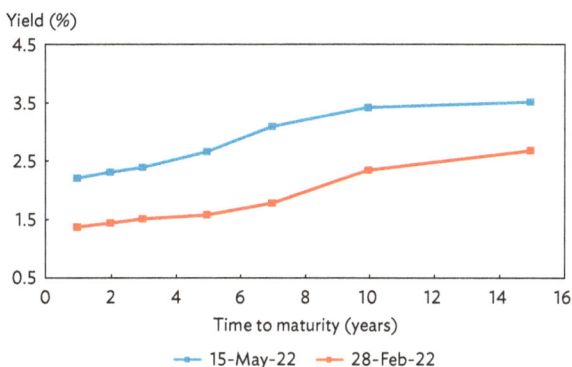

Source: Based on data from Bloomberg LP.

is expected to persist from the impact of the Russian invasion of Ukraine on global commodity prices and supply chain disruptions resulting from COVID-19 mobility restrictions in the People's Republic of China.

Viet Nam's economy expanded 5.0% y-o-y in the first quarter (Q1) of 2022, decelerating from 5.2% y-o-y growth in the fourth quarter (Q4) but up from the 4.7% y-o-y increase in Q1 2021. The domestic economy managed to post high growth despite the surge of COVID-19 cases early in the year. All major economic sectors—primary, industry, and services—expanded during the quarter, with corresponding growth rates of 2.5% y-o-y, 6.4% y-o-y, and 4.6% y-o-y. The government has set an annual gross domestic product growth target of 6.0%–6.5% for full-year 2022.

The Vietnamese dong depreciated against the US dollar by 1.3% from the start of the year through the middle of May, trading at VND23,095.0 per USD1.0 on 15 May. The weaker dong followed the trend in regional currencies as investors sought safe haven in the US dollar amid interest rate hikes by the Federal Reserve and global economic uncertainty.

[13] *Viet Nam News*. 2022. "Loose Monetary Policy Forecast to Continue Despite Inflation Pressure." April. https://vietnamnews.vn/economy/1174858/loose-monetary-policy-forecast-to-continue-despite-inflation-pressure.html.

Size and Composition

Viet Nam's LCY bond market grew 2.4% quarter-on-quarter (q-o-q) to VND2,138.6 trillion (USD93.6 billion) at the end of Q1 2022, slowing from the previous quarter's growth of 9.8% q-o-q (**Table 1**). The overall deceleration was due to slower expansion in both government and corporate bonds outstanding. On an annual basis, the bond market grew 28.9% y-o-y during the quarter, up from an increase of 25.5% y-o-y in Q4 2021. Viet Nam's LCY bond market largely comprises government bonds, which accounted for a 70.7% share of the total at the end of March, although this was slightly down from 71.3% at the end of December 2021. Corporate bonds' market share increased to 29.3% from 28.7% during the same review period.

Government bonds. The government bond market expanded 1.5% q-o-q in Q1 2022 to VND1,511.5 trillion, down from growth of 5.3% q-o-q in Q4 2021. The decline in government-guaranteed and municipal bonds outstanding partially offset the expansion in Treasury bonds and central bank bills outstanding.

Treasury bonds outstanding increased 1.8% q-o-q to VND1,373.8 trillion in Q1 2022, following an increase of 5.7% q-o-q in the preceding quarter. The slower expansion was due to lower debt sales from the State Treasury of Vietnam, alongside relatively more maturities in Q1 2022. The State Treasury of Vietnam raised VND41.3 trillion during the quarter, compared to VND100.0 trillion in Q4 2021, accounting for about 39.0% of the planned issuance in Q1 2022.

Outstanding government-guaranteed and municipal bonds declined 4.6% q-o-q to VND133.3 trillion due to maturities and the absence of any issuance in this government bond segment in Q1 2022.

SBV bills outstanding amounted to VND4.4 trillion at the end of March. In Q1 2022, SBV issued central bank bills comprised of 14- and 28-day bills totaling VND31.7 trillion.

Corporate bonds. Total debt outstanding in the corporate sector amounted to VND627.1 trillion at the end of March, with growth falling to 4.6% q-o-q in Q1 2022 from 22.7% q-o-q in Q4 2021 on slowing corporate bond issuance.

The amount of bonds outstanding of the top 30 corporate issuers totaled VND367.6 trillion at the end of March, comprising 58.6% of the total corporate bond market (**Table 2**). Banks and property firms were the most prolific issuers with outstanding bonds amounting to VND279.6 trillion and VND56.9 trillion, respectively, together comprising a 91.5% share of the top 30's outstanding bonds. The Bank for Investment and Development of Vietnam remained the largest issuer of bonds at the end of Q1 2022 with VND40.9 trillion, up from VND37.2 trillion at the end of Q4 2021.

Corporate issuance in Q1 2022 was less active compared to the previous quarter. Debt sales from the sector totaled VND31.3 trillion, or only about one-fourth of issuance in Q4 2021. This can be traced to Circular No. 16 of the SBV, effective 15 January 2022, that set

Table 1: Size and Composition of the Local Currency Bond Market in Viet Nam

| | Outstanding Amount (billion) | | | | | | Growth Rate (%) | | | |
| | Q1 2021 | | Q4 2021 | | Q1 2022 | | Q1 2021 | | Q1 2022 | |
	VND	USD	VND	USD	VND	USD	q-o-q	y-o-y	q-o-q	y-o-y
Total	1,659,262	72	2,089,053	92	2,138,634	94	(0.3)	18.8	2.4	28.9
Government	1,364,303	59	1,489,606	65	1,511,514	66	(1.1)	6.5	1.5	10.8
Treasury Bonds	1,220,377	53	1,349,811	59	1,373,782	60	(0.6)	23.2	1.8	12.6
Central Bank Bills	0	0	0	0	4,387	0	–	(100.0)	–	–
Government-Guaranteed and Municipal Bonds	143,927	6	139,796	6	133,346	6	(4.9)	(6.1)	(4.6)	(7.4)
Corporate	294,959	13	599,446	26	627,120	27	3.3	156.0	4.6	112.6

( ) = negative, – = not applicable, q-o-q = quarter-on-quarter, Q1 = first quarter, Q4 = fourth quarter, USD = United States dollar, VND = Vietnamese dong, y-o-y = year-on-year.
Notes:
1. Bloomberg LP end-of-period local currency–USD rates are used.
2. Growth rates are calculated from local currency base and do not include currency effects.
Sources: Bloomberg LP and Vietnam Bond Market Association.

Table 2: Top 30 Issuers of Local Currency Corporate Bonds in Viet Nam

	Issuers	Outstanding Amount		State-Owned	Listed Company	Type of Industry
		LCY Bonds (VND billion)	LCY Bonds (USD billion)			
1.	Bank for Investment and Development of Vietnam	40,863	1.79	Yes	Yes	Banking
2.	Vietnam Prosperity Joint Stock Commercial Bank	29,050	1.27	No	Yes	Banking
3.	Ho Chi Minh City Development Joint Stock Commercial Bank	28,768	1.26	No	Yes	Banking
4.	Vietnam International Joint Stock Commercial Bank	26,950	1.18	No	Yes	Banking
5.	Lien Viet Post Joint Stock Commercial Bank	24,090	1.05	No	Yes	Banking
6.	Asia Commercial Joint Stock Bank	21,900	0.96	No	Yes	Banking
7.	Orient Commercial Joint Stock Bank	18,535	0.81	No	No	Banking
8.	Tien Phong Commercial Joint Stock Bank	17,649	0.77	No	Yes	Banking
9.	Masan Group	16,900	0.74	No	Yes	Finance
10.	Vietnam Joint Stock Commercial Bank for Industry and Trade	13,389	0.59	Yes	Yes	Banking
11.	Saigon - Ha Noi Commercial Joint Stock Bank	11,250	0.49	No	Yes	Banking
12.	An Binh Commercial Joint Stock Bank	10,500	0.46	No	No	Banking
13.	Vinhomes JSC	9,935	0.44	No	Yes	Property
14.	Vietnam Maritime Joint Stock Commercial Bank	8,999	0.39	No	Yes	Banking
15.	Sovico Group Joint Stock Company	8,550	0.37	No	Yes	Property
16.	Saigon Glory Company Limited	8,000	0.35	No	No	Property
17.	Bac A Commercial Joint Stock Bank	6,140	0.27	No	Yes	Banking
18.	Southeast Asia Commercial Joint Stock Bank	6,077	0.27	No	Yes	Banking
19.	Golden Hill Real Estate JSC	5,701	0.25	No	No	Property
20.	Vietnam Technological and Commercial Joint Stock Bank	5,600	0.25	No	Yes	Banking
21.	Vingroup	5,425	0.24	No	Yes	Property
22	Military Commercial Joint Stock Bank	5,216	0.23	No	Yes	Banking
23.	NoVa Real Estate Investment Corporation JSC	5,207	0.23	No	Yes	Property
24.	Mediterranean Revival Villas Company Limited	5,000	0.22	No	No	Property
25.	Ho Chi Minh City Infrastructure Investment Joint Stock Company	4,879	0.21	No	Yes	Construction
26.	Bong Sen JSC	4,800	0.21	No	No	Manufacturing
27.	Thai Son - Long An JSC	4,600	0.20	No	No	Property
28.	Vietnam Bank for Agriculture and Rural Development	4,600	0.20	Yes	No	Banking
29.	Trung Nam Dak Lak 1 Wind Power JSC	4,500	0.20	No	No	Energy
30.	Phu My Hung Corporation	4,497	0.20	No	No	Property
	Total Top 30 LCY Corporate Issuers	**367,569**	**16.10**			
	Total LCY Corporate Bonds	**627,120**	**27.46**			
	Top 30 as % of Total LCY Corporate Bonds	**58.6%**	**58.6%**			

LCY = local currency, USD = United States dollar, VND = Vietnamese dong.
Notes:
1. Data as of 31 March 2022.
2. State-owned firms are defined as those in which the government has more than a 50% ownership stake.
Sources: *AsianBondsOnline* calculations based on Bloomberg LP and Vietnam Bond Market Association data.

strict regulations for credit institutions in transactions related to corporate bonds. Notably, bond issuance amounted to VND25.9 trillion in January before dropping to VND1.8 trillion in February and only slightly rebounding to VND3.6 trillion in March.

Such regulations were expected to slow bond issuance activity at the early stage of its effectivity as the market adapts to the new guidelines, similar to what happened in the past when there were new and amended regulations regarding corporate bonds. Over the long run, improvements in information transparency and regulatory compliance are expected to contribute to the sustainable development of Viet Nam's LCY bond market.

Bonds have become an attractive channel for firms to raise funds as the capital market develops and the dependence on bank credit is reduced. The fast-growing corporate bond market has attracted much interest from individual and institutional investors; however, there are potential risks if there is a lack of transparency in the market, low quality of issued bonds, and inaccurate information provided by the issuer. The authorities are closely monitoring compliance to regulations among debt issuers and working on plugging legal loopholes in these regulations. In March, the State Securities Commission canceled nine bond issuances from companies in the Tan Hoang Minh Group, amounting to VND10.0 trillion, that were issued from July 2021 to March 2022. The cancellation was due to the group disclosing false

information and concealing information when issuing a private placement.[14]

Even as the target of new regulations and amid the aforementioned controversy, the property sector dominated bond sales in Viet Nam in Q1 2022, totaling VND15.6 trillion and comprising 50.0% of all corporate issuances during the quarter. Construction firms were next with a market share of 25.3% (VND7.9 trillion) and banks with 14.3% (VND4.5 trillion). The notable bond issuances during the quarter listed in **Table 3** were all from either property or construction firms, with Eagle Side Development and Investment JSC having the singe-largest issuance at VND3.9 trillion.

Table 3: Notable Local Currency Corporate Bond Issuances in the First Quarter of 2022

Corporate Issuers	Coupon Rate (%)	Issued Amount (VND billion)
Eagle Side Development and Investment JSC		
1-year bond	–	3,930
Tuong Khai Construction Investment JSC		
1-year bond	–	2,990
Minh Truong Phu Construction JSC		
1-year bond	–	2,950
Hung Thinh Investment JSC		
7-year bond	–	2,000

– = not available, JSC = Joint Stock Corporation, VND = Vietnamese dong.
Source: Vietnam Bond Market Association.

Figure 2: Local Currency Government Bonds Investor Profile

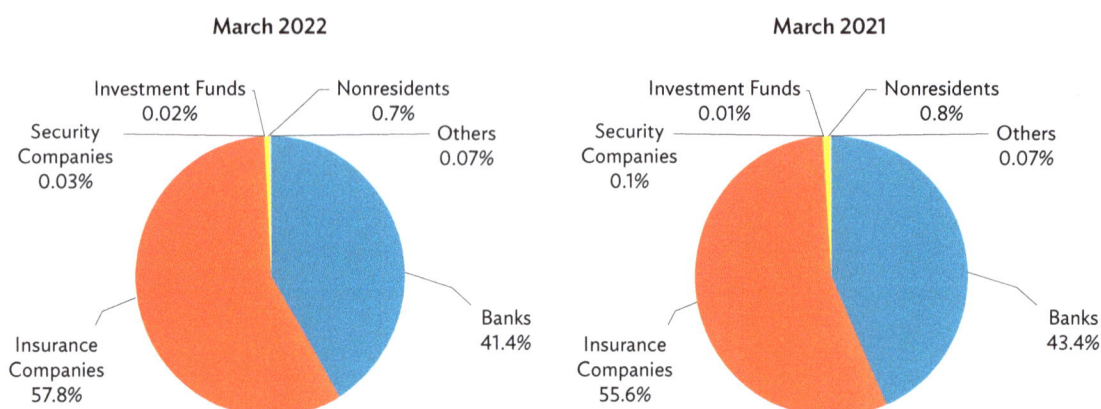

March 2022

Investment Funds 0.02%
Nonresidents 0.7%
Security Companies 0.03%
Others 0.07%
Banks 41.4%
Insurance Companies 57.8%

March 2021

Investment Funds 0.01%
Nonresidents 0.8%
Security Companies 0.1%
Others 0.07%
Banks 43.4%
Insurance Companies 55.6%

Source: Ministry of Finance, Government of Viet Nam.

[14] *Viet Nam News*. 2022. "9 Bond Issuances Worth $439 Million Cancelled." April. https://vietnamnews.vn/economy/1171497/9-bond-issuances-worth-439-million-cancelled.html.

Investor Profile

The combined holdings of insurance companies and banks accounted for nearly all government securities outstanding at the end of March, with holdings shares of 57.8% and 41.4%, respectively (**Figure 2**). The holdings share of insurance companies increased from 55.6% a year earlier, while that of banks decreased from 43.4%. The remaining 0.8% of outstanding government bonds were held by securities companies, investment funds, offshore investors, and other investors, which was down marginally from these investor groups' cumulative holdings in March 2021. The slide in the foreign holdings share is attributable to global economic uncertainty triggering offshore investors to seek safe-haven assets.

Ratings Update

On 28 March, Fitch Ratings affirmed Viet Nam's sovereign credit rating at BB with a positive outlook, noting strong medium-term growth prospects despite COVID-19 pandemic risks and the economic implications of the Russian invasion of Ukraine, as well as sound external finance metrics. The ratings agency stated that contingent liability risks associated with the large state-owned enterprise sector and structural weaknesses in the banking sector continued to constrain the credit rating.

On 26 May, S&P Global Ratings raised Viet Nam's sovereign credit rating to BB+ from BB with a stable outlook. The upgrade reflected Viet Nam's strong economic prospects, sound external position, and improvements in the government's administrative processes. S&P Global Ratings noted that the stable outlook was supported by the economy's recovery from the pandemic's impact, which would in turn strengthen its external and fiscal positions.

Policy, Institutional, and Regulatory Developments

Viet Nam Prime Minister Calls for Law Revision on Corporate Bonds

In April, Prime Minister Pham Minh Chinh issued Directive No. 304, which includes instructions for the Ministry of Finance to revise regulations on the corporate bond market in order to enhance efficiency in enforcing greater transparency and ensuring safety in the market. The directive stated that the focus should be placed on companies with a large amount of bond issuance, high-interest rates, and those having unfavorable business performance without sufficient guarantees. This follows the growing number of cases in Viet Nam of unlawful practices related to corporate bond issuance.[15]

---

[15] *Hanoi Times.* 2022. "PM Chinh Urges Strict Punishment for Violations in Corporate Bond Market." April. http://hanoitimes.vn/pm-chinh-urges-strict-punishment-for-violations-in-corporate-bond-market-320472.html.